The Economics of Information

b

The Economics of Information

LYING AND CHEATING IN MARKETS AND ORGANIZATIONS

IAN MOLHO

Blackwell Publishing

First published 1997
Reprinted 2001
Transferred to digital print 2003

Blackwell Publishers Ltd
108 Cowley Road
Oxford OX4 1JF
UK

Blackwell Publishers Inc.
350 Main Street
Malden, Massachusetts 02148
USA

British Library Cataloguing in Publication Data

A CIP catalogue record for this book is available from the British Library.

Library of Congress Cataloging-in-Publication Data

Library of Congress data has been applied for.

ISBN 0–631–20152–1, ISBN 0–631–20666–3 (pbk.)

Commissioning Editor: Tim Goodfellow
Desk Editor: Valery Rose
Production Controller: Lisa Parker
Text Designer: Lisa Parker

Typeset in 10 on 12 pt Sabon
By Best-set Typesetter Ltd, Hong Kong

Printed and bound in Great Britain by
Marston Lindsay Ross International Ltd,
Oxfordshire

Contents

List of Figures

List of Tables

Preface

Imperfect information has come to occupy a central place in current economic analysis. Unfortunately, the massive literature on this topic is rather diverse and textbooks in the area are rather difficult. The purpose of this book is to present an accessible course on key aspects of the economics of imperfect information.

The book focuses on problems of asymmetric information in general, and adverse selection and moral hazard in particular. The models I use are simple, and often go back to the original journal papers (e.g. of Akerlof and Spence). To academics who know the area, these models might seem dated. To my mind, however, the principal advances that have occurred since the publication of these early papers are mainly ones of *understanding* of the fundamental processes driving the results which can be obtained with the early models. I have therefore attempted to highlight these advances in understanding without the use of more difficult models.

The book is based on a final-year module on 'the economics of information' which I teach at the University of Newcastle upon Tyne, UK. I have added material and pointers to further work in keeping with my belief that a course text ought to be richer than a set of lectures (this means that most students ought to be able to follow the lectures; the brighter and more studious can then glean extra points and insights from the book). Each chapter forms the basis of one (sometimes two) lectures.

The book is divided into 'parts' which are organized by broad issues relating to the role of information in markets. Each part includes an outline of the basic models, and a guide to further developments in the literature. These 'guides' are non-technical, even though the literature they refer to is often analytically rather tough (references to what I judge to be the most difficult papers are indicated by an asterisk, e.g. Wilson (1980)*). The aim here is to cover extensions, developments, applications and elaborations of the basic models and arguments, and to provide the interested reader with a 'way-in' to the more advanced literature. Key further readings are indicated in the Reference lists in bold type, e.g. **Kreps (1990)**.

I have borrowed material from other texts, at various junctures. I have done this largely because there are certain fields of the economics of information in which there has *never* (to my knowledge) been a simple accessible presentation in the journals. Hence I have pieced together material from other texts, and tried to add to or embellish them myself. I make clear my debts to other authors at each stage.

I have included extended discussion of experimental evidence in the book. This is partly because much of the literature on imperfect information is heading this way; partly because in my experience students find that placing issues in an experimental context often helps to bring out the underlying processes more fully and make them more concrete; partly because the evidence is useful in assessing the theory; and lastly because I have found that such material often provides a much needed break and antidote to theory when giving the course.

The emphasis of the book is on processes, rather than on building fully articulated models of particular markets. In the 'real world', the role of information in any one particular market tends to be highly complex. In order to highlight the impact of specific issues, I use simple examples that look at different kinds of information problems separately (e.g. adverse selection in the used-car market, or moral hazard in organizations). The examples are largely incidental – they merely give some motivation and concrete illustrations for discussing information problems.

The book is intended for third-year undergraduates, though arguably it could be used for second years also. Some basic mathematics is used but it is genuinely low level, and I have tried to give verbal/diagrammatic explanations of the algebra as far as possible. Some chapters rely on a knowledge of expected utility theory, and a little game theory is called upon occasionally. For the benefit of the uninitiated (and as a reminder to the initiated) I have included a brief discussion of these in an appendix.

I would like to thank Douglas DeJong, Paul Dolan, Simon Hayes, Tony Miller, Martin Robson and Daniel Seidmann for their helpful comments on preliminary chapters of the book. Finally, thanks to Linda Smith for her rapid and accurate word-processing, patience in dealing with all the changes, and for telling me what she thought of my book.

CHAPTER 1

Introduction: Private Information and Hidden Action

Lying and cheating are facts of life. They pervade all aspects of human existence. Books, TV shows, films and newspapers thrive on stories of deception and betrayal. Pop songs are full of tales of broken-hearted lovers who have been taken in by their partners. Half-lies and downright falsehoods are the stock-in-trade of politicians, diplomats, business executives, lawyers, accountants and ordinary everyday people. A glance through the pages of the Bible would be enough to show that this state of affairs goes back to time immemorial (think of all those tales of intrigue and deception). The mere fear of dishonesty and breach of promise can also do damage, even when in the event people behave truthfully.

This book is about understanding the role of information in situations which potentially give rise to such behaviour, and analysing the consequences for the people involved. Before we go further, we need to define a few terms and concepts. '*Private information*' is economists' jargon for 'I know something you don't know'; it relates to information about given facts, such as whether or not some product has a serious defect. Such information is said to be 'privately observed' by those who have access to it, and '*unobservable*' to those who do not. If a piece of information is known to everyone, then it is called '*public information*' or '*publicly observable*'.[1] The presence of private information creates an '*information asymmetry*'; some people are better informed than others. The term '*hidden knowledge*' is sometimes used instead of 'private information'.

The role of private information is central to an understanding of lying. Say I try to sell you a second-hand car, claiming (perhaps untruthfully) that it is a 'good runner'. The only circumstance under which I might gain from such a lie is when the quality of that car is private information. There would be no point my lying about the colour of the car, say, when you can see it with your own eyes. Private information is a pre-condition for lying.

A further form of information asymmetry may be identified, which relates to the situation where the behaviour of people is unobserved. This situation is often called one of '*hidden action*', as opposed to one of hidden knowledge. For example, an employer may not be able to observe whether or not an employee is shirking at her work. This kind of unobservability creates the potential for cheating. Say a politician agrees to abide by some nuclear test ban or trade sanctions; if the international community cannot observe the behaviour of his/her country, (s)he might well be tempted to cheat on the agreement (since the costs to that person of such an action are likely to be lower when the action is unobserved by others).

A further source of potential for cheating may also be identified. Say that an action by one party is observable to the other party to an agreement. The former might still 'cheat' (take an action counter to the agreement) if the action is '*unverifiable*' in a court of law. You may know that your wife/husband is cheating on you, but be unable to prove it in the divorce courts. Unverifiability is, of course, itself a special kind of information problem; it relates to the inability to credibly inform a third party.

People do not always lie or cheat when they have an information advantage. They tend to do so only if they perceive that they have something to gain by such behaviour – e.g. to get a better price for a second-hand car. This book proceeds on the basic tenet that underlies most of economic theory, which is that people are greedy; they will do anything that yields a payoff (e.g. in terms of utility or profit), even if it involves lying and cheating. As Machiavelli advised his prince:

> A wise ruler, therefore, cannot and should not keep his word when such an observance of faith would be to his disadvantage and when the reasons which made him promise are removed. And if men were all good, this rule would not be good; but since men are a contemptible lot and will not keep their promises to you, you likewise need not keep yours to them. (*The Prince*, Chapter xviii)

Some people may find this approach morally repugnant, but it seems to provide the most obvious working assumption if we are to begin to understand lying and cheating in the real world.

Classic Examples of Lying and Cheating in Economic Theory

There are many areas of economics where these kinds of issues arise, although the words 'lying' and 'cheating' may not be explicitly used. Some examples follow.

1   *Free riders*: consider a good which has the attribute that it is 'non-excludable' in consumption, such as national defence, or public TV broadcasting such as the BBC in Britain. Suppose some decision-maker (the government perhaps) has to choose how much to produce of the good for public consumption, and how much to charge (e.g. through taxation). A basic problem that the decision-maker faces is that she does not know how much people *value* the good; their preferences are private information. The usual price system does not work to extract that information, due to the non-excludability problem: once the good is produced, you cannot stop people consuming it for free. Simply asking people to state their valuation and charging them accordingly will not work either, since people have an incentive to misrepresent their preferences (i.e. to lie); they free ride by stating a value of zero (or less, if possible) to minimize the amount they are charged. If everyone behaves this way then a potentially valuable good may not be produced at all. See virtually any text on public economics for further discussion.

2   *Tactical voting*: say several people place votes on some decision, such as which political party to elect to government; Labour, Conservative, or Liberal Democrat (in the US we might have Republican, Democrat or independent). Then some voters who might actually prefer Liberal Democrat may decide to vote Labour instead, if they see Conservative as the worst outcome and Labour as the only viable alternative (given everyone else's likely voting pattern). Once again, this is a situation involving private information, in this case in relation to voter preferences. Extracting truthful information about each voter's preferences is problematic, because of these kinds of incentives to misrepresent (lie). In fact, a famous theorem in social choice theory (the Gibbard–Satterthwaite theorem) states that there are incentives to misrepresent in every conceivable voting procedure one might try, under a wide set of circumstances (as long as there are more than two alternatives to choose from). See any text on social choice theory for further discussion.

3   *Cartels*: consider some kind of coalition, such as an industrial cartel. The purpose of the cartel is to co-ordinate the decisions of its members and then to share out any surplus that it makes as a result of that co-ordination. For example, OPEC (the Organization of Petroleum Exporting Countries) might impose production quotas on its member states to keep the price of oil high, such that all its members benefit. Forming and sustaining a cartel is beset with problems, many of which involve private information. One such problem arises in deciding how much oil each state should produce. In bargaining over a quota allocation, each member state may find it in their interests to misrepresent their production costs (say), since if they claim they can produce very cheaply they may win a higher production quota. This is a case of private information concerning each state's costs, with no obvious mechanism to extract truthful revelation.

A second problem is that of cheating. The member states may come to some agreement, but will they stick to it? The incentive to cheat arises as a basic free-rider problem of the kind outlined above, since the benefits of a high price are non-excludable (if one producer lowers output to raise price, all producers benefit). Say behaviour was publicly observable. Then the cartel would have to devise some credible system (e.g. of fines) to prevent cheating. But if behaviour was not publicly observable (or at least unverifiable) then the problems of preventing cheating would be multiplied. See any text on industrial economics for a discussion.

These are but a few examples. This book is about the role of asymmetric information in strategic situations such as these, where people may lie and/or cheat. The purpose of this introduction is to explain where these sorts of issues fit into economic analysis, and to outline in general terms the sorts of consequences that follow. The rest of the book sets out stylized models and evidence to flesh out and back up these arguments.

Asymmetric Information in Economic Theory

In order to get an overall perspective on 'lying' and 'cheating' in economic behaviour, it is worth stepping back for a moment to consider some fundamental principles. Perhaps the most basic question which economic analysis attempts to address is 'how to organize the system of production and transaction of goods, to best satisfy peoples' wants and needs, from scarce resources?' To answer this question we must first consider what we mean by 'best'. Economists use the criterion of '*Pareto-*

efficiency' for judging social welfare outcomes. An outcome is Pareto-efficient if the welfare of no single person or group can be improved without reducing the welfare of some other person or group. If an outcome does not satisfy this criterion then it is said to be inefficient. In many situations, there can be several (possibly a large number of) Pareto-efficient outcomes.

The Pareto criterion has the virtue of almost universal acceptance in the sense that most people would agree that 'if some individuals are made better-off and others are no worse-off', such a change would constitute a social welfare improvement. Some people might like to go further and argue, for example, that 'if a large number of individuals are made better-off, and only a very small number worse-off', that also would constitute a social welfare improvement. Such a view is unlikely to gain universal acceptance however – even if it is only the 'very small number' made worse-off that would disagree.

What sort of economic system is likely to yield Pareto-efficient outcomes? A basic economic 'fact of life' is that in most activities there are usually some production gains to be made by specialization. In order to take advantage of these, people must interact via transactions, which are completed through 'contracts'. These contracts may be explicit legally binding agreements in the conventional sense; but in economists' jargon they relate also to implicit agreements, understandings, etc., without the backing of legal force.

Given the potential gains from interactions, the basic problems that an economic system has to solve are to *motivate* and to *co-ordinate* activity. An activity may be desirable in terms of the Pareto criterion, but the individual(s) who are in a position to undertake it must themselves have some incentive to carry it out, otherwise the opportunity for welfare improvement will be lost. Furthermore, if a transaction between people is desirable then the economic system must also solve the problem of co-ordination such that trade takes place. For example, a buyer and seller must be brought together in some sense.

We may distinguish between two broad types of economic systems or '*mechanisms*' which attempt to solve these problems (Williamson, 1975). Firstly, there are *market-based* systems. There are many such systems from traditional street markets to auctions, etc., but broadly they all work via *price signals*. Traders supply goods and services if the market price exceeds their own valuation or cost of production; they demand them if their valuation exceeds the market price. It is easy to see intuitively how, in principle, such a system can 'solve' both co-ordination and motivation problems. One of the outstanding intellectual achievements of traditional economic theory has been to show that under certain conditions the outcome of such a system is Pareto-efficient.

The alternative type of system (or mechanism) is one based on *hierarchies*. These may also take various forms, from the central planning system of the old Soviet Union to the management systems that exist within modern large corporations. In this approach, information, on resources on the one hand and aims and objectives on the other, is fed to decision-makers through the hierarchy. A plan is then devised to advance the organizational aims as best as possible given the resource constraints. A system based on *authority* in the hierarchy is then used to implement the plan.

Both types of systems involve the interaction of people. In the market system they interact as traders, in the hierarchy they interact as agents within an organization. And in both systems these interactions occur as transactions via contracts in the economic sense. A system based entirely on hierarchies would ultimately organize all activity within one all-encompassing structure, e.g. one firm that produces all goods in an economy. At the opposite extreme, a purely market-based system would involve the organization of every economic interaction within the market. (To imagine this, think of the production of any item, e.g. a car, at every stage of production of every component, a price would have to be set and a transaction completed, until finally the car reached the end-user.)

In practice, both market- and hierarchy-based systems co-exist in modern economies. We have open markets, but we also have large organizations such as the modern joint-stock company. Coase (1937) argued that one could think of each system as involving '*transaction costs*' in the organization of activities and economic interactions. These are costs to transacting in a very general sense, which might include, for example, the costs of writing all the contracts that take production of the car through its various stages to the end-user. At a fundamental level, transaction costs are the costs involved in solving the co-ordination and motivation problems alluded to above.

There are two main factors that are likely to affect the level of transaction costs in a system. The first lies in problems of 'bounded rationality'. For example, even if you gave a central planner all the information relevant to some problem, (s)he might still fail to come up with the optimal solution, due to the sheer complexity involved relative to the limited capacity of human beings to comprehend and solve such problems. The loss of social welfare that arises reflects a form of transaction cost inherent in that centralized system.

The other major source of transaction costs is the problem of information. A whole range of information issues arise in relation to the problem of co-ordination, in that both market- and hierarchy-based systems require that decision-makers have good and timely information if they are to function properly. These are important issues. The focus of this book, however, is on issues of asymmetric information and the consequent strategic problems that arise in constructing contracts as the basis for transactions.

At a fundamental level, the problem of motivation may be solved if contracts can be completely specified and enforced. By a complete contract we mean one that specifies an outcome for every possible eventuality. This means that, whatever happens, the parties must know what the situation is, they know what the contract specifies in that case, and they must not be able to renege or re-negotiate the deal. That is a very tall order. But if it can be satisfied (and the contract can also be enforced), then where there are gains to be made from trade it ought to be possible to design a contract such that all the parties are motivated to do the deal. A simple intuition for this is that where 'gains from trade' exist, so the complete contract need only ensure that some share of these gains goes to all parties who require motivation.[2]

The existence of asymmetric information can destroy this desirable state of affairs, because it raises the possibility of opportunistic behaviour, which we call 'lying' and 'cheating'. Complete contracts cannot be specified when some information that is relevant to the deal is private to a subset of the people involved, and/or some action is unobservable. One alternative is to (try to) trade on the basis of an incomplete contract, i.e. a contract written in terms of that subset of knowledge that is public. But an incomplete contract may be an imperfect substitute for a complete contract. The car I wish to sell you may very well be fine, but remain unsold simply because I cannot convince you of its quality – a verbal assurance from me could easily be a lie. To take another example, I might be willing and able to complete some valuable task for you (e.g. repair a fault in your car), but if you cannot observe my action you may not hire me – I might cheat on you by botching the job. The major point that flows from this intuitive argument is that asymmetric information may cause Pareto-inefficiency; a mutually beneficial trade may not take place. Such inefficiencies will be a major theme of this book.

Asymmetric information problems and resulting opportunistic behaviour arise in all systems, whether market- or hierarchy-based; a supplier may cheat on product specification, a manager may slack on the job etc. Coase (1937) and others (notably Williamson, 1975) argued that economic activity would come to be organized in a way that minimized overall transaction costs. For example, organizations such as firms would grow so long as it was more efficient to absorb activities within the firm rather than trade in the market. If it happened to be efficient to produce some component 'in-house' say (in order to avoid opportunistic suppliers perhaps) then so be it; if it were more efficient to sub-contract, then that system would be adopted instead, and so on.

Coase's view is controversial and this is not the place to rehearse all the relevant arguments.[3] From our point of view we would wish merely to claim that transaction costs can be seen to at least potentially *influence* the organization of economic activity. Why *should* more efficient systems of organization replace less efficient ones? Roughly speaking, Coase's argument is that more efficient systems increase the cake or 'surplus' generated through transacting (by virtue of the lower transaction costs), and this provides the potential for incentives to the transactors to introduce a more efficient system (once again, we are appealing to Coase's theorem, as mentioned in note 2).

The major point that flows from this argument is that, in so far as information problems lead to transaction costs, these can affect economic organization. If the information problems involved in a market transaction are too great, then hierarchy-based systems may evolve instead, or vice versa. Such issues also affect how the firm is organized, and/ or how the market may be structured. There are many different hierarchical systems in terms of the organization of seniority, supervision, divisionalization of production and so on; the choice of some specific system as opposed to another in some situation may be seen as a response to the existence of transaction costs in general, and information problems in particular.[4] Likewise, market institutions may develop as a counter to such problems. I might offer a warranty on my car to assure you of its quality; another trader might develop a reputation for honesty through repeated trades; a market may develop for independent firms to verify the quality of the product, etc.

Moral Hazard and Adverse Selection

The problems generated by private information and unobservability (or unverifiability) of actions have specific names in economics; these are respectively '*adverse selection*' and '*moral hazard*'. In its pure form, adverse selection is a problem of '*precontractual opportunism*' in that the presence of private information provides people with the opportunity to lie prior to contract taking place. Moral hazard is a problem of '*postcontractual opportunism*', in that the presence of some unobservable (/unverifiable) action provides people with an opportunity to cheat after the deal is signed.[5]

The terms 'adverse selection' and 'moral hazard' originated in the insurance industry, and this serves as a good example with which to illustrate their effects. The former term derives from the sort of insurance market outcome that arises when people have private information (or hidden knowledge as it is sometimes called). Say there is a pool of customers seeking insurance. Some customers may be inherently high-risk (e.g. they are prone to medical problems, or by nature live a dangerous life-style), others are low-risk. If knowledge of these risks is private to the individuals concerned and unobservable to the insurance companies, then the latter must offer everyone insurance at the same premium. But such a company is likely to end up with predominantly high-risk customers on its books, since the people who know they are prone to illness (say) are the ones who take the medical insurance. Private information in this case means customers can lie about how bad a risk they are; and the outcome from the insurance companies' point of view is that they get an 'adverse selection' of customers on their books, i.e. they end up with the bad risks.

The term 'moral hazard' relates in the insurance industry to the phenomenon that once people take out an insurance policy, they deliberately take more risks as a result. A person who insures his house, for example, has less incentive to look after it as a result. He may not check quite as carefully that all the fires are switched off when going out, as he would have done without insurance, for example. If the house burns down, he can pick up the insurance pay-out. In some extreme cases, people might even deliberately start a fire to claim on the insurance. There is 'hidden action' here in that the insurance company cannot observe the effort people take to prevent the accident. The firm faces the 'hazard' that its customers might behave 'immorally'.

It is quite possible for both moral hazard and adverse selection problems to be present in some particular situation. For example, a manager may take actions that are unobserved by the firm's shareholders *and* have private information about the running of the firm and the policy choices it faces. Different specific real world situations such as this often involve elements of both these problems.

Lying is the abuse of private information to further one's own interests. Such lies can be quite subtle. We are all familiar with lies in the literal sense. But there are also many situations in which non-verbal 'signals' may be sent which also purport to convey information. For example, someone's body language might (seem to) say 'I like you', and that can be a lie. Another example might be the subject of the Kinks song 'Lola', who 'walked like a woman, but talked like a man . . .' In a more obviously economic sphere, a central bank may use various market devices to dupe speculators into believing (wrongly) that an interest rate cut is imminent. Houses and cars are widely fitted with burglar alarms these days, but in amongst the genuine alarms there are many fakes – dummy systems with a box and a flashing light, perhaps, but little else. We shall treat these all as 'lies' of a kind.

Economic models of adverse selection usually assume that people cannot 'get away with' lying forever. The idea is that if someone systematically lies, he may fool you once or twice, but eventually you learn that their communications are not to be trusted. This assumption accords with the old saying 'you can fool some people sometimes, but you can't fool all the people all the time'. In the context of economic modelling it amounts to a form of 'rational expectations' – people make correct assessments *on average* (e.g. about the likely quality of a used car) although they may be wrong in specific cases. With this assumption in place, the consequence of having 'liars' present in the population (who may be try to pass off bad cars as good, say) is ultimately to degrade the information content of the communication ('this is a good car'), conceivably up to the point where it becomes meaningless. The claim 'I love you', for example, is often perceived as meaningless, since everyone can make the claim when it serves their purpose, true or not. In equilibrium, therefore, the end result of lying is not to systematically fool people but to weaken or destroy a mechanism that conveys private information. The informed party can end up as much a loser from this as the uninformed.

A similar argument applies to moral hazard/cheating. As mentioned earlier, you may never find out that you have been cheated in some particular instance; but experience, general observation and common sense will tell you when it is likely to happen. In equilibrium, people are assumed to spot the danger, and to presume that the other (informed) party will cheat on them if it is to that person's advantage (you do not need to observe the act, you can take it on trust that if the other person has the opportunity and the incentive, he/she will cheat on you). Given this, people are likely to seek ways to prevent or minimize the scope for the informed party to cheat. And that may again mean that both parties end up the losers (for example, you might hire someone to watch over the other party, which may be costly to you, and distasteful to the other person).

Part 1 of the book is devoted to a discussion of adverse selection problems. These problems arise when private information is present. In Part 2 we look at signalling mechanisms whereby private information might be communicated between individuals. In Part 3 of the book we consider moral hazard problems.

Information and Mechanism Design

Thus far, the material we have discussed is largely 'positive' in the sense that it uses economic principles to predict likely real-world outcomes in the presence of asymmetric information. There is, however, also a 'normative' branch in the literature which attempts to prescribe the 'best' way of dealing with some information problem. To take a concrete example, say you wish to auction some item (it might be a painting or antique perhaps; it might even be the sale of some franchise, say). You are faced with a pool of bidders, each of whom has a potentially different private valuation of the item, which is unknown to you. You might consider conducting the sale using an 'English auction' design, say, or perhaps a 'Dutch auction'. As a seller, you would probably wish to know which design of auction is likely to yield the highest price for the good. Alternatively, if you were some impartial and benign social planner, then you would probably wish to know which design of auction is likely to maximize (some measure of) social welfare.

The literature on 'mechanism design' attempts to address such questions. The auction problem cited above revolves around issues of asymmetric information, because the valuations bidders place on the good are private. Say you know how much each person was prepared to pay for the good – then you could extract the highest price with ease by selling the good to the person with the highest valuation for a price given by that value (or maybe just under, to give her an inducement to trade). Under private information, however, the bidder may 'lie' – in the case of an auction, they may submit a bid for the good which is less than their true valuation. Different auction designs yield different bidding incentives, and hence are likely to yield different equilibrium solutions. Which auction design is most likely to yield 'truthful' bids and what do the equilibria look like in terms of prices, welfare etc.?

One could go about trying to answer this question by analysing each auction design in turn to work out the predicted equilibrium outcome, and then compare these outcomes. A decision could then be made as to which design was the best from the point of view of the seller, which was the best for the social planner etc. The problem is that there are innumerable different designs of auction one could consider, of which the English and Dutch auctions are but two examples. It would seem a daunting task to analyse them all. Fortunately, there is a short cut in the form of the 'revelation principle'. In the final part of this book we present this principle and illustrate its application to mechanism design problems. We apply it firstly to a bargaining example where buyers and sellers do not know each others valuation of a good. We then apply it to the case of auctions, described above.

Summary

Economic systems attempt to match peoples' wants and needs on the one hand with available resources on the other. The most universally accepted way of judging the merits of a system is in terms of the Pareto-efficiency of the outcomes it generates. Advantages that arise from specialization imply that economic systems which involve some inter-action or transactions between people yield potential efficiency gains. Those transactions may be organized in (some combination of) market- and hierarchy-based systems. Transaction costs arise in any system, and relate to problems of co-ordinating and motivating activity. The problem of motivation could, in principle, be solved by complete enforceable contracts which specify all aspects of the deal in all eventualities.

The presence of private information and/or unobservability of behaviour is one major obstacle to this, which forces agents to work with incomplete contracts. This raises the possibility of opportunistic behaviour, which contributes to transaction costs due to motivation problems, and hence causes efficiency losses. Opportunism may arise at the pre-contract (lying) or postcontract stage (cheating).

Adverse selection problems are generated by the presence of private information or hidden knowledge. In its pure form, adverse selection is an important form of precontractual opportunism, whereby hidden knowledge allows the informed party to lie prior to a deal. Lies can take many forms, apart from straightforward verbal statements. Nobody is taken in forever by lies (of whatever kind); eventually the recipient will learn to discount the communication. Both sender and receiver of the communication may suffer as a result, since an inability to convey private information may cause a transaction of potentially mutual benefit to fall through.

Moral hazard problems are generated by the presence of un-observability or unverifiability. Moral hazard is an important form of postcontractual opportunism, whereby if one party cannot observe/verify the other's actions after the deal is agreed, then the latter may cheat. People do not usually allow cheats free rein; they try to anticipate the problem and introduce worthwhile mechanisms to safeguard their interests. The resulting outcome may be worse for both parties than if full information prevailed.

It may be argued that economic systems adapt to transaction costs in general, including those due to asymmetric information. This may be achieved by appropriate structuring of transactions within and between market and hierarchies. On Coase's (positive) view, observed 'real world' mechanisms might be expected to minimise transaction costs. On a normative view, the revelation principle allows economists to identify mechanisms which may be recommended for use in the 'real world'.

Some Themes of the Book

Game theory provides the appropriate theoretical 'toolkit' for handling issues of strategy.[6] The decision that an individual has to make in a situation of asymmetric information is to choose between various strategies (e.g. 'cheat' versus 'not cheat'). Each person typically makes that choice with the intention of advancing their own objectives. But in a strategic situation (or game), the payoff that an individual gets typically depends not only on their own strategy, but also on the strategies chosen by other people. The main concepts from game theory which we shall employ in this book are (see the appendix at the end of the book for more discussion):

(a) *Dominance*: one strategy (strictly) dominates another from the point of view of some player, if it yields a higher payoff no matter what other players do.[7] A rational player ought never to intentionally play a dominated strategy.

(b) *Nash equilibrium*: This is a situation where each player chooses a strategy that yields that person their highest payoff given the strategies chosen by the other players. Players play mutual 'best responses' (for example, player 1's strategy is a best response to player 2's, and vice versa). No player can profit by unilateral deviation from their equilibrium strategy.

In certain market situations where there are large numbers of traders, it may be possible to analyse asymmetric information problems using the more traditional tool of economic theory called 'Walrasian equilibrium', i.e. by identifying the point where supply equals demand. This is because with enough traders the strategic problem facing any one buyer or seller becomes trivial, they merely have to decide whether they want to buy or sell at the 'going market price'. In this context, Nash equilibrium and

Walrasian equilibrium amount to the same thing. We shall use the Walrasian concept extensively in the first part of the book. Where there are fewer players, the issue of strategic interaction comes to the fore, and the concept of Nash equilibrium will be applied. (Indeed we have implicitly made use of it already – references to 'equilibrium' made in this chapter actually mean 'Nash equilibrium').

Experimental evidence: empirical evidence is the 'test-bed' to assess existing theories, try out new ones, and to refine and improve them. The traditional approach to empirical work has been to fit econometric models to real-world data, and apply hypothesis tests. This approach has many strengths, but it does suffer form the drawback that in the real world there may be all sorts of factors that might have influenced decisions which we cannot observe or control for.

The experimental approach to empirical work attempts to create (as far as possible) a controlled laboratory-type environment within which to observe behaviour. Subjects are put in specific situations with clear-cut decisions to make, and incentives that are controlled by the experimenter. This is done by giving subjects cash payments, depending on the choices they make. With non-trivial amounts of money riding on their decision, each subject has an incentive to think through and make genuine choices. These decisions may then be compared with the predictions of theory. Further, one can compare choices made in different environments – for example, do people make the same choices if their identities are known and publicly observed, as compared to conditions of anonymity? Experimental techniques are 'a natural' for testing theories of asymmetric information. In the experimental laboratory one can closely control the knowledge available to each subject, and observe differences in behaviour that arise as the information structure varies (e.g. knowledge of identity, as above).

Organization of the Book

To recap, the book is organized into four main parts. Part 1 examines adverse selection problems due to the presence of private information. The example (already mentioned) of the market for used cars is used by way of illustration. Part 2 considers the role of 'signals' in markets with private information. The example of job market applicants using education as a signal of their productivity to prospective employers is used. Part 3 relates to moral hazard problems due to unobservability (or at least unverifiability). This is illustrated in terms of an example of shareholders and managers; shareholders own the firm but cannot observe the daily activities of the managers who run it. Part 4 looks at mechanism design issues. The revelation principle is presented, and then applied firstly to a bargaining problem, and then to the case of auctions where the value each bidder places on the good on offer is private information.

NOTES

1   The concept of 'public information' is related to what is called *'mutual knowledge'* and also to *'common knowledge'*. If 'everyone knows' something, that is called mutual knowledge of the *first* degree; if 'everyone knows that everyone knows' something, that is called mutual knowledge of *second* degree, and so on. If 'everyone knows that everyone knows that everyone knows . . .' and so on an infinite number of times, that is called common knowledge.

2   This is the essence of the 'Coase theorem', which is one of the most celebrated ideas in economics. See Milgrom and Roberts (1992) for extensive discussion.

3   Two specific difficulties are that the theory seems to assume, firstly, that transaction costs can be treated separately from production costs and, secondly, that there are no wealth effects (see Milgrom and Roberts, 1992, for further discussion). More generally, the theory may be seen to be so general as to verge on the meaningless – any outcome can be seen as consistent with Coase's view, as long as transaction costs are interpreted sufficiently generally; it also has a strongly 'Dr Panglossian' flavour ('everything is for the best in the best of all possible worlds') in that it suggests that whatever we observe must be optimal.

4   Alchian and Demsetz (1972) go so far as to suggest that the concept of 'the firm' itself arises out of an information problem. In many situations there are productivity gains from working in *teams*. An inherent problem in teamwork, however, is that individuals may have an incentive to shirk (e.g. two people are loading cargo; each may try to let the other take most of the strain). Shirking is often unobservable (or at least unverifiable). Monitoring of behaviour may be cost-effective in that it may deter shirking to an extent that outweighs the costs. But 'who monitors the monitor'? Alchian and Demsetz's argument is that giving *ownership* to the monitor provides that person with the right motivation, since the owner claims the returns after paying employees. The monitor is the owner, i.e. the boss. Hence the classical firm is born from a fundamental information problem. The idea can be generalized to encompass alternative forms of firm organization.

5   The terms 'adverse selection' and 'moral hazard' are used differently by different authors. The definitions used in this book and described in the text are consistent with Williamson (1975; 1985, for example, see pp. 80–5) and

what appears to be an emerging consensus in the more recent literature, such as Hart and Holmstrom (1987) and Milgrom and Roberts (1992).

6   A subtle distinction exists in the literature on game theory between 'games of incomplete information' and 'games of imperfect information'. The latter relates to situations where players may be imperfectly informed about the history of play of the game up to the point where they must make a decision. The former concerns situations where players are not fully informed about the basic structure of the game, e.g. the rules or the payoffs. Incomplete information games cannot be modelled directly. Harsanyi (1967) showed, however, that they could be transformed into games of imperfect information (which can be modelled), by redefining the game. This book deals with games of imperfect and asymmetric information.

7   One strategy weakly dominates another if it yields the same payoff for certain choices by the opponent player, and a higher payoff for others.

REFERENCES

Alchian, A. and Demsetz, H. (1972), 'Production, Information Costs and Economic Organisation', *American Economic Review*, **62**, pp. 777–95.

Coase, R. (1937), 'The Nature of the Firm', *Economica*, **4**, pp. 386–405.

Harsanyi, J. (1967), 'Games with Incomplete Information Played by Bayesian Players – I: The Basic Model', *Management Science*, **14**, pp. 159–82.

Hart, O. and Holmstrom, B. (1987) 'The Theory of Contracts', in T. Berley (ed.), *Advances in Economic Theory, Fifth World Congress* (Cambridge: Cambridge University Press).

Milgrom, P. and Roberts, J. (1992), *Economics, Organisation and Management* (Englewood Cliffs, NJ: Prentice Hall).

Williamson, O. (1975), *Markets and Hierarchies: Analysis and Anti-trust Implications* (New York: Free Press).

Williamson, O. (1985), *The Economic Institutions of Capitalism* (New York: Free Press).

Part I

Adverse Selection: The Market for Lemons

In the following three chapters, we consider theory and evidence relating to situations where one party to a transaction has private information (e.g. about the quality of a product) that is unavailable to the other party. We consider situations where there is no credible way of transmitting the relevant information (verbal assurances are useless, because the people who lack information cannot tell whether the assurance is a lie or not). This yields an equilibrium where only the poor-quality products ('lemons') are traded – that is, there is an 'adverse selection'. The next part of the book proceeds to consider situations where agents can credibly transmit 'signals' which convey the relevant information.

CHAPTER 2

Quality Uncertainty and the 'Market for Lemons'

It is often remarked that if you buy a new car, drive it for a mile or two, and then try to sell it, you may have to take a large cut in price. Several reasons may be advanced to explain this observation; one argument, for example, would turn on the role played by warranties. We shall defer that argument for a while and concentrate in this chapter on an alternative explanation proposed by Akerlof (1970). He argues that the observation can be understood in terms of an underlying information asymmetry – the owner of the used car is better informed about its quality than a potential buyer (at least prior to purchase);[1] the car might, in American parlance, be a 'lemon'. The quality of the used car is private information, and this is the source of the adverse selection problem.

Say for the sake of argument that buyers have no way of finding out the quality of a specific used car. Since used cars 'look alike' to buyers, so good cars and lemons will all trade at the same price. The more poor quality cars there are on the market, the lower the average quality, and so the lower the price will be for used cars. Hence, it becomes difficult to sell a good used car at a fair price.

Faced with this situation, the owners of the best used cars may decide that it is not worth trying to sell their car. The average quality of used cars (put up for sale) will accordingly be lower as a result, and so will the price. Given this, the owners of used cars that are 'second best' in quality may also decide to withdraw from the market, and so average quality and price will be lower still, and so on for the third best , fourth best, etc. This sort of process might lead to the market unravelling entirely; or, somewhat more plausibly, the system may find an equilibrium in which the only viable market that remains is quite literally the 'market for lemons' – only the poorest quality cars are traded.

This sort of process is potentially applicable to any market in which private information is present. The used car market is a convenient example with which to introduce the idea. In the next section we present a model which captures the process of adverse selection in this context (the model we present is slightly different to that used by Akerlof; an appendix to this chapter explains the differences, should readers be interested). The model is highly stylized, and is not intended to be realistic. The purpose of the model is to demonstrate how problems of imperfect information can disrupt the efficient operation of markets. Some features of the model are deliberately made rather extreme, in order to make this point as forcefully as possible. We follow the presentation of the model with a general discussion of adverse selection problems in markets.

The Model

The market for used cars is taken to involve two groups of traders. Each trader in group 1 owns a used car and must decide whether to sell; group 2 traders do *not* own used cars, and decide whether to buy. The model is constructed so that potential gains from trade exist, in that group 2 (the potential buyers) are taken to value used cars more highly than group 1 (the potential sellers). Buyers and sellers each make their decisions on a conventional expected utility maximizing basis; the main feature of the model is that sellers make their decision in the knowledge of product quality, but buyers have to make the best choices they can without that knowledge. We find the market clearing equilibrium under these conditions.

Group 2: demand for used cars

The preferences of a group 2 trader (a potential buyer) are represented in the following utility function:

$$U_2 = M + \left(3/2\right)q \cdot n.$$

In this equation, n is an indicator which takes the value 1 if the trader 'consumes' a used car, and 0 otherwise; q is the quality of that car; and M is consumption of other goods apart from used cars. All these factors would give utility to a group 2 individual.[2]

Group 2 traders each face a budget constraint:

$$y_2 = M + p \cdot n \quad \text{or} \quad M = y_2 - p \cdot n$$

where y_2 is the income of a group 2 trader, p is the market price for used cars, and n indicates whether the individual decides to buy a used car or not, as above.[3] The price of 'other goods' is taken as numeraire and fixed at 1 (that is, p measures the *relative* price of used cars). This budget constraint says that consumers' expenditure (be it on cars, other goods, or both) is equal in total to their income.

Buyers are assumed to be unable to observe the quality of any specific car they might buy. This is the adverse selection problem. It also explains why there is only one price p in the market for used cars; buyers cannot observe differences in quality prior to purchase, hence all cars are traded at the same price. Buyers are, however, taken to know the *average* quality of cars supplied on the used car market. This is a kind of 'second-order' knowledge; buyers do not know if a specific car is any good, but they can make an informed guess on the basis of their knowledge of average quality in the market place.[4]

Given the uncertainty on quality, each buyer's decision must be made on the basis of *expected* utility ($E(U_2)$) rather than actual utility. This is given as (see the appendix to the book):

$$E(U_2) = M + (3/2)E(q) \cdot n = M + (3/2)\mu \cdot n$$

where $\mu = E(q)$ = average (or expected) quality of used cars on the market. Substituting in the budget constraint (given earlier) for M in this equation yields

$$E(U_2) = y_2 + \left[(3/2)\mu - p\right]n.$$

The decision the trader must make is whether to buy a used car ($n = 1$) or not buy ($n = 0$). If $[(3/2)\mu - p] > 0$ then setting $n = 1$ may be seen to *increase* expected utility in the above equation, so the trader is better off buying than not buying. If $[(3/2)\mu - p] < 0$, however, then setting $n = 1$ would *decrease* expected utility, and so the trader is better off not buying. Finally, if $[(3/2)\mu - p] = 0$ then the trader is indifferent. Maximizing expected utility leads to the 'demand rule' for group 2 traders of:[5]

'only buy if $(3/2)\mu \geq p$'.

Intuitively, these traders will only buy if the expected quality of used cars is high enough relative to the price.

Group 1: supply of used cars

Traders in this group each own one used car, and must decide whether to sell it or not (see note 3). This decision is also made as a utility maximizing choice. The utility function and budget constraint of each group 1 trader are similar to those for group 2 traders, and given as:

$$U_1 = M + q \cdot n,$$ utility function;
$$y_1 = M + p \cdot n \quad \text{or} \quad M = y_1 - p \cdot n,$$ budget constraint.

A key point here is that consuming a used car ($n = 1$) raises utility of individuals in this group by q (the quality of that car), whereas for group 2 traders the same car would raise utility by $(3/2)q$; group 1 traders *own* the cars, but they get less utility from a car of given quality than group 2 and hence there are potential gains from trade. The budget constraint here allows for the possibility that group 1 traders may *sell* their car, and use that income to buy more of 'other goods' M. (If they sell, then $n = 0$ and $y_1 = M$; if they keep the car then part of their income is locked up in it, leaving them ($y_1 - p$) to spend on other goods.)

Group 1 are taken to know the quality of their car, prior to selling it. This is the information asymmetry at the heart of the model. The reason for this asymmetry presumably lies in the fact that owners have had some previous experience with their car which allows them to know its quality. Given that knowledge, sellers face no uncertainty and hence their supply decision is based on maximizing actual rather than expected utility. Substituting the budget constraint into the utility function yields:

$$U_1 = y_1 + (q - p)n.$$

Thus if $(q - p) > 0$, then keeping the car ($n = 1$) increases utility. If $(q - p) < 0$, then the trader is better off selling ($n = 0$). If $(q - p) = 0$, the trader is indifferent. Utility maximization therefore leads to the 'supply rule':

'only sell if $p \geq q$'.

In order to proceed further, we need to know more about the quality of used cars that group 1 traders own. Akerlof makes the specific assumption that the quality of used cars follows a uniform distribution, with minimum quality 0 (the worst possible, as bad as having no car at all) and maximum quality 2 (the best possible, a mint condition car with

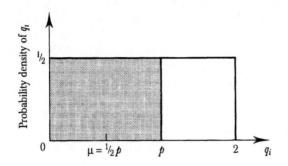

Figure 2.1 The distribution of car quality

no faults). The assumption of a uniform distribution means that if you pick a used car at random from the entire stock, then you are just as likely to get a top quality one as a bottom quality one, or indeed one of any quality level in-between.

The distribution is depicted in figure 2.1. Loosely speaking, one can think about this diagram in terms of a car park. At the extreme left of the car park are the worst quality cars; as we move rightward so the quality of cars improves until we reach the best quality cars on the extreme right (the potential buyers, of course, do not know from what part of the car park the car is selected). To be more precise, to get the probability density shown in the diagram we must divide the number of cars at each quality level by the total stock of used cars. The probability that a car chosen at random out of the stock of cars will be of some given quality or less is then given as the area under the distribution to the left of that quality level. For example, the chances that a car is of quality less than the point p in the diagram is given as the shaded area (if you are rusty on probability densities, see the technical appendix at the end of the book).

The uniform probability density is $1/2$; to see this, note the following. There is a probability of 1 that a car is of quality between 0 and 2. This probability is represented in the diagram as the entire area under the distribution. The distribution is in the shape of a rectangle, with area given by distance up the vertical axis times distance along the horizontal. The latter takes the value of 2 for the whole distribution, so for the entire area to equal 1, the distance up the vertical (i.e. the density) must be $1/2$.

Each group 1 owner has one car; the quality of that car is a random draw from this distribution (so some owners will be lucky and have good quality cars, some will be unlucky). Each owner decides whether to sell his/her car using the 'supply rule' outlined above (i.e. 'only sell if $p \geq q$'). Say the market price p was ($^1/_2$); then all the cars of quality less than a half would be sold. In terms of the diagram, we could draw a line across the 'car park' at $q = p = (^1/_2)$; all cars to the left of that line would be put up for sale, whilst all cars to the right of it would be kept by their group 1 owners. The probability that a car chosen at random out of the stock of cars will be one of the ones put up for sale is then the area under the distribution between 0 and the price for used cars p. This area can be calculated as 'distance up the vertical axis times distance along the horizontal (up to price p)', which is given as $(^1/_2) \cdot p$. The total supply of used cars put up for sale is then given as '(the probability that a car chosen at random is sold) times (the total stock of cars available for sale)'. Say there are N group 1 traders each with exactly one car; then the probability times stock calculation gives total supply S for $p \leq 2$ as:

$$S = \left(^1/_2\right)p \cdot N.$$

Now consider the average quality of cars supplied. In the diagram, only the cars in the shaded area are put up for sale (these are the ones at the low quality end of the car park). The average quality of these cars, given the market price $p \leq 2$, is indicated on the diagram and given as:

$$\mu = \left(^1/_2\right) \cdot p.$$

This follows because the point $\mu = (^1/_2)p$ on the diagram is halfway between 0 and p; at this point, half the cars put up for sale are of quality less than μ, and half are of quality greater than μ. Hence μ gives the average quality of cars for sale.

Market equilibrium under adverse selection

Given demand and supply determined in this way, where is the (Walrasian) 'supply equals demand' equilibrium?[6] We know that group 2 traders only buy cars if $(^3/_2)\mu \geq p$. We also know that the supply decisions of group 1 are such that $\mu = (^1/_2)p$. For any positive price, it is impossible to satisfy the former condition, without violating the latter equation. Hence there can be no equilibrium at positive prices.

In fact, an equilibrium does exist in this model, and it arises where $p = 0$. The only cars that may be supplied at this price are those with the very lowest quality, $q = 0$. Sellers whose cars have quality $q = 0$ are in fact indifferent about selling at $p = 0$, and buyers are indifferent about buying

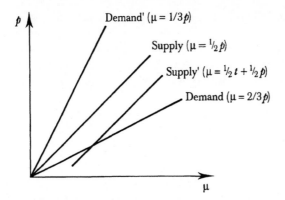

Figure 2.2 Price and quality equilibrium in the used-car market

when $(3/2)\mu = p = 0$. An equilibrium arises when the quantity of cars supplied = quantity demanded at $p = 0$ with $q = \mu = 0$. Given the uniform quality distribution depicted in figure 2.1, we know that the chances of a car having quality of exactly zero are virtually nought anyway (probability $(q \leq (p = 0) = \frac{1}{2}p = 0)$, hence the equilibrium at $p = 0$ results in effectively zero trade (supply = demand = 0).

This outcome is illustrated in figure 2.2 (not drawn to scale). The line $\mu = \frac{1}{2}p$ represents average quality of cars in the market, reflecting the decisions of suppliers. Demand is positive at any point to the *right* of the $\mu = (\frac{2}{3})p$ line, reflecting the decisions of consumers. The zero trade equilibrium arises because for any positive price, the 'supply line' lies always to the *left* of the 'demand line' – the two only cross at the origin.

The underlying logic driving the result is as follows. Sellers want systematically to sell poor quality cars, so if a car is up for sale the buyer reasons 'I want to buy a car, but if you want to sell me this particular car then it can't be very good, so I won't buy it.' Akerlof likens this result to Gresham's Law 'bad money drives out the good'; here bad cars drive good cars out of the market. The logic is also reminiscent of Groucho Marx's famous joke 'I wouldn't join a club that would have me as a member'; and the outcome of zero trade is, of course, also the same.

Market equilibrium under perfect information

Consider, by way of contrast, a perfectly competitive market with fully informed buyers and sellers. Say for simplicity that there are at least as many buyers as sellers. Then for any given car i with quality q_i there is a range of prices $q_i < p_i < 1\frac{1}{2}q_i$, where sellers would be willing to sell and buyers to buy (e.g. if $q_i = 1$, then a price anywhere between 1 and $1\frac{1}{2}$ will do). Hence the entire stock of cars is transferred, at (possibly) different prices for each quality level of car. The cars wind up with those individuals who value them most highly – quite a difference from the outcome under adverse selection!

Discussion

We note below a number of points about Akerlof's model, and about adverse selection problems in general.

1 The first and most obvious point is that the adverse selection problem leads in this case to *total market failure*. The utility functions of the traders are, of course, rather unusual, but one would still expect a properly functioning market to be able to exploit fully the potential gains from trade. The outcome under adverse selection in this case is that none of the gains from trade are realized. Apart from the information problem, this market is perfectly competitive (for example no traders have market power to influence the price). The factor which impedes mutually beneficial trade is the presence of imperfect and asymmetric information. The zero trade solution of the model is Pareto-inefficient; and the source of the inefficiency lies in the information structure.

2 The zero trade solution of the model analysed above is rather special. With a few small amendments, we can easily construct a version of the model so that *positive trade* does in fact take place in equilibrium. Say the utility function of a group 2 trader was $U_2 = M + 3qn$ then the demand rule would be to 'only buy if $3\mu \geq p$'. Since supply decisions yield average quality supplied such that $\mu = (\frac{1}{2})p$ for prices less than 2, then positive prices yield average quality such that both buyers and sellers will, in that case, trade in the market.[7] In terms of figure 2.2, the 'demand line' now becomes $\mu = (\frac{1}{3})p$, and demand is positive at any point to the right of this line; since the 'supply line' $\mu = \frac{1}{2}p$ is indeed to the right of the new demand line, so we can find prices at which buyers and sellers will be willing to trade.

Alternatively, different assumptions about the distribution of car quality could also lead to positive trade equilibria. In particular, Akerlof allows minimum car quality $q = 0$, and this has important (though not immediately obvious) consequences. Say instead that car quality was uniformly distributed between minimum quality level $t > 0$ and maximum quality 2. The uniform density would then be $1/(2 - t)$, and average quality for any given market price would be $\mu = (^1/_2 t + ^1/_2 p)$, defined for $p \geq t$. Demand is positive as long as $(^3/_2)\mu > p$ using the original utility functions. A little manipulation shows that this condition is satisfied as long as $t \leq p < 3t$ which is possible for $p > 0$ since $t > 0$. In terms of figure 2.2, the 'supply line' becomes $\mu = ^1/_2 t + ^1/_2 p$ as indicated, and this lies to the *right* of the original demand line at least for a range of low prices. We can conclude from this that under Akerlof's assumptions (minimum quality = 0) the market unravels completely; but if the worst used car has quality $t > 0$ then we can get the market to potentially 'reravel' (i.e. we can find prices such that the average quality of cars that sellers are willing to supply is high enough for buyers to want to buy them, at those prices).

3   As long as some cars are traded, however, then *it is systematically the poor quality cars that are put up for sale*. Sellers do not put a random sample of cars on the market; they sell if $q \leq p$, i.e. they put a biased (low quality) sample or 'adverse selection' on the market. Hence, even if we manage to get some trade, only the lower quality cars get traded. This really is a 'market for lemons'.

This brings us back to the point made in the introduction about the low price of second hand cars (issues of warranties etc. aside). When dealers sell *new* cars from their showrooms, they do not keep the good cars supplied from the manufacturer for themselves, and just sell the bad ones (they may not even know if a specific car is good or bad). When buying new, therefore, the consumer is just as likely to get an above average quality car as a below average one. Hence new cars sell for a market price that reflects the average quality of all new cars (good and bad). There is no 'biased sample' or 'adverse selection' in the market for new cars.

It is only in the second hand market that sellers become selective about which cars to keep and which to sell. The market price in this market then reflects the average quality of cars put up for sale, i.e. the average quality of the 'lemons'. Since the average quality of lemons is obviously less than the average quality of all cars, so the price on the second hand market is dramatically less than on the new market.

This argument may be illustrated in terms of the model, as follows. Say sellers *cannot* observe the quality of their car, and hence cannot be (quality) selective in their supply decision. Their expected utility would be

$$EU_1 = M + E(q)n = M + \mu n$$

where average quality is now a random draw from the distribution of all used cars and so takes the value $\mu = 1$. Substituting in $\mu = 1$ and the budget constraint yields

$$EU_1 = y_1 + (1 - p)n$$

and expected utility maximization dictates 'only sell if $p \geq 1$'. Compare this with the demand rule for group 2 'only buy if $3/2\mu \geq p$', which with $\mu = 1$ now reads as 'only buy if $p \leq 3/2$'. Suppose for simplicity that there are at least as many potential buyers as sellers. Then the whole stock gets sold at a price satisfying:

$$1 < p < 1\tfrac{1}{2}.$$

This solution tells us that *without* adverse selection, we get positive prices (and sales). Our earlier analysis showed that *with* adverse selection we get $p = 0$. Hence adverse selection causes the market price to fall.

4   Another way of thinking about the problem, which is in the 'spirit' (if not the letter) of the model, turns on the idea of *arbitrage*. Consider what could happen if prices were not lower on the used car market. Then the buyer of a new car which turned out to be a lemon could put that car on the used-car market and get the same price for it as for a new car. Having sold his lemon, he could go back to buy another new car, and keep that car if it turned out to be in perfect condition, or else sell it. In principle, he could keep doing this, until he eventually got himself a top quality new car. In the presence of asymmetric quality information, therefore, if the price of used cars was the same as new cars then there would be arbitrage opportunities of this kind which traders could exploit until used car prices are indeed driven below those of new cars.

5   One could criticize the analysis on the grounds that there are characteristics of used cars that are in reality observable to the buyer, e.g. the age and model of the car. Hence we get different prices for 3-year-old Ford Escorts as compared to 7-year-old Vauxhall Cavaliers. In principle, this need not undermine the validity of Akerlof's argument, however, since *a 'market for lemons' can exist within each market segment*. Thus there are good quality 3-year-old Escorts, and bad quality ones; if buyers cannot tell them apart, then the bad quality ones will drive out the good. The basic underlying point driving this conclusion is that the seller almost always knows more about the quality of his car than the prospective buyer.

6   The root of the market failure in Akerlof's model lies in the fact that the *market price plays a dual role*; it determines average quality of cars on the market, *and* it serves to equilibrate the quantity of cars demanded and supplied. This is rather like having to hit two targets with one bullet. Looked at in this light, it is perhaps not surprising that the market functions rather poorly.

7   One aspect of the model which is intuitively attractive is that in equilibrium, *prices are positively correlated with average quality* ($\mu = \frac{1}{2}p$). In Akerlof's model, buyers know average quality. In the 'real world', people often try to *estimate* the likely quality of a good in relation to the price charged for it, on the basis of this positive correlation (this idea is explored further in the paper by Wolinsky (1983)* discussed at the end of chapter 3).

8   One can think of asymmetric information in the market as the cause of an externality. If there were full information and a seller brought a high quality car to the market place, then he would receive the full benefit in terms of a correspondingly high price for his car. Under imperfect information, however, the effect is merely to raise average quality by some tiny amount and hence cause a marginal increase in the prevailing market price for all used cars. The benefits of this accrue to all sellers, not just the seller of the extra high quality car.

9   There are many *other examples* where adverse selection problems arise apart from the used car market. The example of insurance was cited in chapter 1. A further example (discussed in more detail in chapter 3) would be credit markets. Lenders may not know the credit-worthiness of borrowers, and offer loans to all borrowers at the same rate. If so, then they may attract mainly 'bad borrowers', i.e. those most likely to default on the loan.

10   Returning to the example of the used car market, say a seller actually tries to sell a good quality car in the second hand market; a potential buyer cannot observe its quality and hence will only pay the same price for that car as for any other in the second hand market. The seller might try saying 'this is honestly a very good car so it is worth a bit more', but why should the buyer believe him – after all, it is in every seller's interests to say this whether or not it is true. The buyer cannot distinguish which sellers are telling the truth from those that are lying. The seller's claim lacks *credibility*.

Under certain circumstances, it may be possible to overcome or at least alleviate the information problems. The heart of the problem lies in the inability of buyers and sellers to contract on quality. The problem would be solved if buyers had recourse to an effective *legal system* to protect them from fraudulent sales; then if they found the car they had bought was of poorer quality than that which was claimed, they could take the seller to court. The difficulty with this solution, of course, is that in reality it may be difficult to prove in court that you had been mislead. Alternatively, some sort of *regulation*, e.g. in the form of quality standards, might alleviate the problem (see chapter 4).

A further possibility is that if trade is repeated in the market then sellers may be able to build a *reputation* for selling good quality goods, and hence be able to price accordingly (this does not happen in the Akerlof model, since buyers and sellers are anonymous and trade only occurs for one period). We shall discuss this issue in the 'guide to further literature' at the end of the next chapter, and in the experimental work presented in chapter 4. Finally, there may be some credible way of informing the buyer about quality, and this might well reflect one of the roles played by warranties. Say a seller offers some kind of warranty which says 'I'll pay for the repair of any defects observed over the next year' – then the buyer may reason 'sellers of lemons are unlikely to offer warranties, so this car is probably good quality'. The message is made credible because the costs of repair are likely to accumulate to greater amounts for a seller of lemons than for a seller of good cars. This kind of argument is an example of *'signalling'* where the seller can transmit potentially credible messages, and it is the subject of the next part of this book. For the time being, though, we have a couple of other chapters to get through before we can look at these sorts of arguments in depth.

NOTES

1   When a potential buyer cannot tell quality purely by inspecting a good, such goods are sometimes called 'experience goods'.
2   Traders are implicitly assumed to be risk-neutral and to have a constant marginal rate of substitution between car quality and other goods. These assumptions make it easier to highlight the adverse selection process in the model.
3   For simplicity we assume that all potential traders can engage in at most one trade in the market. Potential buyers choose whether or not to buy one car, and potential sellers choose whether or not to sell their (one) car.
4   The assumption that buyers know the average quality of cars available in the market place amounts to assuming 'rational expectations', as discussed in chapter 1; buyers do not make systematic mistakes in estimating values for variables over which they have imperfect information, at least in equilibrium.

5   We assume that individuals can afford to buy used cars, i.e. that $y_2 > p$.
6   We use the Walrasian equilibrium concept on the assumption that the numbers of group 1 and group 2 traders are both very large. Under these circumstances, Walrasian equilibrium corresponds to the game-theoretic concept of Nash equilibrium; each buyer and each seller makes a choice which is a 'best response' to the choices of all other buyers and sellers.
7   For example, say the price was 1, then average quality supplied would be $\mu = \frac{1}{2}$. Group 2 buy cars if $3\mu \geq p$ and with $\mu = \frac{1}{2}$ and $p = 1$, this condition is satisfied and demand is now positive. The intuition is that if potential buyers want used cars badly enough, then they will still buy even though they know that most used cars for sale are lemons.

Finally, we might note that if we were to use a more general utility function for group 2 of the form $U_2 = M + \beta qn$, then positive trade occurs for any $\beta > 2$ (we used the case $\beta = 3$ in the main text). This is because the condition for group 2 to buy (given this utility function) is $\beta\mu \geq p$ and this is true for $\beta > 2$ since $\mu = (\frac{1}{2})p$.

Appendix: Comparison with Akerlof

In the version of the model presented here, potential sellers own one car and decide whether or not to sell it, whilst potential buyers own no cars and decide whether or not to buy one. In Akerlof's original version, both groups of traders could own (and get utility from) several cars. He assumed a constant marginal rate of substitution between consumption of used cars (of given actual or expected quality) and other goods. The consequence of this difference is that (a) Akerlof had to model the demand for used cars by group 1 (we dispense with that piece of analysis), and (b) his formulation lead to corner solutions where people either devoted all their income to used cars or none (our version is more intuitive in that people potentially devote only a fraction of their income to used cars). Finally, our formulation is convenient in that it fits more easily with the Wilson (1979) model given in the next chapter.

CHAPTER 3

Adverse Selection: The Wilson Model

Akerlof (1970) made specific assumptions in his model of adverse selection, in particular about the tastes of buyers and sellers and about the quality distribution of the good. We have argued that this approach is valid in so far as Akerlof is able to make good points and valuable insights within this framework. Wilson (1979, 1980*) showed that there are further valuable and interesting insights to be gained by relaxing some of these assumptions. Wilson's analysis does not undermine the main results to emerge from Akerlof. He was able to show however, that when (i) buyers differ in their preferences and (ii) the quality distribution of used cars might be other than uniform, then the following *further* results obtained:

(a) There may be *several* different points at which supply and demand are equalised (i.e. there may be multiple Walrasian equilibria).

(b) These equilibria can be *ranked* using the Pareto criterion. Contrary to conventional intuition, Wilson showed that all traders prefer the *highest price* equilibrium (a rather surprising result, since we normally think of buyers preferring to trade at lower prices).

(c) Even at the highest price equilibrium, all traders may prefer the price to go still higher; that is, they may prefer to trade at prices where supply and demand are not equal. In the absence of a Walrasian auctioneer to guide the market to a point of market clearing, therefore, competitive pressures may not generate a 'supply equals demand' solution in these markets.

In sum then, Wilson shows that the presence of adverse selection can destroy many of our conventional ideas about the way markets operate.

At the end of the chapter we give a guide to further developments in the literature on the theory of adverse selection, going beyond the Akerlof and Wilson studies.

The Wilson Model

There is a stock of used cars that may potentially be put up for sale. These cars vary from some minimum quality q_1 to some maximum q_2. The distribution of car quality in between these two points is described by a density function $f(q)$.[1] *Owners* of cars (and hence potential sellers) have tastes described (as in the previous chapter) by the utility function:

$$U = M + q \cdot n.$$

They face a budget constraint:

$$Y = M + p \cdot n.$$

The utility maximizing decision rule for potential suppliers is:

'only sell if $p \geq q$'

exactly as in the previous chapter. As a result, both the quantity supplied and the average quality of the supply rise as the price of used cars rises. This is because an increase in price induces the owners of marginally better cars (than those already on the market) to sell.

The preferences of non-owners (and hence potential buyers) are represented by utility function:

$$U = M + t \cdot q \cdot n,$$

where t is the marginal rate of substitution (MRS) of car quality for consumption goods. Non-owners are taken to vary in their value of t: some people have a stronger preference for quality in used cars than others (Akerlof assumed $t = 3/2$ for all buyers). The lowest value of t for any individual in the population is t_1; the highest value is t_2. The remainder lie somewhere between these two points. The higher a person's value of t, the greater their valuation of used cars. The distribution of t between t_1 and t_2 is described by a (continuous) density function $h(t)$.[2] Non-owners face budget constraint $Y = M + p \cdot n$, and hence $M = Y - p \cdot n$, as before. Substituting into the utility function, we get:

$$U = Y + (tq - p)n.$$

Non-owners do not know the quality of a car prior to purchase, all they know is the average quality of cars for sale μ, which depends on price ie $\mu = \mu(p)$.[3] Hence, expected utility (relating to expected quality) is given as

$$E(U) = Y + (t \cdot \mu(p) - p)n.$$

Now, if $t \cdot \mu(p) > p$ then it is worth buying a car (ie setting $n = 1$), since purchase raises expected utility by an amount $(t \cdot \mu(p))$ more than it costs (p); if $t \cdot \mu(p) < p$, then it is not worth buying the car (hence the trader sets $n = 0$); and $t \cdot \mu(p) = p$ then the trader is indifferent. Thus we get the decision rule 'only buy if $t \cdot \mu(p) \geq p$'. This means that an individual non-owner is more likely to buy a car the higher is average quality relative to price in the market, and the higher is that person's valuation of car quality (given by t, the MRS).

Multiple Walrasian equilibria

We know from the analysis of the car owners' decision rule that supply increases with market price, and that the average quality of the cars supplied also rises with market price. What happens to demand as price rises? Non-owners only buy if:

$$t \cdot \mu(p) \geq p.$$

As price rises, so the right-hand side of the inequality (i.e. the price) gets bigger; but the left-hand side gets bigger too, since average quality $(\mu(p))$ rises with price. Say the distribution of used car quality at the current price is such that a small increase in price would bring a large number of extra cars into the market – cars whose quality is higher than those currently for sale. Then that small increase in price could raise average quality quite substantially. Now note the following two conditions.

(a) If average quality rises *more than proportionately* with price over some range (i.e. $\mu(p)$ rises faster than p) then the condition $t \cdot \mu(p) \geq p$ is *more* likely to be satisfied as price rises over that range.[4] Hence the demand curve over that range will be upward sloping.

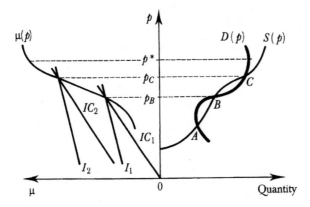

Figure 3.1   The Wilson model: demand and supply/price and quality

In conventional markets, the effects of price changes on demand are considered *holding everything else constant*. In this case, however, the average quality of cars on the market is *not* a constant, and it is this feature which drives the result. Average quality can rise to such an extent in response to a price rise, that demand rises also.

(b)   **If there are enough non-owners who are induced to buy as a result of the price rise, then demand may not merely increase with price, it can increase faster than supply.**[5]

With both these conditions satisfied, we can get a situation such as that depicted in the right-hand panel of figure 3.1 – the demand curve $(D(p))$ rises over a certain range, and intersects with the supply curve $(S(p))$ at three points (ignore the left-hand panel for the time being). Hence we have, in this example, three Walrasian equilibria $(D(p) = S(p))$, given by points A, B and C.

Pareto ranking of the Walrasian equilibria

Compare points B and C in the diagram. Sellers obviously prefer to trade at point C. This is because people who were willing to sell at the lower price of p_B will be even more willing to sell at the higher price p_C – they are getting more money for the same car. As for the extra sellers induced by the high price, they still have the option at p_C of holding on to their cars but have chosen voluntarily to sell at the higher price, and hence must be better off by selling at p_C than not selling at all. Thus,

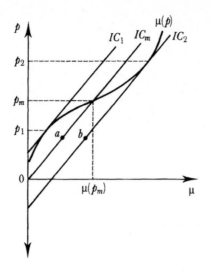

Figure 3.2 Consumer indifference curves and average quality supplied

sellers clearly prefer the high price equilibrium (a similar argument works for equilibrium *A* compared to *B* also). If we can establish that buyers *also* prefer point *C*, then we can say that everyone is better off at *C* than at *B*, and hence that equilibrium *C* ranks higher than *B* on the Pareto criterion.

The argument for buyers is, unfortunately, rather more complicated, and we will need to set up some extra apparatus to establish this. The preferences of a typical potential buyer may be represented in an indifference map of the kind given in figure 3.2 (ignore the $\mu(p)$ curve for the time being). Recall that the expected utility function may be written $E(U) = Y + (t\mu(p) - p) \cdot n$, and assume for the moment that $n = 1$ (the individual buys). This implies that a buyer's indifference curves (in terms of price mapped against average quality) are straight lines with slope t. The curves slope upwards, because as price rises so the buyer needs more quality to compensate. They are straight lines because the buyer's willingness to substitute quality for price does not change as the consumption pattern changes; it is the number t which is fixed for each individual. People prefer to be on indifference curves to the right of the diagram, rather than those to the left. Thus, for example expected utility is higher on IC_2 as compared to IC_m, since a point such as b involves more quality for the same price as compared to a. The value of t varies across individuals. Those with a higher t (and hence higher valuation of used cars) have more steeply sloped indifference curves.[6]

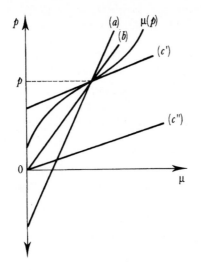

Figure 3.3   Indifference curves and average quality supplied

Figure 3.2 superimposes the relation between average quality and price prevailing in the market ($\mu(p)$) on the indifference map. This shows average quality of cars traded on the market rising with price, reflecting the supply decisions of sellers. If a potential buyer were *not* to buy a used car, then this would leave him at the origin of this diagram – the point where $p = 0$ and quality consumed = 0 (non-purchase). This yields utility consistent with indifference curve IC_m. In order to persuade the potential buyer to enter the market, the price/quality combination would have to make him better off than at IC_m. If the market price were p_1 say (and average quality $\mu(p_1)$) then entering the market would leave the buyer on IC_1 – but this involves less utility than IC_m (it lies further *in* than IC_m), and so the individual would not buy. At price p_m, (quality $\mu(p_m)$) the individual would be exactly indifferent between buying or not, since he attains IC_m either way. If price were p_2, however, then purchase would leave the buyer on IC_2, which is preferred to IC_m and hence the individual *would* buy. In general, the buyer will enter the market if doing so puts him on an indifference curve that cuts the vertical axis *below* the origin (and hence lies further *out* than IC_m).

Figure 3.3 illustrates the preferences for a *number* of potential buyers, at some prevailing market price p. Individual (*a*) has a relatively steep indifference curve (high *t*), and will enter the market at price p (since this puts him on an indifference curve that cuts the vertical axis below the origin). Individual (*b*), with somewhat lower value for *t*, is indifferent at this price – this person is a *marginal buyer* (the slightest change in price and/or quality can make up his mind either way). Individual (c) would *not* buy, since purchase leaves him on c' (which cuts the vertical axis *above* the origin) whereas non-purchase puts him on a preferred indifference curve, c''.

Armed with this apparatus, we are now in a position to compare the Walrasian equilibria in the right-hand panel of figure 3.1. The left-hand panel of the same figure depicts the average quality function $\mu(p)$ prevailing in the market,[7] and the indifference curves of some buyers. We shall now compare equilibria B and C from the buyers' point of view (an identical argument holds for the other equilibrium at A compared to B). I_1 gives the indifference curve of a typical (actual) buyer at price p_B. Moving from equilibrium B to C yields an increase in price to p_C which raises average quality, such that this same buyer can now attain indifference curve I_2, which is further out than I_1 (more quality for any given price) and hence yields more utility. Clearly, such a person is better off at equilibrium C than at B.

What about people who did not buy at equilibrium B? IC_1 depicts the indifference curve of a marginal buyer at equilibrium B. The shift to equilibrium C is enough to make this person's mind up – he could attain IC_1 initially, but at the new equilibrium he can achieve higher utility on IC_2 and hence he definitely enters the market. The point is that any person that enters the market voluntarily in the move from B to C must be better off doing so, since the option of non-purchase is still open to them if they wanted to take it. Finally, potential buyers who do not buy at either equilibrium are obviously unaffected by the change, and hence are no worse off.[8]

To summarize then, we know that sellers prefer the high price equilibrium, because they like to sell their cars (of given quality to them) at high prices. The above analysis shows that buyers also prefer the high price equilibrium, because the improved quality of cars in the market more than compensates for the high prices. Thus everyone is better off, and the high price equilibrium ranks above the low price one on the Pareto criterion. If the market happened to settle at a low price equilibrium, that outcome would in a sense, reflect a co-ordination failure. A benign planner could then step in to guide the market to the Pareto dominant high price solution.[9]

Buyers and sellers may prefer prices above market clearing levels

Finally, consider a price such as p^*, which lies above p_C. The corresponding average quality which we call $\mu(p^*)$ may be found by taking a horizontal line across from p^* until it intersects the $\mu(p)$ curve. Once again, buyers attain indifference curves that are further out and hence yield higher utility at this point, as compared to those attained with equilibrium C (this is true as long as $\mu(p)$ rises faster than p, and hence the demand curve keeps rising). Since supply exceeds demand at p^*, it is also true that no buyer is rationed out of a deal at this point. Hence buyers prefer p^* to p_C.

Sellers obviously like the higher price at p^* – the only problem from their point of view is that with supply outstripping demand at this price, some sellers will be rationed out of a deal, i.e. they may get no buyer at all. Sellers face a trade-off as price rises above p_C, therefore, between the higher price of cars sold and the lower probability of getting a sale. Wilson (1979; 1980*) shows that as long as the probability of getting a sale does not fall too much, then sellers also *ex ante* prefer the higher price.[10] For example, say the demand curve kept on rising after p_C and very nearly kept pace with the supply curve – then sellers might enjoy a large increase in price and still be able to sell with very high probability. Given their risk neutrality, it is easy to see that they would accept such a trade-off as worthwhile.

Of all the Walrasian equilibria points (A, B and C) available, we know (from the earlier argument) that C is the most preferred. Now we see that a point of disequilibrium between supply and demand such as at price p^* may be preferred to C (and hence also to A and B) by all traders in the market. Hence, a Walrasian auctioneer that guided the market to a point where supply equals demand may do the market traders no favours. More to the point, if the market happened to be at a point such as at p^* and no Walrasian auctioneer were present, then there is no obvious reason ex ante for buyers and/or sellers to drive the price down to p_C – the market may stay perpetually at a point of excess supply.

Summary

Akerlof demonstrated that when buyers lack information on the quality of specific goods, so (a) the market comes to be dominated by trade in low quality goods, and (b) that potential gains from trade are not fully exploited in a Walrasian equilibrium. Wilson's work must be seen as a development of Akerlof's arguments. He shows that relaxing some of the restrictive assumptions built into Akerlof's model yields further insights into market processes with asymmetric quality information.

Firstly Wilson shows that multiple Walrasian equilibria can arise (in stark contrast to Akerlof, where the equilibrium was unique). The reason for this lies in the (more-or-less) unrestricted distributions of car quality and of buyers tastes used by Wilson. As car prices rise so the average quality of cars supplied rises also, in the normal way. Over some price ranges, there may be relatively large numbers of marginal cars that are added to the stock of cars up for sale, generating very substantial increases in the average quality of cars supplied. Large numbers of potential buyers may be attracted into the market as a result, such that demand increases with price. Given the possibility of upward sloping demand over certain ranges (and downward sloping over other ranges) it is possible for the demand curve to cut the supply curve more than once, and hence we find multiple Walrasian equilibria.

The second point is that where multiple equilibria exist, so the high price equilibria Pareto dominate the low price ones. Sellers prefer the high prices because they get more money for selling the same car. Buyers prefer the high prices because the higher average quality more than compensates for the extra money that they have to pay. With both sides of the market preferring the higher prices, the Pareto criterion yields a clear judgement in favour of the high price equilibrium.

The final point is that all parties might (jointly) prefer the market price to go still higher than the highest price equilibrium. As long as the demand curve is still rising, buyers prefer to pay more because of the higher average quality; sellers may also prefer higher prices, as long as the advantage to them of the generally higher price outweighs the disadvantage of not always finding a buyer for the car they have brought to market. Hence buyers and sellers may prefer to trade at a point of permanent excess supply, rather than see the market return to market clearing levels.

A Guide to Further Theoretical Work on Adverse Selection

Point 1   Credit-rationing

Stiglitz and Weiss (1981)* suggested that one explanation for credit-rationing by lenders (banks, etc.) could be in terms of lemons problems. This kind of observed behaviour is hard to explain in conventional economic theory, where we would expect well-behaved markets to respond to excess demand by raising price until the market 'clears'. But consider a bank that has to lend out money under conditions of limited liability, not knowing exactly the credit worthiness of each borrower. Some borrowers might be low risk in the sense that they want the money for a sound project that yields stable if unexciting returns, hence the chances that they will default on the loan are low. Others might have more speculative projects in mind, however which *could* 'hit the jackpot' and make a fortune but they might just as easily fail. These latter borrowers are high risk; they are 'lemons' in the sense that as far as the bank is concerned they are more likely to default.

Say the bank faces excess demand for loans. If it were to raise its interest rate to 'clear' the market, this may have the unfortunate 'adverse selection effect' of also driving away its low-risk borrowers. Marginal borrowers of this kind (with stable low-return projects) will no longer be viable at the higher interest rate. The high-risk lemons stay, however; if their project fails they will just default on the bank, but they still have an incentive to take out the loan because they might yet 'hit the jackpot' in which case a somewhat higher interest rate is negligible in comparison.

From the bank's point of view, raising the interest rate lowers the 'quality' of its portfolio of borrowers therefore.[11] This unfortunate side-effect of raising rates could well leave the bank worse-off (in the sense that it made more money at low interest rates with high quality loans than at high interest rates with poor quality loans). Hence, it may prefer to respond to the excess demand by credit rationing instead, i.e. keep interest rates where they are (preserving the quality of loans) and simply refuse loans to some customers. This kind of rationing solution may be applicable to many markets with adverse selection problems.

Point 2   Multiple Walrasian equilibria

The paper by **Rose (1993)** bears directly on Wilson's result (outlined above) that multiple Walrasian equilibria can arise. We have seen here that this depends on the demand curve sloping upwards over one or more ranges, and that this in turn depends on the distribution of car quality. Rose analysed the properties of Wilson's model under a *variety of specific distributions for car quality*. Under most 'standard' distributions (e.g. gamma, chi-squared, exponential, log-normal) he used numerical methods to show that the demand curves are, in fact, always downward sloping, and hence multiple Walrasian equilibria cannot arise. One prominent exception to this rule was the normal distribution, where he found it was possible at low prices for the demand curve to be upward sloping. Wilson's multiple equilibria result can also, of course, apply if the distribution of car quality is not well-approximated by the 'standard' distributions used by Rose.

Point 3   Reputation effects

This issue was first raised by **Heal (1976)** in a comment on Akerlof's paper (see also Akerlof's (1976) response to Heal). Heal cast the lemons problems in terms of a prisoner's dilemma. Two players (A and B) trade goods with each other. Each agent decides on the quality of good to sell – 'high' or 'low'. It is in the interests of agent A to sell low quality, given the quality agent B sells him, and vice versa. Hence in a standard 'one-shot game' (i.e. they trade once only), the Nash equilibrium is for both to sell low quality – even though they jointly prefer to trade high quality. This is equivalent to the outcome where both prisoners confess in standard game theory. As Heal points out, however, in an infinitely repeated game (i.e. they trade with each other again and again *ad infinitum*) it is possible for the co-operative outcome (both A and B sell high quality) to be a Nash equilibrium, as long as the agents do not discount the future too heavily. (This argument seems broadly consistent with the experimental results on reputation effects discussed in the next chapter.) The theory of reputation effects in prisoners dilemma games has since been extensively analysed, see in particular Kreps *et al.* (1982)*.

Point 4   Maintenance expenditure

Kim (1985)* analysed an adverse selection market involving two periods, where a car is new in the first period and used in the second. People can incur maintenance expenditures on the car while new, to improve its quality in the first and second periods – hence the quality of used cars is endogenous. Within this context it is possible for the quality of *traded* used cars to be greater than non-traded cars (contradicting Akerlof). As an illustration of this, consider people who have a very high preference for quality cars. They may be inclined to buy new, maintain the car (to improve its current as well as subsequent performance) and then sell it and buy another new car next period. People with a lower preference for quality in cars may be inclined to buy new, not maintain it to any great degree, but still keep the car when used. Then the quality of cars that are kept may be lower than those that are sold, since they have not been so well maintained.

Point 5   Price signals of product quality

Wolinsky (1983)* looks at cases in between the Akerlof/Wilson extreme of 'no quality information', and the perfectly competitive extreme of complete information. Consumers shop around by visiting firms, and they bear a search cost for each visit, though not in acquiring the (imperfect) quality information on the firm's product when they are there. Some consumers have a greater preference for quality than others, and sellers find it more costly to produce better quality goods. In this context, Wolinsky shows that it is possible in equilibrium for product prices to exactly signal quality (that is, there is an equilibrium in which consumers can tell just by looking at the price of a product what the quality of that specific product will be).

The equilibrium works as follows. Consumers 'shop' by picking a price that they are willing to pay for the product, and sampling firms that charge that price (sampling is one at a time). Consumers form an expectation of the quality of the product from the price charged. A firm could try to 'rip the customers off' by supplying a product of lower quality than expected – but some customers will find them out (via the imperfect information available on product specific quality) and go elsewhere. Hence the firm must weigh the higher margin from supplying low quality against the loss of sales – and in this equilibrium identified by Wolinsky, they will find it most profitable to supply the quality the customer expects.

Wolinsky shows that the equilibrium price of a product is greater than the marginal cost of producing a good of that quality. Firms do not compete prices down to marginal cost (as one would expect under perfect competition), because lowering prices would be interpreted by customers as implying lower quality. The poorer the product specific information available to consumers, in the market, the higher the mark up of price over marginal costs. In the absence of fixed costs, Wolinsky shows that as the product specific quality information gets so good as to approach perfect information, so prices approach marginal costs (the competitive solution); as information gets worse so eventually we approach the 'no trade' solution identified by Akerlof.

Point 6   Lemons in the labour market

Greenwald (1986)* developed a 'lemons-type' model of the labour market. His analysis involved new workers being hired by employers in an 'entry-market'; at this stage employers do not know the specific abilities of each worker, and hence hire all comparable workers at the same wage. After hiring, employers find out which workers are high ability, and they try to retain those workers. Hence, people that change jobs are perceived in the market as 'lemons' – in the same way as used car sellers keep the good cars and sell off the bad ones. Thus, when a worker changes job, (s)he is labelled a lemon, and so the wage rate (price of labour) is low on the 'second hand' labour market. The consequences of this in Greenwald's model are that adverse selection reduces turnover *across* firms in the labour market; further, employers prefer to fill jobs from internal (to the firm) pools of labour, rather than hiring on the second hand market where labour quality is low, and hence turnover *within* firms is high. Greenwald saw adverse selection in this context as potentially explaining the existence of:

(a)   internal labour markets (for the above reason);

(b)   primary and secondary labour markets (the primary labour markets are for able workers who employers wish to keep, characterized by stable job histories and internal career paths; the secondary market is for the 'lemons' who get the bad jobs, unstable job histories, and trade in the 'second hand' market); and

(c)   general human capital accumulation (there is a standard argument that private firms will not invest in the general (or transferable) human capital of their workers, because the investment is lost to the firm when the worker leaves; Greenwald argues that with the presence of adverse selection workers will not leave since they would be perceived as 'lemons' if they did, and hence it becomes worthwhile for the firms to invest in general human capital).

NOTES

1   This density may be interpreted in exactly the same way as the uniform density used by Akerlof (we likened it in chapter 2 to a car park). The only difference here is that the shape of the distribution need not be rectangular as in figure 2.1 – it could take any arbitrary shape one might care to specify. The interpretation in terms of a probability range as the area underneath the density is the same as before.

2   Note that car owners implicitly have a value of $t = 1$. For there to be possible gains from trade, we require that $t_2 > 1$, that is some non-owners value cars more highly than owners.

3   The notation $\mu = \mu(p)$ simply means that average quality is a function of the market price. The form of this function in Akerlof was $\mu = \frac{1}{2}p$; here the

functional form may be different because the stock of used cars need not have the uniform quality distribution assumed by Akerlof.

4   A numerical example might help us here. Say $t = 3/2$ for some individual, and initially we have $p = 1/2$, and $\mu(p) = p^2$. Then $t \cdot \mu(p) = (3/2) \cdot (1/2)^2 = 0.375$ and clearly $t \cdot \mu(p) < p$, hence the decision is not to buy. If price rose to a value of 1, however, then $t \cdot \mu(p) = (3/2) \cdot (1^2) = (3/2)$ and now $t \cdot \mu(p) > p$, so the individual buys at the higher price. Note that because $h(t)$ is a continuous distribution, there will always be *someone* whose demand will increase under the condition (a) in the text, and so market demand must rise (it cannot stay the same).

5   Whether this condition is satisfied or not depends on the distribution of t across the non-owning population (i.e. the form of $h(t)$).

6   That is, the greater a person's valuation of quality in used cars, the more they would be willing to pay in terms of higher prices, for some given increase in quality.

7   Note that between p_B and p_C (for example), average quality rises faster than price, consistent with the upward sloping demand curve.

8   Note that it is impossible for someone to want to *withdraw* from the market in the move from equilibrium B to C. The marginal buyer at C has indifference curve going through the points $(p_C, \mu(p_C))$ and the origin; the only people who definitely do *not* enter the market at C are those with flatter indifference curves than this, such that they go through $(p_C, \mu(p_C))$ and cut the vertical axis above the origin. But such a person would not enter the market at B either, since if we draw their (parallel) indifference curve through $(p_B, \mu(p_B))$ we find that it must cut the vertical axis above the origin also.

9   Game theorists might like to know that in a two-stage game where sellers first announce offer prices and then buyers decide which buyer to buy from (if any), then the pure strategy subgame perfect Nash equilibria yield the highest price competitive equilibrium returns (Mas-Colell et al., 1995, chapter 1.3). The concept of subgame perfection is briefly discussed in the appendix to this book (see p. 254).

10   A sufficient condition for sellers to prefer the higher price is that the difference between the elasticity of supply and the elasticity of demand be less than one.

11   Stiglitz and Weiss (1981)* note that moral hazard problems may also be present, aside from the adverse selection issue described in the text. The idea here is that each borrower may have a range of projects to choose from, where some are higher risk/higher return than others. The bank may be unable to observe the choice made by the borrower (a moral hazard problem). As the banks interest rate changes it is possible that the same group of borrowers may seek loans (i.e. no adverse selection) but each borrower changes their choice of project, thus affecting the quality of the banks loan portfolio.

CHAPTER 4

Lemons Problems:
Experimental Evidence

In the introductory chapter we noted that economists have increasingly turned to using experimental techniques in order to test the predictions of theory. In this chapter we illustrate the experimental approach in relation to the work of Lynch, Miller, Plott and Porter (1986) (henceforth LMPP) on 'lemons' problems. LMPP is not the only experimental study relevant to lemons problems. By concentrating on the LMPP study, however, we hope to introduce readers to experimental techniques, and provide a clear focus for this chapter. Further empirical literature is cited at the end of the chapter, including studies of a non-experimental nature.

It is very difficult to test for adverse selection effects on 'real-world' data, because there are so many unobserved and uncontrolled factors which affect that data. Observations of peoples' behaviour in a controlled environment might, however, tell us if the model is right or not; LMPP pursued this idea in their experiments. Two of the authors (Lynch and Porter) were from the Federal Trade Commission (FTC), and much of the LMPP paper considers lemons problems from a regulatory point of view. They argue that:

> The 'lemons' model itself is of more than academic interest to the FTC. The FTC Staff (1978) explicitly referred to and used this model to argue the merits or lack thereof of . . . the proposed Used Car Rule. The model has also been explicitly involved in various housing warranty cases. Less explicit but quite conscious use of the main theme of this model appeared in the Staff Report on Life Insurance (1979).   (LMPP, p. 251)

Clearly, unsuspecting buyers of used cars, houses etc. can get 'ripped-off' in a lemons framework – they may pay high prices hoping for good quality goods, and be badly disappointed. Worse, they may be seriously misled by the lies of sellers; and in equilibrium *both* buyers and sellers may be worse-off *ex post* as a result of this possibility. These situations may reasonably be regarded as cases where some form of market regulation might be deemed appropriate. Ultimately, LMPP wanted to investigate in their experiments 'under what conditions are regulations penalising deceptive or misleading seller claims, or government mandated disclosures or standards likely to improve market performance?' (LMPP, p. 251).

Designing an Experimental Market

Buyers and sellers traded in fictional goods. Incentives were constructed as follows. Buyers were given 'redemption values' (RVs). After purchasing the 'good', the buyer claimed the RV for that good from the experimenter. Usually, the buyer had to pay a price to the seller for the good – so if the price was x and the RV was y then the buyer made $y - x$ from the deal. This amount $y - x$ is analogous to 'consumer surplus' in economic theory – it is the gain or 'surplus' that the buyer makes from trading in the market. It is in the buyer's interest to trade in the market in a way that gives him/her maximum surplus.

Sellers were in a symmetrical situation. They were given a cost of producing a unit, i.e. an amount they must pay to the experimenter if they decide to 'make' the good. They charge a price to the buyer for the sale of the unit; the excess of this price over the cost represents the 'producer surplus' from the trade, i.e. it is the net return to the seller.

The experiments conducted by LMPP typically involved eight buyers and six sellers. Sellers could supply units that were graded either Super or Regular (i.e. high or low quality).[1] The experimental market consisted of a series of trading periods. Sellers were restricted to supply no more than two units in each period (i.e. two Supers or two Regulars, or one of each). Transactions were conducted in a medium of exchange called francs (these converted into dollars at a rate which yielded average returns to subjects of around $5–7 per hour in the experiments). The constant cost to sellers of 'producing' each Regular was 20 francs, and for each Super it was 120 francs. The redemption values for buyers are given in figure 4.1. Thus, buyers would get 180 francs from the experimenter for the first Regular they bought, 165 for the second, and so on. Given that buyers' RVs exceed sellers' costs there are obviously potential gains from trade to be made. In effect, these gains involve buyers and sellers making money out of the experimenter, through trading with each other.

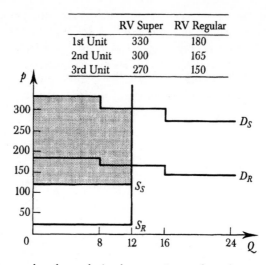

	RV Super	RV Regular
1st Unit	330	180
2nd Unit	300	165
3rd Unit	270	150

Figure 4.1   Demand and supply in the experimental market

Figure 4.1 also plots the demand and supply curves for Supers and Regulars, given the design of the market. With six sellers, each restricted to a maximum sale of two units, the maximum supply is 12 units, and hence the supply curves are vertical at this point. Sellers would only consider supplying Regulars if the price exceeded marginal costs of 20; they would only consider supplying Supers if the price exceeded MC of 120. The maximum price buyers would consider paying for Regulars is 180 (the RV for the first unit); and they would only consider paying this for their first Regular. With eight buyers, the demand curve for Regulars is therefore flat at a price of 180 francs for the first eight units, after which it falls to 165 (the RV for the second Regular) and so on.

If the market operates such that only Supers are traded, then the equilibrium price is 300 francs (and quantity is 12). This yields a total surplus (to buyers and sellers) generated by trade given by the shaded area in the diagram, which may be calculated as:

$$8 \times 330 + 4 \times 300 - 12 \times 120 = 2400 \text{ francs.}$$

This is the amount of money which trade in Supers extracts from the experimenter.

On the other hand, if only Regulars are traded then the equilibrium price is 165 (quantity is 12), and the market surplus can be calculated as 1860. Clearly, the trade in Supers is more beneficial to the market participants, and under full information (where buyers and sellers can immediately recognize Supers and Regulars prior to trade) this is the solution one would expect to observe, in theory.

What would we expect to happen under asymmetric information, where buyers cannot tell whether the good is a Super or a Regular until after they have bought it? For any prevailing market price, sellers have an incentive to make Regulars and supply them at that price, since Regulars are cheaper to produce (i.e. producing and selling Regulars rather than Supers is a dominant strategy). Sellers might actually manage to rip-off buyers once or twice by charging the high price (300 francs) and palming their customers off with Regulars; eventually, however, buyers would in theory realise they are being ripped off and come to expect sellers to supply Regulars. Ultimately, therefore, the 'lemons' model predicts that we are likely to end up at the equilibrium in which Regulars are traded at price 165 (given the demand and supply curves used in this particular experiment). Asymmetric information results in a loss of surplus to traders as compared to the full information solution; the subjects of the experiments do not make as much money out of the experimenter as they might have done.

Organization of the Experiment

The experimental subjects were students at Boston University, at California Institute of Technology and at Pasadena City College. Each experiment lasted around 3 hours and consisted of a series of trading periods. Twenty-one experiments were conducted. The subjects were randomly allocated the role of either buyer or seller.

Initially, the experimenters read out instructions to all the subjects to inform them of the design of the market etc. Those subjects allocated the role of buyers then occupied one room and sellers were taken to another room. Each room had an experimenter in it, and these communicated with each other by Citizens Band (CB) radio. Trading was by 'double auction'. That is, sellers could make offers, which buyers could accept (if they rejected then sellers could progressively lower the asking price); and buyers could also make bids which sellers could accept (if sellers rejected the bids, then buyers could progressively raise the bid price). Sellers could, for example, communicate offers to the experimenter in their room, who would transmit the offer via the CB radio to the experimenter in the buyer's room, who in turn would write the information down on a blackboard. When a buyer wanted to accept some offer, they would

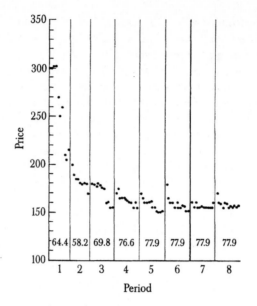

Figure 4.2   Some experimental results (*note*: numbers are market efficiency values)

indicate acceptance to the experimenter, who would radio back to the sellers. Say buyers do not know whether they are getting a Regular or Super – then they find this out after the deal is done (or sometimes at the end of the trading period).

Results

LMPP measured market performance in terms of an 'efficiency index', calculated as the actual earnings of subjects in the market as a percentage of maximum possible earnings. The full information solution given earlier yields 100 per cent efficiency; the 'lemons solution' yields 78 per cent efficiency. Figure 4.2 gives detailed results in terms of prices and efficiency for a typical experimental market (this is LMPP's experiment 1). Buyers did not know the grade of the good being supplied. A few trades initially took place at around the equilibrium price for Supers. Seemingly, the sellers took the high prices but supplied Regulars, and so we see the price tumbling down to around the 165 level consistent with an equilibrium in which Regulars are traded. The market stabilizes at this level.

Market efficiency levels out at the 78 per cent mark, as predicted by the lemons model (ignore periods 7 and 8 for the time being).

These detailed results relate to only one of the 21 experiments LMPP conducted. The average market efficiency for all the markets which traded under these conditions was 72 per cent. Under these circumstances, 399 units were traded and 384 (96 per cent) of these units were Regulars. Average prices were in most cases within 5 francs of that predicted by the lemons model (165 francs) by the fourth period of trading. This looks like pretty convincing evidence in support of the lemons model.

Alternative Treatments: Reputation

LMPP proceeded to investigate the market performance under alternative environments. One idea which they investigated concerned the possibility that reputation might alleviate the lemons problem (some relevant theory on reputation effects is discussed at the end of chapter 3). In the basic treatments discussed above, buyers and sellers traded anonymously (i.e. when offers were transmitted via the CB radio, for example, buyers did not know which individual seller might have made that offer). LMPP therefore ran some experiments where the sellers were given numbers, and buyers could identify sellers by that number. With identification possible, sellers might be able to establish a reputation for selling Supers, and attain the maximum efficiency equilibrium.

In the event, the results of these treatments were unpredictable. For example, in the last two periods of experiment 1, shown in figure 4.2, seller identification was allowed, and clearly it made no difference to the results. In other experiments, traders did seem to be able to improve efficiency over the lemons solution. Also, some of the subjects seemed to establish reputation effects more successfully than others (e.g., those from the California Institute did better than those from the Pasadena College in this respect).

Sellers seemed to encounter two problems in using identification as a means to overcome the lemons problem. Firstly they had to win the confidence of buyers in their 'reputation'. Sellers might have to sell Supers at low prices for a while before buyers were convinced of the sellers' reputation; indeed, on some occasions the buyers seemed suspicious of such behaviour by sellers (the buyer might believe the seller to be irrational or perhaps trying to trap them by selling Regulars at Super prices at some later date). Even after a good reputation was established, however, sellers encountered the second problem of achieving price adjustment – raising the price of Supers to the equilibrium price of 300 francs. Given the potential costs of establishing a reputation and the uncertainty of the reward in terms of higher returns in later trading periods, it is perhaps not surprising that allowing seller identification did not always succeed in overcoming the lemons problem.[2]

LMPP used their experimental markets to investigate the conditions under which reputation effects were most likely to succeed. They found that lowering the difference in marginal cost between Supers and Regulars led to more successful reputation effects (since this reduces the costs the seller has to bear when attempting to establish reputation). Also, the way in which the information on grade of purchase was revealed seemed to matter. in the standard 'lemons experiment' discussed above, individual buyers were informed privately about whether the unit they had bought was a Regular or a Super. Reputation effects worked more successfully (after controlling for differences in the subject pool) however, if this information was made public (such that *all* buyers in the experiments were told the grade of every unit traded).[3]

Alternative Treatments: Advertising

LMPP also looked at the role of advertising in their experiments.[4] In these treatments it was possible for sellers to advertise the quality of the unit for sale. In some treatments the advertisement was optional (sellers could advertise quality if they wanted to) and in other treatments it was mandatory. In addition, in some treatments truthful advertising was 'enforced' – that is, if a seller advertised a Super, then the experimenter would ensure that the unit traded was indeed a Super. In other treatments, however, false advertising was allowed, i.e. sellers could get away with advertising a Super and supplying a Regular.

When truthful advertising was enforced, market efficiency improved dramatically to levels in excess of 95 per cent. This result held up regardless of whether the sellers' identities were known. It also held up regardless of whether advertising was mandatory or optional. Seemingly, sellers take the opportunity of advertising (enforced as truthful) and selling Supers even if they have the option of not advertising at all. The (enforced truthful) advertising is used voluntarily to overcome the information problem in the market; more on this in the next section. From a regulation point of view, however, LMPP interpret this finding to imply that mandatory disclosure of information on quality standards is unnecessary; all that is required to establish 'good' market performance is that where information is provided (e.g. via advertising) that it be monitored for its veracity. Truthful advertising (i.e. monitored effectively by an independent body) serves to overcome the lemon problem.

In treatments where advertising was allowed but was not enforced to be truthful, the outcome reverted to that predicted by the lemons model. In some cases, sellers were able to temporarily mislead buyers about quality by making false claims, but buyers soon learned to ignore such claims. Market efficiency settled down at the 78 per cent consistent with the lemons theory.[5]

The effects of 'false' advertising are not beneficial – but they were not particularly harmful either, in these experiments at least. As LMPP put it:

> People are not misled. They simply dismiss all sellers' claims so that advertising fails to provide effective information which could enhance efficiency. This last finding may provide some insight into the advertising industry's strongly voiced support for the FTC's advertising substantiation program. (LMPP, p. 299)

Summary

This chapter illustrates how experimental markets can be set up and conducted. Buyers preferences are induced via cash incentives in the form of redemption values. Sellers costs are constructed via fees for the units they decide to trade. Incentives on both sides of the market are controlled by the experimenter, and sellers and buyers interact to determine prices and qualities traded under a variety of market environments. The particular study by LMPP investigated the role of information on product quality (part of the market environment) in affecting outcomes.

LMPP's experimental markets confirm the main points of Akerlof's arguments, that when buyers lack specific information on product quality:

(a) it is the lower quality goods that are traded in equilibrium; and

(b) the market fails to exploit fully the potential gains from trade.

They also demonstrate that under certain circumstances, the market failure can be overcome by:

(i)   Allowing sellers to reveal information (e.g. by advertising) backed up by some agency to ensure truth telling. Without the backing of the agency to ensure veracity, this mechanism was useless. But with it, mandatory disclosure of quality information was unnecessary; sellers volunteered the information anyway.

(ii)   Reputation effects: these can work to overcome market failure, but are less reliable than the advertising mechanism. Reputation is more likely to work when the differential in costs of producing better quality goods is small, and when the information on the quality of the good sold is publicly (rather than privately) revealed.

Further Empirical Literature on Adverse Selection

Further experimental evidence

1   The LMPP study was conducted in a 'double auction' context. A further study by **Holt and Sherman (1990)** tested for lemons problems in the context of a *'posted offer' market*. Rather than sellers/buyers announcing offer/bid prices and allowing each to respond to the other (as in a 'double auction'), in a posted offer market sellers place a 'price tag' on the product and buyers shop around choosing which goods they want. Holt and Sherman allowed for many possible quality grades for the good (up to eighteen), rather than just having Regulars and Supers. Sellers costs and buyers redemption values depended on the quality grade. The grade that yielded the maximum trading surplus for buyers and sellers (i.e. extracted the most money from the experimenter) was *not* the highest, making it possible for trade to occur at inefficiently *high* grades. Holt and Sherman (1990) found that when trade was conducted under full information conditions (buyers and sellers could observe quality prior to trade), then 84 per cent of the maximum gains from trade were realized and the average grade of units traded was near the surplus maximizing level. Under asymmetric information conditions (buyers could not observe quality), however, the average grade was inefficiently low and only 46 per cent of the gains from trade were realised.

2   In another study **Plott and Wilde (1982)** constructed experiments on the *market for expert advice*. Say a patient comes to a doctor – the doctor can tell what is wrong with the patient (since (s)he is an 'expert'), but the patient is uninformed; the diagnosis is private information. Suppose there

are two drugs the doctor can recommend; drug X is appropriate for certain illnesses, and drug Y for others. Say, however, that it always pays (i.e. makes more profit for) the doctor to recommend drug Y – would the expert 'rip-off' patients by recommending drug Y regardless of whether it was appropriate? (Similar issues arise in all markets where customers have to rely on expert advice.) Plott and Wilde allowed the uninformed buyer (e.g. the patient) to consult several experts. They found that buyers tended to get several expert opinions, and reject those which deviated from the norm. This behaviour helped buyers to avoid being misled.

'Real-world' evidence

1   The first study to test the lemons hypothesis on real world data was **Bond (1982)** who analysed the *market for used pick-up trucks* in the US. Bond compared the maintenance requirements for trucks bought second hand, against that for trucks that had never been traded. He argued that, if the lemons model was right, the former should require more maintenance on average than the latter, since used trucks are more likely to be lemons. He found that after controlling for observable quality characteristics of the model year and lifetime mileage (things which buyers can be expected to know about before purchase), there was no difference in the maintenance requirement of used and non-traded trucks, contradicting the lemons hypothesis. Bond suggested this might be due to the efficacy of counter-acting institutions (reputation and the like) in overcoming lemons problems. **Pratt and Hoffer (1984)** challenged his empirical analysis; from **Bond's (1984)** response it would appear that the maintenance required for very old trucks (older than 10 years) was indeed greater for used as opposed to non-traded trucks, in line with the lemons model.

2   **Genesove (1993)** performed rather more sophisticated tests, based on the *wholesale used car market* (WUCM). This market was used by car dealers to manage their stock – i.e. they bought and sold cars on this market in order to achieve a balanced 'portfolio' in their stock of cars for sale. Cars were traded very quickly on the market (each car being 'on the block' for about 90 seconds), suggesting that imperfect quality observation was likely to arise. No warranties were provided. Genesove noted that the market consisted of dealers who sometimes traded only in used cars (UCD's), and dealers who traded in both new and used (NCD's). Buyers could observe whether the seller was an NCD or a UCD. Genesove argued that with adverse selection present, the dealer-type (i.e.

UCD or NCD) that traded a higher proportion of their cars in the WUCM would get a higher average price. The underlying argument for this is that if NCD's (say) badly want to get rid of cars on the WUCM, then they will sell off some of their good cars along with the bad; hence the average quality of the cars they sell will be higher, and so the price paid by buyers to NCDs would be higher also. Genesove found some empirical support for this hypothesis.

3 **Gibbons and Katz (1991)** present an empirical application of the lemons model to the *labour market*. They argue that workers that have been laid-off by their employers are more likely to be 'lemons' (and perceived as such by the market) than workers who have been displaced through plant closure, in line with Greenwald (1986)* discussed above. This is because employers get the chance to be selective about who they lay off, whereas in the case of plant closure all workers lose their jobs. To test this idea, they look at the pre- and post-displacement wages of white collar workers. They found that, all other things being equal, workers displaced by lay-off suffered a loss in wages five and a half percentage points greater than workers displaced by plant closure. They also found that laid-off workers suffered longer unemployment spells following displacement. These findings are consistent with the lemons model.

4 In an unusual application, **Greenwald and Glasspiegel (1983)** looked at lemons problems in the *market for slaves*. The argument was that slave-owners were likely to be better informed on the quality of their slaves than potential buyers, and systematically to sell off their poorest quality slaves. Their analysis of the slave market in pre-Civil-War New Orleans suggested that traded slaves may indeed have been 30–40 per cent lower quality than average, and that 'good' slaves were around three times less likely to be traded than 'bad' ones.

5 **Copeland and Galai (1983)** analysed bid–ask spreads in options markets in terms of adverse selection effects. Market-makers in asset markets quote different prices at which they are willing to sell, as compared to those at which they are prepared to buy. The difference between the two (the bid–ask spread) is often greater than one would expect in terms of the usual transaction costs. This phenomenon may reflect an adverse selection problem. Market-makers trade on the basis of their information on the market; they deal with many traders, some of whom may be better informed than them about particular assets (and others may be less well informed). The bid–ask spread must be large enough to cover the likely losses in dealings with better informed traders, as compared to likely profits from deals with less well informed traders.

NOTES

1   Note that in Akerlof (1970) the quality distribution of the *stock* of cars is exogenous, whereas here sellers decide on the quality of goods to produce hence the quality distribution of the stock is endogenous. The important point of similarity, though, is that the quality distribution of cars *traded* is endogenous in both cases.

2   It is perhaps worth noting that LMPP's experiment 1 only allows two periods for reputation effects to work. The subjects did not know exactly when the experiment would end, but presumably had a fair idea that little time was left at this stage. Hence, sellers had very little time to establish a reputation and then benefit from the higher prices, and it is not surprising that they appeared not to even try. In some other experiments, however, seller identity was known from the start, and still the lemons equilibrium was observed.

3   This finding is consistent with the view that the expected returns to the seller of establishing a reputation are greater with public as opposed to private revelation. A publicly established reputation attracts buyers from a wider pool of potential customers.

4   LMPP also provide an interpretation of these experiments in terms of warranties. I shall stick to the advertising interpretation, partly because it is (in my opinion) clearer, but also to avoid the danger of confusion. Mention of the word 'warranties' might suggest a standard signalling game is being played, of the kind hinted at at the end of chapter 2. In fact, the strategic structure of the game is more subtle – see note 5.

5   These results fit in remarkably well with theory. Costless advertising without enforcement of truth-telling is a form of 'cheap-talk'; and given the conflicting interests in these experiments, it is not surprising that in equilibrium no information is conveyed (see chapter 7). Enforcement of truth-telling changes the strategic structure into that of a 'verifiable message game'; and, as we note in chapter 7, the equilibrium here involves a strategy for buyers which is to 'assume the worst'. In this case that means that if a seller advertises the unit as a Super you must believe him (the claim is verifiable); but if he makes no advert then you assume it is a Regular. Sellers respond by supplying Supers, because they cannot make Regulars and pass them off as Supers (they cannot make a false advert, and 'no advert' is interpreted by buyers as meaning that the good is Regular), and because it is more profitable to (truthfully) sell Supers rather than Regulars. Mandatory disclosure of the grade is unnecessary because, by 'assuming the worst', buyers force sellers to volunteer the information ('this is a Super') anyway.

References for Part I

Difficult readings are marked by an asterisk (*).

Akerlof, George (1970), 'The Market for Lemons: Quality Uncertainty and the Market Mechanism', *Quarterly Journal of Economics*, 84, pp. 488–500.

Akerlof, George (1976), 'Reply to Professor Heal', *Quarterly Journal of Economics*, 90, p. 503.

Bond, Eric (1982), 'A Direct Test of the "Lemons" Model: The Market for Used Pick-up Trucks', *American Economic Review*, 72, pp. 836–40.

Bond, Eric (1984), 'Test of the Lemons Model: Reply', *American Economic Review*, 74, pp. 801–4.

Copeland, Thomas and Galai, Dan (1983), 'Information Effects on the Bid–Ask Spread', *Journal of Finance*, 38, pp. 1457–69.

Genesove, David (1993), 'Adverse Selection in the Wholesale Used Car Market', *Journal of Political Economy*, 101, pp. 644–65.

Gibbons, Robert and Katz, Lawrence (1991), 'Layoffs and Lemons', *Journal of Labour Economics*, 9, pp. 351–80.

Greenwald, Bruce (1986),* 'Adverse Selection in the Labour Market', *Review of Economic Studies*, LIII, pp. 325–47.

Greenwald, Bruce and Glasspiegel, Robert (1983), 'Adverse Selection in the Market for Slaves: New Orleans, 1830–1860', *Quarterly Journal of Economics*, 98, pp. 479–99.

Heal, G. (1976), 'Do Bad Products Drive Out Good?', *Quarterly Journal of Economics*, 90, pp. 499–502.

Holt, Charles and Sherman, Roger (1990), 'Advertising and Product Quality in Posted-Offer Experiments', *Economic Inquiry*, 28, pp. 39–56.

Kim, Jae-Cheol (1985),* 'The Market for "Lemons" Reconsidered: A Model of the Used Car Market with Asymmetric Information', *American Economic Review*, 75, pp. 836–43.

Kreps, D., Milgrom, P., Roberts, J. and Wilson, R. (1982),* 'Rational Cooperation in the Finitely Repeated Prisoners' Dilemma', *Journal of Economic Theory*, 27, pp. 245–52.

Lynch, Michael, Miller, Ross, Plott, Charles and Porter, Russell (1986), 'Product Quality, Consumer Information and "Lemons" in Experimental Markets', in P.M. Ippolito and D.T. Scheffman (eds), *Empirical Approaches to Consumer Protection Economics* (Washington, DC: Federal Trade Commission, Bureau of Economics), pp. 251–306.

Mas-Colell, Andrea, Whinston, Michael and Green, Jerry (1995),* *Microeconomic Theory* (Oxford: Oxford University Press).

Plott, Charles and Wilde, Louis (1982), 'Professional Diagnosis vs Self-Diagnosis: An Experimental Investigation of Some Special Features of Markets with Uncertainty', in Vernon Smith (ed.), *Research in Experimental Economics*, vol. 2 (Greenwich, CT: JAI Press), pp. 63–112.

Pratt, Michael and Hoffer, George (1984), 'Test of the Lemons Model: Comment', *American Economic Review*, 74, pp. 798–800.

Rose, Colin (1993), 'Equilibrium and Adverse Selection', *Rand Journal of Economics*, 24, pp. 559–69.

Stiglitz, J. and Weiss, A. (1981),* 'Credit Rationing in Markets with Imperfect Information', *American Economic Review*, 71, pp. 393–409.

Wilson, Charles (1979), 'Equilibrium and Adverse Selection', *American Economic Review*, 69 (papers and proceedings), pp. 313–17.

Wilson, Charles (1980),* 'The Nature of Equilibrium in Markets with Adverse Selection', *Bell Journal of Economics*, 11, pp. 108–30.

Wolinsky, Asher (1983),* 'Prices as Signals of Product Quality', *Review of Economic Studies*, L, pp. 647–58.

Part 2

Signalling

This part of the book deals with situations where it is possible to credibly transmit private information from the informed to the uninformed party via the use of publicly observable 'signals'. A detailed labour market example is set out, where employers cannot observe workers' productivity before hiring them, but they can observe each worker's education level which may act as a signal of productivity. Two versions of 'signalling' are considered. In the standard signalling model the informed party initiates the sequence of events; for example, the worker chooses an education level and employers respond with wage offers. In the alternative version (called 'screening') the uninformed party initiates the sequence of events; for example, employers offer workers a choice of contracts (which name the wage they will offer for a specified education level attained by the worker) and the workers respond by selecting their preferred contract.

CHAPTER 5

Job Market Signalling

Say employers are recruiting workers. Employers assess the likely productivity of each applicant and offer each a corresponding wage. The problem is – how are employers to know which are the good quality workers? Say, in the extreme, all the applicants 'look alike' (that is, the productivity of the worker is private information). Then if it were left up to the applicants, each would claim to be 'high productivity', and employers would end up paying them all the same wage.

This is another adverse selection problem therefore. But now we shall change the story slightly. Say that the job applicants can, in principle, be distinguished in terms of levels of educational attainment. Some might have left school with no qualifications, some might have A levels, some degrees etc. Good quality job applicants might realise that to get a well paid job they need to 'stand out' in the recruitment process, and hence they invest in a high level of education. Employers might then correctly guess that those applicants with higher attainment are likely to be the more productive workers, and offer them the higher wages.

Why don't *all* the job applicants invest in education to the level required in order to get well paid job offers? The answer to this question, and the reason why the education signal might 'work', lies in the premise that there are costs involved in signalling[1] which are greater for the low ability applicants. (This might be because it is harder in some sense for low ability people to 'make the grade' in education, for example.) As a result, low ability applicants may be deterred from investing in education where the high ability ones are not. The presence of differences in signalling costs for workers of different quality makes the signal of 'education' potentially credible. Thus signalling behaviour may serve to generate information for employers as an endogenous market process.

It is also quite possible, however, for signalling to lead to an equilibrium in which *no* information is transmitted in the market. It is even possible in certain circumstances (as we shall see in subsequent chapters) that no equilibrium exists *at all*.

In order to demonstrate these points, however, we need to look at a more rigorous model of signalling behaviour. This part of the book requires very little maths but the *logic* is rather demanding in parts; if you find it heavy going then I recommend you ignore the footnotes in this (and the next) chapter.

Signalling Equilibria

The classic article in this area is Spence (1973). In this chapter we present a slightly revised and reworked version of his model. The heart of the analysis lies in the idea of a signalling equilibrium. The signalling process works as follows:

(1) Job applicants decide on how much education they wish to invest in to signal to employers, and they pay the corresponding signalling cost.

(2) Employers cannot observe each applicant's productivity, but they can observe the signal (i.e. the former is private information to the applicant, the latter is public).[2] They form probabilistic beliefs about the relationship between the observed signal and unobserved productivity, and make wage offers on that basis. After hiring, employers can observe the worker's actual productivity.

Note the 'order of the moves' here. In this story the applicants move first by making their signalling decision; employers then respond with wage offers.

A *signalling equilibrium* arises when:

(a) Job applicants have no incentive to change their signalling decision, given the signalling costs on the one hand and the wage offers available to people with differing education levels on the other. (That is, the signal they have chosen is the one that yields the highest net return available to them.)

(b) The employers (i) make competitive wage offers, and (ii) they find their beliefs are confirmed. 'Competitive wage offers' imply that employers end up making expected normal profit from the transaction.[3] 'Confirmation of beliefs' means that employers interpretation of the signal turns out to be true;[4] for example, if an employer believed that an applicant was high productivity on the basis of the observed signal, then in equilibrium (s)he would find after hiring that this was true (if the beliefs were found to be *false*, then the employer would want to change the wage offer).

A signalling equilibrium as set out above is also a Nash equilibrium, in the language of game theory.[5] This is because each of the players in this 'signalling game' is choosing a strategy which is a 'best response' to the other players' strategies. The applicants are choosing education levels which maximize their net return, given the wages on offer and the signalling costs. Each employer chooses wage offers which maximize profits given their beliefs, the strategies of the other employers, and the signalling decisions of the applicants. In equilibrium, none of the players wants to change their decision, given the decisions of the other people.

A Numerical Example

Now we get down to specifics. The following example serves a very similar purpose to the Akerlof (1970) used car market example. That is, it is not (and is not meant to be) realistic as a model of the labour market, but it makes a point very simply and effectively about the sorts of things that can happen in a market where signalling behaviour is prevalent.

Employers and job applicants are taken to be risk neutral. There are two types of job applicants:

type L: productivity = 1, proportion in the population = q,

type H: productivity = 2, proportion in the population = $1 - q$.

That is, it is just worth it to a firm to pay type L (low ability workers) a wage of 1, and type H (high ability) a wage of 2.[6] By the term 'just worth it' we mean that such wage offers would leave firms making normal profit.

Note that the productivity of each worker is assumed to be fixed; the amount of education they receive, for example, does not affect productivity. This helps to keep the numbers simple, and to focus attention on the signalling role of education; it is not difficult, however, to generalize the model to allow for education to affect productivity (see, for example, Spence, 1974; Kreps, 1990*).

We shall also assume that the returns to any worker who did not accept a job of some kind are so low that no worker would voluntarily choose that option (e.g. their productivity if they just stayed at home was zero). The point here is to avoid any 'lemons' problems; if workers could choose not to accept employment, then firms might receive a 'selective sample' of workers. We wish to avoid that issue here to focus attention on the signalling problem.

We now outline two benchmark cases, with which the signalling solutions can be compared.

(A) *Perfect information*: say employers could observe each worker's productivity. Then they would pay each worker their marginal product, so

type L workers would get a wage = type L productivity = 1,

type H workers would get a wage = type H productivity = 2.

This is the classic solution of traditional economic theory, along the lines of perfect competition.

(B) *Imperfect information, no-signalling*: what would happen if employers could not observe productivity and job applicants could not use signals as a way of informing employers? In these circumstances, the only thing employers can do is to give all applicants the same wage (since all applicants 'look alike'). That wage would be given by the (weighted) average level of productivity of the applicants:

$$w = \left(\text{productivity of type L}\right) \cdot \left(\text{proportion of type L}\right.$$
$$\left.\text{in population}\right) + \left(\text{productivity of type H}\right) \cdot \left(\text{proportion of}\right.$$
$$\left.\text{type H in population}\right)$$
$$= 1 \cdot q + 2 \cdot \left(1 - q\right)$$
$$= 2 - q.$$

The more type Ls there are, the nearer is q to 1, and so the nearer is w to 1. Employers make normal expected profits as a result of this wage offer (that is, they make positive profits if the worker turns out to be type H, negative profits if he is type L, and zero profit on average).

Signalling equilibria: separating solutions

Now we allow workers to signal ability via education. As hinted earlier, there are different kinds of signalling equilibrium. Here we deal with the most famous kind, called separating equilibria for reasons that will become apparent. The equilibrium loosely sketched out in the introduction to this chapter was of this kind.

Suppose educational attainment is measured by some number y. For type L workers, the costs of acquiring education rise one-for-one with the level of attainment, that is $c_L = y$. For type H, signalling costs are $c_H = y/2$, that is it costs type H workers half as much to reach any given level of education as it costs type L. Crucially then, it costs more for low ability workers to send the signal than it costs high ability workers. This is called the 'single crossing property' in the literature, and is a precondition for informative signalling, as noted in the introduction.[7]

Costs to education may be monetary and/or psychic. To calculate the monetary *benefits* to education we turn next to an important part of the signalling equilibrium, concerning employers beliefs. Say employers believed that only applicants with some *particular* level of educational attainment (which we will call y^*) or more are high productivity, and the rest are low productivity. That is, if employers observed an applicant with level of education y which had value $y < y^*$ then they would believe that person to be type L and offer him/her a wage $w = 1$; if they observed an applicant with education y which had a value $y \geq y^*$ then they would believe that person to be type H and offer him/her a wage $w = 2$.

These beliefs generate a wage offer schedule of the kind drawn in figure 5.1. Wage offers vary with education hence we write $w(y)$, that is 'wages as a function of education', where in this case we can see $w(y)$ is a 'step function' (jumping from $w = 1$ to $w = 2$ as education reaches y^*). Superimposed on this wage schedule, we have drawn the signalling cost functions $c_L = y$ for type L, and $c_H = y/2$ for type H.

Remember that the first 'move' or decision to be made in this signalling model comes from the job applicant. He/she must choose an education level given the incentive of a higher wage for higher education on the one hand, and the disincentive of the signalling cost on the other. For both type L and type H individuals there is no point in setting their education at any level other than 0 or y^*; signalling $y = 0$ elicits a wage

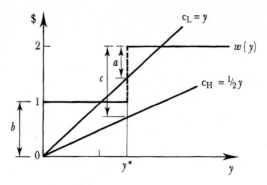

Figure 5.1 A separating equilibrium

offer of $w = 1$; signalling $y = y^*$ elicits a wage offer of $w = 2$. Any other level of the education signal would merely incur signalling costs without any corresponding increase in the wage offer. Both type L and type H workers therefore choose between setting $y = 0$ and setting $y = y^*$ in order to maximize their net return (w – signalling costs).

Consider the situation for type L in the diagram. As we have drawn it, setting education y at the level $y = 0$ yields net return given by distance 'b', whereas setting $y = y^*$ yields net return given by distance 'a'. Since 'a' is less than 'b' we can conclude that it is best for type L people to set $y = 0$, i.e. they do not invest in education. For type H people, however, setting $y = y^*$ yields net return given by distance 'c' (since their signalling costs are lower), whilst $y = 0$ still only yields 'b'. Since 'c' is greater than 'b', it is best for type H people to set $y = y^*$.

Say job applicants signal along these lines, and employers respond with job offers in accordance with their beliefs. Will those beliefs turn out to be confirmed? Employers believed that applicants with $y < y^*$ would all be type L and indeed that is true – the only applicants who have $y < y^*$ actually set $y = 0$, and these are all type L. Employers also believed that applicants with $y \geq y^*$ would all be type H and indeed that is true also – the only applicants who have $y \geq y^*$ actually set $y = y^*$, and these are indeed all type H.[8]

Hence we have satisfied all the conditions for an equilibrium; job applicants are choosing their optimal signal, wages are set at a level equal to expected productivity (implying normal profits), and employers' beliefs are confirmed. This equilibrium holds given the way the diagram is drawn, but in general what are the circumstances under which an equilibrium of this kind holds? To answer this we must find out under what circumstances type L people set $y = 0$, and under what circumstances type

H people set $y = y^*$.[9] The conditions for this are given by the following two 'self-selection constraints':

type L people set $y = 0$ if $w(y = 0) \geq w(y = y^*) - c_L(y = y^*)$

that is,

$1 \geq 2 - y^*$

which implies

$y^* \geq 1$ (5.1)

Type H people set $y = y^*$ if $w(y = 0) \leq w(y = y^*) - c_H(y = y^*)$, that is

$1 \leq 2 - \tfrac{1}{2}y^*$

which implies

$y^* \leq 2.$ (5.2)

A signalling equilibrium holds given the employers beliefs, as long as $1 \leq y^* \leq 2$. The main features of such an equilibrium are as follows.

1   It is a 'separating equilibrium' in the sense that type L and type H applicants are clearly identified or 'separated out' in the solution. Type L choose $y = 0$ whereas type H choose $y = y^*$. The signal is informative, and the employers reward workers with wages corresponding to productivity.

2   The equilibria are not unique. Any value of y^* between 1 and 2 will sustain the solution, given the employers beliefs – hence there are actually an infinite number of equilibria!

3   The different equilibria can be ranked on the Pareto criterion. The closer is y^* to 2 the worse off are type H people, whilst type L people and employers are unaffected. This is because higher values for y^* involve higher signalling costs to type H workers – they end up having to over-invest in the education signal. Type L still get a wage of 1 and employers get normal profit, however, for any y^* between 1 and 2. The equilibrium that yields the Pareto-efficient (separating) outcome (i.e. that which is a Pareto improvement on any other of these separating equilibria) is where $y^* = 1$, since here signalling costs are at the minimum level necessary to separate out the two types of applicants, given the imperfect information in the market.

4   The results do not depend on the proportion of low productivity workers in the population (i.e. q). There could be just a handful of poor workers (q small) and the vast majority of good workers would still incur signalling costs to distinguish themselves from that handful, in this equilibrium.

5   The full information solution outlined above (case (A)) Pareto-dominates all the imperfect information separating equilibria. This is because the wages received by each worker are the same under full information as under (imperfect information) separation; but in the former case no signalling costs are incurred at all (equivalent to everyone setting $y = 0$), whereas in the latter case type H workers must set education at least to level $y = 1$.

6   The 'no-signalling' benchmark case outlined above (case (B)) can also Pareto-dominate some of the separating equilibria. To see this, note the following.

Type L workers are better off with no-signalling: recall that with no-signalling, all applicants get wage $w = 2 - q$. By comparison, in the separating equilibria identified above, type L applicants get $w = 1$ and pay no signalling cost. Clearly, as long as $q < 1$ (there are some type Ls in the population) then the no-signalling wage $w = 2 - q$ is better than a wage of 1, and hence we can conclude that type L would prefer the no-signalling outcome. The reason for this is that in the separating equilibria they get paid their marginal product of 1, but with no-signalling they get a bit more than that because employers think they might be type H (high ability).

Type H workers can be better off with no-signalling: in the separating equilibrium, type H workers' net return (wage minus signalling cost) is $2 - y^*/2$. For them to be better off with no-signalling means the following has to hold:

$$2 - q > 2 - y^*/2$$

which rearranges to yield

$$y^* > 2q$$

For example, say q (the proportion of type Ls in the population) is equal to $\frac{1}{2}$; then if $y^* > 1$, so high ability workers would prefer the no-signalling equilibrium. The intuition for this is that although high ability workers get a higher wage in the separating equilibria, they also pay signalling costs which can outweigh the higher wage.

Employers are indifferent: they make expected profit of zero (normal profit) in all equilibria.

Thus we can conclude that the no-signalling outcome Pareto-dominates many separating equilibria. Once the players are *in* a separating equilibria, however, there is nothing any one person can do unilaterally to 'get back' to the no-signalling case.

7   Education results in negative externalities, in the sense that the marginal private benefit may be positive (that is why type H people invest in it), but the marginal social benefit is always zero since it does not affect the total output of the goods produced in the economy. Education is unproductive, but people still invest in it.

Signalling equilibria: pooling solutions

So far, we have dealt with situations in which the two types of workers end up getting 'separated'. There is a further logical possibility, however, that the workers end up getting 'pooled' – i.e. they send the same signal and get the same wage offer.[10] Can job market signalling generate equilibria in which the workers get pooled in this way? We show here that the answer to this question is 'yes'.

Consider the following example. Say employers held the following probabilistic beliefs:

(i)   If a job applicant has education below y^*
      (s)he is type L for certain.

(ii) If a job applicant has education at level y^* or above,
      (s)he is type L with probability q, and
      (s)he is type H with probability $1 - q$.

That is, employers think that low education means low ability for sure, but when an applicant with high education arrives they think it is possible that applicant is high ability, but they might still be low ability. Given competition amongst employers for workers, the belief (i) above means that all workers with $y < y^*$ get offered a wage $w(y < y^*) = 1$; the belief (ii) means that all workers with $y \geq y^*$ get offered a wage $w(y \geq y^*) = 1q + 2(1 - q) = 2 - q$.

The initial move comes from the workers, who must decide whether to set $y = 0$ or set $y = y^*$ (there is no point in setting education at any other level). Say y^* happened to be rather low (we will be precise in a moment), so that all workers decided to set $y = y^*$. That is, for all workers the following is true:[11]

net return from setting $y = y^* \geq$ net return from setting $y = 0$.

For type L workers, this means:

$$w\left(y = y^*\right) - c_L\left(y^*\right) \geq w\left(y = 0\right)$$

that is

$$2 - q - y^* \geq 1$$

and so

$$1 - q \geq y^*. \tag{5.3}$$

For type H workers, it means:

$$w\left(y = y^*\right) - c_H\left(y^*\right) \geq w\left(y = 0\right)$$

that is

$$2 - q - \tfrac{1}{2}y^* \geq 1$$

and so

$$1 - q \geq \tfrac{1}{2}y^*. \tag{5.4}$$

In fact, if we look at these inequalities we see that inequality (5.4) is redundant – if (5.3) is satisfied then (5.4) will automatically be satisfied also (since y cannot be negative). As long as employers' beliefs are such that the former inequality is satisfied ($1 - q \geq y^*$), then both type L and type H job applicants will set $y = y^*$. This situation is captured in figure 5.2. The wage offer would be 1 for all education levels below y^*, jumping to $2 - q$ for $y \geq y^*$, consistent with employers' beliefs. The distance 'a' gives the net return to type L workers at $y = y^*$, and this is clearly more than distance 'b' which is the net return at $y = 0$. The distance 'c' gives the net return to type H workers at $y = y^*$, and this is also more than 'b'.

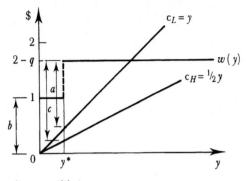

Figure 5.2   A pooling equilibrium

It is in the interests of both worker types to signal $y = y^*$ in this situation. Employers respond by offering all applicants a wage of $2 - q$, consistent with their prior probabilistic beliefs. Are the beliefs confirmed? Belief (i) above is never wrong, since no workers set $y < y^*$ and hence this belief is never tested. Belief (ii) above is shown to be right at least in so far as observing applicants with $y = y^*$ employers will find that such workers are type L with probability q, as expected. This is because all workers set $y = y^*$ so the probability that any individual worker will turn out to be type L is the same as that from a random draw from the population, and the proportion of type L workers in the population is exactly q. Employers beliefs are confirmed. Furthermore, they make normal expected profits since wage offers equal productivity on average. Hence, we can conclude that we have an equilibrium in which workers are pooled, each sending the same signal (y^*) and receiving the same wage $2 - q$.

We said earlier that y^* had to be 'low' for this to work. By this we meant that inequality (5.3) above

$$1 - q \geq y^*$$

had to hold. So if $q = \frac{1}{2}$ for example (half the population is type L, the other half is type H), then y^* would have to be no more than a half.

Say y^* was actually fixed at a value of $y^* = 0$ (which trivially satisfies $1 - q \geq y^*$). Then the outcome would exactly reproduce the 'no signalling benchmark' case – all workers receive the same wage $w = 2 - q$, and no signalling costs are incurred. However, it is also possible to have $y^* > 0$ and still satisfy the condition $1 - q \geq y^*$. In this event, it is individually rational for workers to pay the signalling costs, and yet overall no one benefits. Workers still get a wage $2 - q$ which is exactly what they would have got in the absence of signalling, but they suffer the 'pain' of getting education (i.e. pay the costs). And in this case, no useful information is transmitted to the employers by the signal. The employers' beliefs are confirmed but the signal is completely useless, since all workers invest in it to the same level and hence it yields no power for distinguishing between good and bad applicants. The employers are quite literally no better informed than they would have been if the signal had not existed.

Overall then, the example set out above has the following properties:

1   It yields 'pooling equilibria', in the sense that all workers send the same signal y^* and get the same wage ($w = 2 - q$). Type L workers successfully mimic the behaviour of the type Hs by sending the same signal, degrading the information content of the signal until it is as worthless as the verbal assurance of the used car seller who says his car is good quality. The signal is uninformative.

2   The equilibria are not unique. Any value of y^* between 0 and $1 - q$ will do to sustain the solution, given the employers' beliefs. Thus there are an infinite number of these pooling equilibrium, as well as the infinite number of separating equilibria identified earlier.

3   The different equilibria are once again not equivalent from a welfare point of view. Higher values of y^* impose costs on both types of workers, without making anyone better off – hence equilibria with y^* closer to $1 - q$ are Pareto-inferior to those with y^* closer to 0.

4   The equilibrium does depend on the proportion of low productivity workers in the population (q). For example, the pooling wage w will be higher, the fewer such workers there are in the population. However, for any value of q such that $0 < q < 1$, a set of pooling equilibria can be found.

5   The full information solution (case (A)) does *not* Pareto-dominate the (imperfect information) pooling equilibria, and vice versa. Type L workers are better off under pooling; they get $2 - q - y^*$ which is at least as much as their full information return of 1 (given that $1 - q \geq y^*$). Type H workers are worse off under pooling; they get $2 - q - \frac{1}{2}y^*$ which is less than their full information return of 2.

6   The no-signalling benchmark (case (B)) (quite obviously) Pareto-dominates the pooling equilibria for any $y^* > 0$. Workers get the same wage $w = 2 - q$ in either case, but with pooling equilibria they have to pay signalling costs and if these are positive ($y^* > 0$) that leaves them worse off than with no-signalling.

7   Once again there is a divergence between the social and the private benefit to education. In this case, however, (unlike in the 'separating' case above) education does not even convey useful information to the employers.

Refinements – Which Equilibrium is 'Right'?

The reader might care to reflect on how we manage to generate so many different solutions for such a simple problem; solutions that vary both qualitatively (some yield 'pooling' others 'separating') and quantitatively (different y^* values). The reason for this lies in the role of employers' beliefs. Different sorts of beliefs can lead to different sorts of outcomes. It is emphatically *not true* that *any* belief can be consistent with equilibrium (say employers believed all workers were type H regardless of the signal, then they would find out otherwise as soon as they hired a type L worker). The sorts of beliefs that can arise in equilibrium are constrained by the fact that they must be consistent with signalling behaviour. Nevertheless, there is still a great deal of room left for manoeuvre, within these constraints.

From one point of view the multiplicity of equilibria that arise in this context seems quite an interesting result, in that it suggests that introducing imperfect information into economic models can have richly varied effects. In the final analysis, however, we are left without much of an idea as to what will happen – and a good theory ought to give predictions as to what is likely to happen and what is not.

In these circumstances it is worth asking whether there is any way of choosing some of the equilibria as being 'more likely' than others. Ideally, it would be nice to have some general rule or criterion with which to choose between equilibria. This is what game theorists call looking for 'refinements' – i.e. using some criterion to select some equilibria as plausible and reject others as implausible.

Most of the standard criteria for refinements existing in the armoury available to game theorists actually turn out to have little or no power in the context of signalling games (that is, most or all of the signalling equilibria turn out to satisfy these criteria and hence we are left with almost as many equilibria as we started with). Academics have therefore ended up looking for refinements that are 'tailor-made' for the signalling models, and a number of these have been proposed. One of the strongest and best known refinements is the 'intuitive criterion' proposed by Cho and Kreps (1987)*.

This material is rather advanced and we cannot do justice to it here (see Kreps, 1990*; Gibbons, 1992*) for more advanced discussion). Broadly speaking, however, these refinements place stronger constraints on the employers' beliefs. In the analysis so far, employers' beliefs could be pretty daft and still support an equilibrium. Refinements select those equilibria that are supported by employers beliefs that seem *a priori* 'sensible', and reject those where the beliefs appear silly.

In particular, refinements in the job market signalling context relate to employers' interpretation of (i.e. their beliefs about) signals that are *not* sent in equilibrium. Consider for example a separating equilibrium as above, where employers observe applicants who either arrive with $y = 0$ or $y = y^*$, where $y^* > 1$. How then would they react if they unexpectedly encountered an applicant with education y' such that $1 < y' < y^*$, i.e. a signal they do not normally observe in the equilibrium?

In terms of the equilibrium specified above, employers would believe that applicant is low ability. Cho and Kreps (1987) suggest, however, that employers may be more sophisticated, and think as follows:

> The most any worker can conceivably get as reward for signalling y' is a wage of 2. If he were *low* productivity that would leave him with a net payoff of $2 - y'$, but that is *less* than their current equilibrium payoff of a wage of 1; that is, $2 - y' < 1$ since $y' > 1$. If he were *high* productivity then signalling y' and receiving the highest possible wage of 2 would leave him with net payoff $2 - \frac{1}{2}y'$ which is *more* than his current equilibrium payoff of $2 - \frac{1}{2}y^*$; that is $2 - \frac{1}{2}y' > 2 - \frac{1}{2}y^*$ since $y' < y^*$. Hence low productivity workers cannot conceivably benefit from signalling y', whereas high productivity workers can. Hence I will take it that this worker is high productivity and offer a wage of 2.

High productivity workers would then do best to respond to such sophisticated employers by signalling y' rather than y^*, and the original equilibrium with y^* is undermined. This new equilibrium can then in turn be destroyed by signalling y'' such that $1 < y'' < y'$ by the same argument, and so on. The same logic works until the signal for high productivity workers is driven right down to $y = 1$ (while type Ls still set $y = 0$). Of all the separating equilibria identified earlier therefore, only the one where y^* is set at $y^* = 1$ passes Cho and Kreps' 'intuitive criterion'.

None of the *pooling* equilibria survive the 'intuitive criterion'. To see this, say initially that a pooling equilibrium held where workers pooled on a signal y^* (which must satisfy constraints (5.3) and (5.4) set out earlier), then employers unexpectedly encountered an applicant who signalled $y' > 1 > y^*$. By the same logic as above, for a *low productivity* *worker* to have any *possibility* of gaining from sending y' rather than y^*, the following must hold:

$$2 - y' \geq (2 - q) - y^*$$

where $2 - q = w =$ the pooling wage. This implies that $y^* \geq y' - q$ but this conflicts with the original constraint (5.3), since $y' > 1$. Hence there is no conceivable incentive for a low productivity worker to deviate from an original pooling equilibrium in which he/she sent y^* (satisfying (5.3)) by sending y' instead, and sophisticated employers would realize this. For a *high productivity worker* to conceivably benefit from sending y' rather than y^*, the following must hold:

$$2 - \tfrac{1}{2} y' \geq (2 - q) - \tfrac{1}{2} y^*$$

which implies that $y^* \geq y' - 2q$, which need not conflict with constraints (5.3) and (5.4).[12] Hence, high productivity workers can conceivably gain by sending y' rather than y^*. Sophisticated employers realize this (according to the intuitive criterion), and so conclude that the applicant who sends y' is type H, and reward him/her with a wage of 2. All type Hs would then send y' to gain the higher wage (and higher net return), and the pooling equilibrium is broken. We have already seen that there is but one *separating* equilibrium that passes the intuitive criterion ($y^* = 1$), hence we are left with just this equilibrium as the predicted outcome, on the basis of the refinement. That equilibrium is the Pareto-efficient separating point.[13]

Summary and Conclusions

In the classic Akerlof (1970) model of the used-car market, it was assumed that there was no way of credibly transmitting information from one side of the market to the other. Sometimes this assumption is appropriate, and then Akerlof's model applies (and/or Wilson's model (1979, 1980*)) as discussed in Chapter 3). In other instances, however, signalling mechanisms may exist and the role of these signals needs to be introduced into the model. The classic example of this is job applicants signalling their ability by investing in education. Spence (1973) investigated this idea, and his work (along with numerous subsequent writers) shows that signalling can have rather surprising effects.

Firstly, different kinds of equilibrium can arise. In particular, it is possible in equilibrium that workers of different abilities are 'separated' in the sense that they signal to different levels, and they get different wage offers. But it is also possible that in equilibrium the workers are 'pooled', i.e. they signal to the same level, and they get the same wage offer. In the former case, the education signal succeeds in transmitting information about productivity; in the latter case it fails.

Secondly, even though education may serve no productive role in these models, in the sense that it does not raise total output, still people rationally choose to invest in it. This would suggest that 'just because we observe people investing in education does not mean it raises their abilities – it could just be a costly signalling process'.

Thirdly for each kind of equilibrium there are many different levels of education that may be consistent with equilibrium behaviour. Equilibria with low education Pareto-dominate equilibria with high education, given the kind of equilibrium (separating or pooling).

Signalling creates a potential for deception, whereby the low ability workers might masquerade as high ability; the irony of this is that in either pooling or separating equilibria the people who suffer are *not* those that might be *deceived* (the employers get normal expected profits in equilibrium, whatever happens); rather it is those that may be *imitated* (the high ability types).

The defining characteristic of a job market signalling equilibrium is that it involves a set of beliefs on the part of employers (about the relationship between signals and productivity) which generate wage offers that are consistent with signalling behaviour which ultimately confirm the original beliefs. The large variety of equilibria that can emerge in this situation (in both number and kind) arise because the definition of an equilibrium imposes very little constraint on the beliefs employers might hold. Much of the subsequent literature on signalling has attempted to select some of the signalling equilibria as more likely to hold in reality than others, on the basis that the 'rejected' equilibria involve beliefs which do not appear to be sensible. The strongest refinement yields a unique prediction, which is the Pareto-efficient separating outcome (i.e. the best separating equilibrium attainable, judging by the Pareto criterion, given the presence of imperfect information in the market).

NOTES

1   Many writers use the alternative spelling 'signaling'. We shall stick to the double 'l'.

2   In the Spence model, employers could also observe what he termed 'indices'. The distinction here is that signals are alterable characteristics such as education, i.e. they are things which the job applicant can do something about. Indices are unalterable characteristics like race or gender, i.e. they are things which an applicant has no power to change (at least not usually!) but which are still observable to the employer.

3   More technically, the employers make simultaneous independent wage offers which in equilibrium are driven to the level of the expected productivity of the workers, as in Bertrand competition. The point of this is to make sure that the (profit maximizing) employers have no monopsony power in hiring labour.

4   For the more technically minded reader, the point here is that employers' beliefs have to be consistent with Bayes' rule. This rule is explained in the technical appendix to the book.

5   The more accurate term 'Bayesian–Nash equilibrium' is sometimes used to reflect the importance of Bayes' rule (in relation to employers' beliefs) in the equilibrium.

6   For realism we might say that wages are measured in tens of thousands of dollars, so that a wage of 1 means $10 000, say. An underlying production function that would generate constant marginal = average productivity as used in this example is $Q = 1 \cdot L1 + 2 \cdot L2$ where Q is the value of the firm's output, $L1$ is the input of type L workers, $L2$ is the input of type H.

7   Broadly stated, the single crossing property is that from any given situation it costs more for low quality types to increase the signal than it does for high quality types, whether the signal is a warranty on a used car, education or whatever. Without this property the signal is bound to fail to communicate information, since there would be nothing to prevent low quality types from imitating high quality types in the signals they send.

8   Employers' beliefs at points other than $y = 0$ and $y = y^*$ are not tested, since no applicant chooses $0 < y < y^*$ or $y > y^*$. Hence we could, in fact, sustain the same outcome with very different initial beliefs and wage schedule. Employers might, for example, believe that all applicants with education level y other than y^* were low productivity, and hence offer a wage schedule that was flat at $w = 1$ for all y, except at the single point y^* where it would be $w = 2$. This would elicit exactly the same choices from applicants as those described in the main text.

9   When $y^* = 1$ the net returns for type L workers of setting $y = 0$ are exactly equal to the net returns at $y = y^*$. We use the convention that in this event, type L workers break the 'tie' by selecting $y = 0$. The point of this is that it allows us to identify $y^* = 1$ as the minimum value of y^* that is necessary and sufficient for a separating equilibrium. When $y^* = 2$ we assume type H workers set $y = y^*$.

10   In fact, 'separating' and 'pooling' do not exhaust the logical possibilities. There are also 'semi-pooling' or 'semi-separating' equilibria. For example, type L workers may strictly prefer the low wage offer, but type H may be indifferent between the low wage (low signalling cost), high wage (high

signalling cost) jobs on offer, and choose at random between them (a 'mixed strategy', in the language of game theory). In this sort of solution, employers would know that a job applicant with high education was definitely type H; but if a job applicant arrived with low education then (s)he might turn out to be type L or (s)he might be type H. This sort of situation is discussed in more detail in advanced texts such as Kreps (1990)* or Gibbons (1992)*.

11 Once again, we break the 'tie' where the net returns are exactly equal in both situations ($y = 0$ and $y = y^*$) by employing the convention that workers set $y = y^*$.

12 Say, for example, $q = 0.5$, $y^* = 0.25$ and $y' = 1.1$. The constraints (5.3) and (5.4) for a pooling equilibrium are satisfied. For a type L worker to conceivably gain, we require $y^* \geq y' - q$ which in this case means $0.25 \geq 1.1 - 0.5$, which is false. For a type H worker to conceivably gain, we require $y^* \geq y' - 2q$ which in this case means $0.25 \geq 1.1 - 1$ which is true.

13 The intuitive criterion yields this unique prediction when there are only two types of workers, L and H. Stronger refinements are needed to generate a unique prediction when there are more types (e.g. say there are low, medium and high productivity workers), see Cho and Kreps (1987)*.

CHAPTER 6

Screening: A Self-selection Mechanism

This chapter deals with an approach to the signalling problem that was pioneered by Rothchild and Stiglitz (1976), and has come to be called 'screening'.[1] At the time that Rothchild and Stiglitz (henceforth we will call them RS for short) wrote their paper, the connections between their work and Spence's work were not fully appreciated. Their analysis related to private information in the insurance market (see chapter 7 for more discussion of this example).

It is now understood that beneath the surface, the information problem in the insurance model outlined by RS is in fact *almost* identical to that in Spence's job market model. There is, however, a subtle and implicit difference in the structure of the signalling game used by RS which led them to rather different results as compared to Spence. In this chapter we point out that subtle difference, and use the job market framework set out in the previous chapter to derive the RS result for screening. In this way we hope to highlight the fundamental underlying issues in terms of comparing conventional signalling *à la* Spence with screening *à la* RS.

Equilibrium in Job Market Screening

The underlying information problem we shall deal with here is still the same – employers do not know job applicants productivity. The sequence of moves in a job market model in a screening context is structured as follows.

(1)   Employers offer a 'menu of contracts' for job applicants to consider. Each contract consists of a *pair* (w, y) – that is, each contract names a wage offer for a specified level of education.

(2)   Each job applicant considers the menu of contracts on offer from employers, and chooses that contract which he/she most prefers.

In screening equilibrium the following conditions hold.

(a)   'No contracts being offered in the market make expected losses.' If a contract made a loss on average, then it would be withdrawn.

(b)   'No contract "*outside*" the market makes expected positive profits.' Say there is some feasible contract which is not being offered in the market (i.e., it is 'outside' the market), and which if it were offered would make a profit on average. Then employers would have an incentive to introduce that contract.

Note that one implication of these conditions is that all contracts make exactly zero (normal) expected profits in equilibrium. Contracts that make losses are withdrawn, and contracts that make excess profits attract rival offers until expected profits are competed down to zero.

A crucial difference between signalling and screening lies in the order of the moves. In *Spence-style signalling*, job applicants made the first move by choosing the level of education to signal. Employers then had to interpret that signal in order to make their wage offers; and they interpreted the signals according to their prior beliefs. Employers were, in a sense, constrained in that they could not initiate the signal – they could not, for example, ask applicants to come up with some different level of signal to that which the applicants had chosen. This generated a kind of rigidity in that model in that from the employers' point of view the applicants' signals were pre-set. The system yielded an equilibrium if employers' interpretation of (beliefs about) the pre-set signal turned out to be true.

Under *RS-style screening*, by contrast, the employers choose both the wage and the education level as part of an offer contract, giving them complete freedom as to the sorts of contracts that they can put on the market. The job applicants then respond by choosing their preferred contract, that is they 'self-select' into contracts.

The consequences of this may be seen in relation to the conditions for equilibrium. In Spence-style signalling, employers made expected normal profit. It is quite possible within that framework that there exist other contracts ((w, y) pairs) which would have made money if offered, but which never get introduced. Employers never get the chance to offer them because they merely respond to applicants signals (y) with wage offers (w).

Under RS-screening, however, employers are free to choose whatever wage/education combinations they please, in the form of an offer contract. Competition amongst employers for job applicants then ensures that if a contract makes money so it is offered, if it loses money so it is not. Hence (b) is a condition for equilibrium under screening, but not under conventional signalling – and as we shall see, condition (b) does a lot of work in the forthcoming analysis.[2]

'No Pooling Equilibrium Exists'

Consider figure 6.1. A contract in the screening model may be identified as a *point* on this diagram; each point specifies a pair (w, y), i.e. the wage offer w for the level of education y. Employers can offer any (and as many) such contracts as they like. There is no 'wage-offer schedule' here. Rather, employers offer sets of contracts/points, which applicants choose between.

The 'break-even lines' may be interpreted as follows. The break-even line for type H workers is constructed such that any contract on this line would make exactly zero ('normal') profit if the only workers who took the contract were type H. Any contract *above* the line would make losses by offering a wage which exceeds type H workers productivity of 2. Conversely, a contract below the line makes positive profits (if only type H take it). The break-even line for type Ls is analogously defined, under the assumption that only type Ls take the contract. The 'break-even (pooled)' line is constructed such that any contract on that line makes zero (normal) profit on average if all workers in the population take it. The exact position of this line depends on the proportion q of type L workers in the population. If q is low then the 'break-even (pooled)' line will lie close to that for type H workers; if q is high it will lie close to that for type L.

Is it possible for a single contract to be offered in a screening equilibrium which all the workers take (i.e. a pooling contract)? RS's answer to this question was 'no'. The argument runs as follows. For any pooling contract to form an equilibrium, that contract must lie on the 'break-even (pooled)' line, by equilibrium condition (a). Consider contract A in figure 6.1 by way of example. Now draw one line through point A and parallel to c_L, and another through A and parallel to c_H. Consider any point to the north east of A between these two lines, such as contract B on the

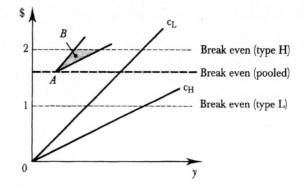

Figure 6.1   Pooling equilibria do not exist

diagram. In comparison with A, B offers a higher wage and demands more education. The increased cost of attaining the higher education is less than the higher wage for type H workers, so they would take B in preference to A. But the reverse is true for type L workers who would be worse-off at B, hence they stick to contract A. Hence the offer of B would 'cream-off' the good workers.

The next question is 'does B make a profit?' If B made a loss, then no employer would want to offer it anyway. But we see that in fact B makes excess (i.e. super-normal) profits in that it attracts only those workers who are high productivity, and it pays them less than their worth of 2 (indeed, any contract in the shaded triangle creams-off the good workers *and* make profits).[3]

Thus contract A does not satisfy condition (b) above and so cannot be a (pooling) equilibrium in a screening model; there is another contract B 'outside' the market which would make profits if offered. The same argument holds for any pooling contract. Using the same logic as that set out above, we will always be able to find another contract around (like B) which separates off the high ability people and makes at least normal profit. Hence we reach the RS result that in a screening model no pooling equilibrium exists.

'If a Separating Equilibrium Exists then it is Unique'

Can the offer of a pair of contracts yield a 'separating equilibrium' in this screening model? Consider the pair of contracts A_H and A_L in figure 6.2.

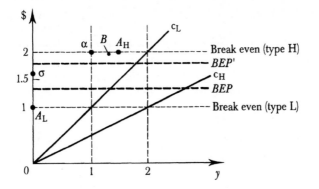

Figure 6.2 A separating equilibrium may exist

This pair is designed to 'separate' the worker types, because type H workers prefer A_H and type L workers prefer A_L (A_H offers higher wages, but the costs of getting education up to the required level are too great for type L workers, since $y > 1$ at A_H). Each contract also breaks even, consistent with equilibrium condition (a); A_H attracts only type H workers and pays them what they are worth, and A_L attracts only type L workers and pays them what they are worth.

The pair of contracts (A_L, A_H) cannot yield an equilibrium, however, because it does not satisfy condition (b). That is, there are other contracts around which would be profitable if offered. To see this, consider contract B in figure 6.2. Type H workers prefer B to A_H because it offers almost the same wage for lower education signalling costs, whilst type L workers would stick with A_L because the signalling costs of reaching B are still high enough to put them off. Thus B attracts only type H workers, and makes profits.

The same argument goes for any contract involving $y > 1$ that is designed to be attractive only to the high ability workers. To be part of an equilibrium, such a contract must lie on the 'break even type H' line. But there will always be another contract around which asks for lower education such that it is attractive to H-types but not L-types, and offer wages infinitesimally less than 2 such that it makes positive profits for the employer. The only contract which cannot be undermined in this way is α (where $w = 2$, $y = 1$), offered alongside A_L. The contract α involves the lowest possible education level that employers can demand of high ability workers, without definitely attracting the low ability workers away from A_L. (Any lower than $y = 1$, and type L workers will want to pool in with type H workers.) And both A_L and α break even.

Do the pair of contracts (A_L, α) yield a (separating) equilibrium? The answer to this question is 'maybe'. Clearly, the pair of contracts (A_L, α) cannot be undermined by any other *separating* contracts. Any other contract that would attract type H workers and not type L (i.e. an alternative to α) would lose money since it would have to offer a wage greater than 2; and any other contract that attracted type L workers and not type H (i.e. an alternative to A_L) would also lose money since it would have to offer a wage greater than 1.

However, it may be possible for the pair of contracts (A_L, α) to be undermined by a *pooling* contract, i.e. one which attracted both types L and H. To see this, note first of all that the net return to type L workers (who take A_L) is the wage of 1; and the net return to type H workers (who take α) is the wage of 2 minus the signalling costs of $c_H(y = 1) = \frac{1}{2}$, leaving $2 - \frac{1}{2} = 1\frac{1}{2}$. Consider now the offer of a contract like σ on the market. The contract σ offers a wage $w \geq 1\frac{1}{2}$, and involves no signalling costs since it asks for zero education. Both type L and type H workers would take it, since the net return of at least $1\frac{1}{2}$ exceeds anything that either type gets with A_L or α (remember α yields exactly $1\frac{1}{2}$ to type H workers). Hence, σ succeeds in pooling the worker types.

The question is 'does σ make profits?' The answer to this question depends on the position of the 'break even (pooled)' line. Say there were more type L workers in the population than type H, so that $q > \frac{1}{2}$; then the 'break even (pooled)' line (defined at $w = 2 - q$) would lie below $1\frac{1}{2}$, as in line *BEP* in figure 6.2. In this case a contract such as σ (which lies above *BEP*) would make losses on average. Pooling would be unprofitable because there are too many low productivity workers in the population. And if contracts like σ (which demand $y = 0$ for a wage $w \geq 1\frac{1}{2}$) are unprofitable so any other pooling contract would also lose money. This is because a pooling contract that asked for $y > 0$ would have to compensate workers for the signalling costs by offering a higher wage and so yielding even lower profits.[4] With $q > \frac{1}{2}$, therefore, the separating pair (A_L, α) cannot be undermined by the offer of a pooling contract. Any contract which managed to pool the worker types would make a loss. Thus condition (b) holds good and the pair (A_L, α) yield a separating equilibrium.

Consider now the case where type H workers predominate in the population, that is $q < \frac{1}{2}$. the break even (pooled) line would lie above $1\frac{1}{2}$, as in *BEP'* in figure 6.2. In this case, a contract like σ not only succeeds in attracting both types of workers, but also makes money, since σ lies below *BEP'* (and hence pays workers less than they are worth on average). In this case the separating pair (A_L, α) can be undermined; condition (b) is not satisfied because we can find other contracts like σ

which would make profits if offered. Thus, no separating equilibrium exists when $q < \frac{1}{2}$. We know that σ itself cannot yield an equilibrium because σ is a pooling contract, and we showed earlier that no pooling equilibrium exists. (The contract σ can itself be undermined by the offer of a contract that creams of the high productivity workers.) With no pooling and no separating equilibrium, we find no equilibrium exists *at all* when $q < \frac{1}{2}$.[5]

In summary, therefore we find that if type L workers predominate in the population ($q > \frac{1}{2}$) then the separating pair (A_L, α) survives and is an equilibrium; but if type H predominates ($q < \frac{1}{2}$) then the pair (A_L, α) are destroyed by the existence of a profitable pooling contract, and no equilibrium exists. Where (A_L, α) do survive, then the equilibrium is unique.

The outcome in this latter case is the same as that found by application of the Cho and Kreps (1987)* refinement of signalling equilibria as set out in chapter 5. That is, type H set $y = 1$ and receive wage $w = 2$; type L set $y = 0$ and receive wage $w = 1$. Separation of the worker types is Pareto-efficient in this case (given the presence of imperfect information) in that the signalling costs imposed on type H are at the minimum level necessary to induce separation ($y = 1$). The outcome is still Pareto-inefficient, however, when compared to full information, since no signalling costs were incurred at all in that case. Finally, we may note that where a screening equilibrium exists, the high ability workers are better off as compared to the benchmark case (chapter 5, case B) where the education screening/signalling device was absent.[6]

Reactive and Anticipatory Equilibria

Some economists have been troubled by the RS result that screening equilibria may not exist, and they have suggested alternative approaches. Riley (1979a)* used an approach based on what he called 'reactive equilibrium'. He argued that pooling contracts like σ in figure 6.2 will not be offered even when they are viable (i.e. $q < \frac{1}{2}$), because employers would realise that if they were to offer σ (which pools both types of workers) then rival employers would offer separating contracts that cream off the best workers away from σ, leaving σ making a loss (in the same way that contract B broke A as a pooling equilibrium in figure 6.1). Hence (A_L, α) would survive as a separating equilibrium.

In general, Riley showed that where employers anticipate the *intro-*

duction of further contracts as a reaction to any contract they might introduce, then the Pareto-efficient separating outcome survives as an equilibrium.

Wilson (1977)* developed yet another approach which he called 'anticipatory equilibrium'. Recall the pooling contract *A* in figure 6.1 – we argued that this cannot be an equilibrium because the offer of a contract like *B* would cream off the good workers and make a profit. Wilson argued, however, that because the offer of *B* would drive contracts like *A* out of business, so it would force *A* to be *withdrawn*; but as soon as *A* goes, the bad workers are left without a contract, and they would have to take *B* for lack of any other option. So *B* ends up with both good and bad workers, rather than creaming off only the good ones, and *B* will go bust (since it offers a wage greater than the workers average productivity of $2 - q$). If employers realize this will happen, then *B* will not be offered, and hence *A* survives as an equilibrium.

In general, Wilson showed that if firms anticipate the *withdrawal* of existing contracts as a reaction to any new contract they might introduce, then a pooling equilibrium always exists (a separating equilibrium may exist also).

Signalling versus Screening

The differences in the results of screening and signalling models are perhaps not quite as dramatic as they might initially seem. Signalling yields many equilibria, but if we are prepared to be selective about which of these is the more likely, then Cho and Kreps tell us that the Pareto-efficient separating equilibrium is the most sensible. Under the RS version of screening, where an equilibrium exists then it is this self-same Pareto-efficient separation that emerges. Thus far the predictions are the same. However, on the one side one might be sceptical of the refinement proposed by Cho and Kreps; and on the other, there may be no RS equilibrium in the screening model.

To the extent that the predictions differ there is an obvious question, which asks: 'which model is "right", signalling or screening?' The answer to this question may sound wimpish, but ultimately it must be 'it depends'. Different market situations involve by their nature different sorts of institutions. In some markets it will be appropriate to assume that the uninformed parties (i.e. the role played by employers in our example) make the first move, and the informed parties (i.e. the role played by job applicants in our example) respond. In these situations, the 'screening' model would appear to be the right one. Certainly this does seem to be the appropriate assumption to make in the RS case of insurance markets – insurance firms offer contracts and customers choose which they want.[7] In other markets it would seem more appropriate to assume that the informed party moves first, and hence the signalling model is 'right'. In the labour market it is arguably more sensible to assume that the applicant first chooses the (education) signal and then employers try to work out the applicants productivity from that signal.

The same point holds also for Riley's and Wilson's variants of the screening model.[8] Say the institutional structure of the market was that employers (the uninformed party) proposed contracts and then, when these offered contracts were made public, they were allowed to *add* further contracts (and if they did, then further contracts could be added, and so on). This kind of market set-up would be consistent with Riley's model, and we would expect his results to apply. If, instead, employers were allowed to propose contracts and then, once these were made public, they could progressively *withdraw* them, then Wilson's model would be applicable.

Summary

In job market *screening* models the employers move first by offering contracts (wage/education pairs); job applicants then self-select into their chosen contract. In *conventional signalling* models, the applicants move first by sending signals (education levels) to employers, who respond by offering wages. In the latter, employers have no control over the level of the signal; they can only interpret the education signal (via beliefs) and offer wages accordingly. In the screening model, however, employers specify *both* the wage and the education level in the contract; they then have an incentive to offer *any* contract on the market that would make profits. This difference means that in a screening equilibrium there are no further contracts that could be introduced to the market that would make profits if offered (condition (b)). In a Spence-style signalling equilibrium, this condition need not apply.

The consequence of this is that the multiple equilibria that arise under conventional signalling are destroyed under screening. No pooling equilibrium exists under screening, because it is always possible to find a profitable separating contract that creams off the good workers. If a separating equilibrium exists then it is unique, and yields exactly the same solution as that identified by Cho and Kreps' refinement of signalling equilibria, i.e. it is the Pareto-efficient separating outcome. But such an equilibrium only exists if low productivity workers predominate in the population ($q > \frac{1}{2}$); otherwise the Pareto-efficient pair can be broken by the offer of a profitable pooling contract, and no screening equilibrium exists at all.

Wilson and Riley have suggested alternative versions of the screening model where equilibria do exist. The appropriateness of the models (i.e. signalling, RS-signalling, Wilson-screening, or Riley-screening) depends on the institutional set-up of the market, which determines the sequence of moves. The question then arises 'what determines the institutional structure of a market?' We shall leave this as an open question in relation to job market processes. In the final part of this book on mechanism design, however, we consider questions of this kind in some alternative settings.

NOTES

1   The term 'screening' was not used by Rothchild and Stiglitz themselves. It is also often used more-or-less interchangeably with the term 'signalling' in the literature. We follow recent precedent (see, for example, Kreps, 1990), however, to use the term 'screening' to refer to the market process identified by Rothchild and Stiglitz.

2   Game theorists might like to know that the order of the moves in the screening game allows us to identify proper subgames. Equilibrium conditions (a) and (b) in the main text then correspond to conditions for subgame perfect equilibria of the screening game (see Kreps, 1990,* p. 694; Mas Colell et al., 1995,* chapter 13). In the Spence signalling game there were no proper subgames, hence all the equilibria were subgame-perfect. See the technical appendix of the book for a brief discussion of subgame perfection.

3   Contract B cannot itself be an equilibrium, since it makes excess profit.

4   A contract offering net return greater than 1 but less than $1\frac{1}{2}$ would only attract type L workers and would lose money because such workers are only worth 1. A contract offering net return less than 1 would attract nobody.

5   Strictly speaking, the RS result on screening in this case is that no *pure* strategy equilibrium exists. There are mixed-strategy equilibria, but they are not very meaningful in this context.

6   Absence of the education device means all workers get $2 - q$. Where a screening equilibrium exists, type H workers get net return 1.5. For type H workers to be better off with no education device, we need $2 - q > 1.5$, that is, $q < \frac{1}{2}$; but we have established in the text that if $q < \frac{1}{2}$ then no screening equilibrium exists.

7   It is difficult to imagine how things could be otherwise in the insurance market. The 'signal' here is customers 'willingness to accept less cover', but customers cannot *initiate* the information transfer process by sending this signal, in the way that workers can by sending the education signal. In the insurance case, the customers can only convey the signal by *responding* to firms' offers with their choice of insurance contract.

8   In a Nash equilibrium, each player plays a best response, holding opponents strategies constant. Superficially, this would appear to be inconsistent with Riley's and Wilson's arguments where players anticipate a *reaction* to a change in their own strategy. Here we alter the structure of the game by introducing specific *sequences* of moves, such that the Riley and Wilson studies do conform with Nash equilibrium.

CHAPTER 7

Further Literature on Signalling Theory

There is now a huge literature on signalling. In this chapter we give a few pointers on the directions subsequent work has taken. In an attempt to organize this literature, we divide this chapter up into two sections. The first section relates to *applications* of the theory to other areas. The next section moves on to extensions of the basic idea to situations that are akin to signalling in that they allow communication between informed and uninformed parties, but the strategic structure is different.

Signalling Theory: Applications

Applications of signalling are too numerous to give an exhaustive list. The following examples are intended to illustrate the flexibility of the basic idea, and its relevance to a wide variety of situations.

Point 1   Biological examples

Signalling is not confined to economic spheres. Evolutionary biologists have noted the role of communication amongst species, e.g. bird song, hackle-raising and tail-wagging in dogs, croaking frogs, etc. All these are signals in the sense that they are intended to convey information from the sender to the receiver.[1] There are clear examples of mimicry amongst certain species, e.g. the appearance of wasps with their yellow and black stripes might signal danger to other species, and hover-flies mimic this appearance; edible insects such as butterflies mimic the appearance of other insects that are distasteful, in order to gain protection for themselves etc. (see Dawkins, 1989, pp. 63–5). There is a strong similarity between such examples and the behaviour of workers in Spence's model. There, low productivity workers have an incentive to mimic high productivity workers by becoming educated to the same level; in some cases the costs of mimicry are too great and the low productivity workers give up the attempt (separating equilibria), whilst in others the mimicry succeeds (pooling equilibria). In the economic sphere, behaviour is driven by incentives, given beliefs. In the biological sphere, it is driven by 'survival of the fittest'; hereditary features (such as evolving black and yellow stripes amongst hover flies) which raise the chances of survival are likely to spread through a population, over time.

An interesting biological example is that of the 'stotting' gazelles, who jump in the air when predators appear. Biologists were puzzled by this behaviour, since a gazelle would seem to be attracting the attention of the predator to itself and away from other gazelles. A signalling explanation due to Zahavi (see **Dawkins, 1989**, p. 171) is that the gazelle is sending the message 'I can jump very high, so I must be fit and healthy, so you will not be able to catch me, so you may as well chase someone else'. By adopting this behaviour the gazelle informs the predator of its type, in a way that advances its own interest in survival. Signalling by jumping up in the air is costly to the healthy gazelle (at least in terms of energy) but it is even more so to unhealthy ones, who presumably find it hard to summon the energy; the latter could try to 'pool in' and mimic healthy gazelles, or else 'separate' and hope that the predator chooses another target.

Point 2   Poker

This can be seen as a complex signalling game (**Binmore, 1992, chapter 12*** gives an analysis). Each player has private information on the quality of his or her own hand, and each sends a publicly observable signal in terms of the stakes they place. A naive approach to the game might be to place low stakes for a bad hand, and high stakes for a good hand; but incentives to mimic can easily confuse the interpretation of the signal. If you have a bad hand you might bluff by placing high stakes, hoping to convince others that your hand is good so that they fold (throw in their hand); but if they call your bluff then you are liable to lose that stake. Interestingly, players with good hands might also try to deceive, by mimicking the signal normally associated with bad hands; by placing a low stake they might tempt others to call rather than fold, hence increasing their winnings from the good hand (this is sometimes called 'sandbagging').

Good poker players usually ensure that the only form of communication they initiate is via their stake (they keep a 'poker face', and 'keep their cards close to their chest'). They tend also to play mixed strategies – e.g. with the very same bad hand they will sometimes bluff and sometimes fold. And it is often said that good poker players tend also to be good at business, where the strategic situations can be quite similar.

Point 3   Entry deterrence

This is an important topic in industrial economics, since one might expect welfare losses to be greater in concentrated (e.g. monopoly) industries that are able to deter new entrants, as compared to equally concentrated industries that are unable to do so. There are many ways in which incumbent firms (i.e. those already established) might be able to deter new entrants, and this is no place to rehearse all the arguments. One particular argument (associated with the work of **Milgrom and Roberts, 1982***) that is of interest here, however, revolves around the idea of imperfect information.

Say an incumbent has a monopoly over a particular market, and a potential entrant is considering setting up a rival establishment. Say the potential entrant does not know whether the incumbent is efficient (has low unit costs) or inefficient (has high unit costs). If the new firm decided to enter and found that the incumbent was actually inefficient, then the entrant would make profits; but if the incumbent turned out to be efficient then the entrant would be unable to compete and would end up making a loss.

Say the (potential) entrant can observe the incumbent's output level prior to the entry decision, though it cannot observe the incumbent's costs. It knows that a low-cost monopolist's profit maximising output in that market is high (Q_H), whilst a high-cost monopolist's profit maximizing output is low (Q_L). Then the entrant might be able to infer the incumbent's type (i.e. high or low cost) from observation of the output level prior to the decision on entry. If the entrant observes Q_L, for example, then the inference might be 'this established firm must be inefficient', and hence the entrant would set-up and expect to make a profit. The observed pre-entry output of the incumbent can be interpreted by the entrant as a signal of the unobserved efficiency of the incumbent.

Now consider the incumbent's decision. An efficient incumbent will produce Q_H. Say, however, that the incumbent happened to be inefficient. Then it could 'separate' by producing low output prior to (the decision on) entry; or it could try to 'pool' by producing high output prior to entry. The former makes maximum profit for an inefficient incumbent in the pre-entry period. The latter strategy is costly (the signalling cost is that it foregoes some profit prior to entry), but it may succeed in 'fooling' the potential entrant into believing it is efficient, and hence stave off entry leading to greater profit in the future.

Consider a pooling equilibrium in which an inefficient incumbent successfully mimics an efficient one by producing high pre-entry output, and deters the potential entrant from coming into the market. Such a successful entry deterring strategy means that consumers lose the benefits which the entrant would have brought, in terms of higher industry output and lower prices.

Point 4   Advertising as information

Firms are selling rival brands of a product. Consumers can only tell the quality of any particular brand *after* they have bought it. The product is also of a kind that is purchased repeatedly. Then costly advertising campaigns may act as a signal of quality (**Nelson, 1974**). The *literal* content of the advert may be meaningless, but the very fact that a firm has engaged in a costly promotion may convey information. The signal may work because sellers of poor quality brands have less to gain from the promotion; customers who have sampled their product once will not buy it again. Hence it is possible to construct a separating equilibrium where only the sellers of high quality brands advertise. Interestingly, the 'single crossing property' in this context relates *not* to differential signalling costs (the cost of an advertising campaign is likely to be the same for all) but to differential *returns*; the low quality firms have less to gain from the campaign.

Point 5   Company profitability, dividends, debt and equity

Say equity investors are poorly informed on the expected profitability of a company. Then numerous authors have argued (e.g. **Bhattacharya, 1979**) that firms may use their *dividend policy* as a signal of their financial strength. This involves signalling costs, partly because there are more tax-efficient ways of distributing money to shareholders and partly because it is costly for firms to raise finance to fulfil dividend commitments. Low profit firms may then find it difficult to match high dividend payments, and hence the more profitable firms can 'separate out' by adopting a generous dividend policy to attract investors. This argument is consistent with the well-documented observation that stock prices rise when companies announce (unanticipated) dividend increases; investors interpret this as a signal of strengthening underlying profitability and hence they buy shares in that company. The implication is that in a signalling equilibrium firms could end up paying *excessive* dividends (i.e. they may over-invest in the signal) in the process.

Similarly, the financial structure of the firm may also be used as a signal of expected profits (e.g. **Leland and Pyle, 1977; Ross, 1977**). Suppose the managers of a firm have preferences such that they like high share prices for their firm and low chances of bankruptcy. Debt finance raises the chances of bankruptcy, but high expected profits reduce it. The managers tend to be better informed about expected profits than equity shareholders. Then managers can use debt as opposed to equity finance to signal high expected profits. Managers of low profit firms would choose equity finance, since debt finance and low expected profits would be too dangerous in inviting bankruptcy. Managers of high profit firms separate out by incurring the signalling cost of risking bankruptcy through debt finance, since this risk is offset by the high expected profit.

This theory predicts that in equilibrium equity investors interpret the issue of debt as signalling strengthening expected profits, causing the share price to rise (the managers' reward for incurring the signalling cost). They interpret issue of equity as signalling weakening profits, causing the share price to fall. Once again, this is in fact a well established empirical pattern, consistent with the signalling model.

Point 6   Insurance (screening)

We noted in chapter 6 that the **Rothchild and Stiglitz (1976)** model of screening was actually developed in relation to an insurance market example. Here we expand on that application a little further.

Say there are two types of customers (potentially) seeking insurance; one type is low risk, the other high risk. Firms operate in a competitive insurance market (such that each makes $\pi = 0$ in equilibrium), but they cannot tell which customers are high risk and which are low when they sign the insurance contract. The firms can offer a menu of contracts, each of which specifies a level of insurance cover for a given premium. Customers choose which contract they want. The 'single crossing property' arises because high risk customers are willing to pay more for insurance than low risk ones, from any given initial state (this follows from expected utility theory; intuitively, the high riskers are more likely to make a claim, and hence will be willing to pay a bit more for the insurance cover).

This situation exactly parallels that described in chapter 6 for the job market model with screening, and the same results follow. Pooling cannot be a (screening) equilibrium, because firms can always cream off the low risk customers by offering a new contract. Pareto-efficient separation *can* be an equilibrium if the proportion of bad riskers in the population is high; if the converse holds then no (screening) equilibrium exists.

Point 7   Age/wage profiles (screening)

Empirical evidence suggests that wage rates increase with age, even after controlling for human capital effects (as productivity increases with experience). **Salop and Salop (1976)** offer an explanation for this in terms of a screening model. Say a firm wants to attract workers who are likely to stay, rather than suffering continual *turnover* in its labour force. Then it offers contracts which provide wages that increase with length of service. Such contracts are likely to be more attractive to 'long-stay' workers than to 'short-stay' workers, who by quitting early would fail to collect the higher wages that come with long service. Hence such contracts serve to screen the population in such a way as to reduce the labour turnover.

Signalling Theory: Developments and Extensions

Cheap talk

Farrell (1995) gives a short but lucid introduction to this area. So far we have looked at costly signalling mechanisms as a means of communicating private information. Signalling costs have been an essential part of the story. Arguably, however, people manage to communicate with each other every day, without incurring any noticeable costs; we talk to each other verbally, as well as using other forms of costless message transmission such as body language. Costless messages such as these are frequently informative and believed.

To be sure, in certain instances costless messages are not enough, and we hear people saying 'talk is cheap', 'actions speak louder than words' etc. In such situations a costly signal is required to convey information, and this is the case in Spence's model where a simple verbal claim (by a worker) to be high productivity will be dismissed as just cheap talk by the employer. The reason that cheap talk conveys no information in Spence's example is that both types of workers want the same response, i.e. they want higher wages.[2]

In many other situations cheap talk can credibly convey information. To take an alternative example, say instead that the two types of workers had different skills, e.g. one type were good managers and the other good computer programmers; both types were equally valuable to an employer, and neither could do (and disliked) the other's work. Then each type of worker might credibly communicate this information by 'cheap talk'. The essential difference with Spence is that there is a common interest here in conveying truthful information. The 'managers' want to be given managerial jobs, and that is where the employer wants to put them; and likewise for the programmers. There is nothing to be gained, and much to lose, from giving false information, and the employer knows this. If a suspicious employer were to say 'prove to me that you are a manager' that person could reply 'why should I lie to you? I want the same outcome as you do'. Cheap talk can yield informative equilibria, when common interests arise.

To understand everyday language and communication as a game of imperfect information would be, of course, a huge and very probably overly ambitious research programme. But there are many specific instances of interest to economists that arguably can fruitfully be analysed in these terms. For example, it has been argued that the monetary policy announcements made by the US Federal Reserve Board can be analysed as part of a cheap talk game (see references in Farrell (1995) for details on this and other examples).

Verifiable messages

Recall the oath that a witness makes in a court of law: they swear to 'tell the truth, the whole truth, and nothing but the truth'. This book is founded on the premise that people are not so honest in real life – they may lie about the quality of their car, or pretend to be high productivity when they are not, etc.

The literature on verifiable messages is a little different, however. It is about situations where people are constrained to tell the truth, because any claims they make can be freely verified, or because the penalties for not doing so are prohibitive. A manufacturer might claim his product meets certain safety or quality standards; consumer groups or legal agents can check this out. A politician tries to back up an argument by citing some historical fact; journalists or opposition politicians can look up the history books and verify it. A university applicant might claim to have made certain grades in an exam; the admissions officer can check out the exam certificates. And so on.

The issue in 'verifiable message games' is not whether the informed party is telling the truth (they *must* do so) but whether they are telling *the whole truth*. The manufacturer's claim about safety standards may be true, but if those standards are very low so *all* products meet them then this is not very informative; and there might be other more stringent standards that the manufacturer conveniently fails to mention and which the product does not meet. The politician's fact may be true, but there might be other facts which he does not cite that are not so favourable to his argument, etc.

Various authors have analysed this sort of situation; our discussion is based on the work of **Milgrom and Roberts (1986)**. Consider first the following situation: there is a decision-maker (DM) who relies on an interested party (IP) for information. The latter makes a verifiable claim to the former, and the former makes a decision on that basis. Then Milgrom and Roberts show that under certain assumptions the DM has a unique equilibrium[3] strategy, which is to (a) 'assume the worst', and (b) make a decision on that basis. The idea here is that in equilibrium a sophisticated DM must view any claims from the IP with extreme scepticism: if a manufacturer claims 'quality is at least x', then the DM must assume 'quality is exactly x'; if a university applicant claims 'I got at least 50 per cent in my exam' the DM must assume they got exactly 50 per cent, etc. In equilibrium, this sceptical attitude will indeed be right, and the decision made on that basis will be the same as that which would arise under full information.

The intuition for this result is fairly straightforward – the IP wants to put himself in the most favourable light, without actually telling a lie. If the university applicant could truthfully claim he got 60 per cent in his exam, then he would make a (verifiable) claim that would leave the DM in no doubt of that. The claim of 'at least 50 per cent' does leave such doubt, implying that the applicant can in fact truthfully claim no more than 50 per cent.

Of course, some DMs may not be so sophisticated – they many naively believe exactly what they are told. In that case, it may pay the interested party to leave some room for doubt (if you claim 'at least 50 per cent', then some sucker may actually believe you might have got 60 per cent). But it is always best for a *sophisticated* DM to 'assume the worst'.

The law gives another nice example. Say a defendant chooses to exercise his right to silence. Then it is often argued that the likely reason for such a refusal is because the defendant has something to hide, suggesting that they are probably guilty. This is equivalent to 'assuming the worst'. The truthful advertising of chapter 4 is another example (see note 5 of that chapter).

As mentioned above, this equilibrium only arises under certain conditions. These conditions include:

(i)   the DM must be sufficiently sophisticated;

(ii) the DM must be informed of the preferences of the IP[4] (if the admissions officer does not know what the applicant is trying to achieve by his claim, then he cannot interpret it);

(iii) the DM must know the factors about which the IP has information (say the applicant failed a second exam, and does not mention this in his claim; if the admissions officer does not know there was another exam then he cannot make the correct inference).

What happens if one or more of these assumptions fails to hold? Milgrom and Roberts show that in the presence of several interested parties with conflicting interests, competition can still yield an equilibrium where the full information decision is reached. Imagine for example a legal contest, where two interested parties have directly opposing interests. If one party neglects to convey a relevant piece of information (since it is unfavourable to them), then the other party will have an incentive to bring it to light, and vice versa. Hence, all decision-relevant information will eventually emerge, and even an unsophisticated DM who may have very little prior information about the IPs preferences can still reach the full information decision. The old maxim 'the truth will out' can apply.

NOTES

1   Many of these examples involve situations where communication is costless. As such they belong to a class of signalling situations called 'cheap-talk games' which we shall discuss later.

2   The implicit cheap talk experiment of chapter 4 also failed to yield informa-

tive outcomes for similar reasons. Sellers of Regulars and sellers of Supers *both* wanted buyers to believe their unit was a Super, to get the higher price – hence the buyer cannot tell them apart, on the basis of the cheap talk message they send. See note 5 of chapter 4.

3 The term 'equilibrium' here actually refers to 'sequential equilibrium' which is a *refinement of* Nash equilibrium (that is, all sequential equilibria are Nash, but the reverse is not true).

4 These preferences must also be monotonic, e.g. the university applicant wants to maximize his chances of acceptance.

CHAPTER 8

Signalling/Screening Behaviour: Experimental Evidence

In this chapter we discuss the methods and results of an experimental study on signalling. In chapter 4 we introduced the idea of using laboratory-style experiments to test the predictions of theories, and we applied it to the theory on adverse selection. Here we do the same for signalling, in relation to the work of Miller and Plott (1985). A guide to further empirical work on signalling, including experimental and non-experimental studies, is given at the end of the chapter.

Clearly, we have had a lot of theory on signalling. The question is, 'what does this theory tell us about how people really behave?' Specifically we want to know:

(i)   If signalling mechanisms are around in some markets, do people use them?

(ii) If so, do they use the mechanisms in such a way that conforms to any kind of signalling equilibrium, of the type we have discussed?

(iii) If so, does signalling lead to equilibria that are pooling, or those that are separating?

(iv) What are the welfare properties of the outcomes? In particular do we observe anything like the Pareto-efficient separating outcome (the unique prediction that survived the Cho and Kreps (1987)* 'intuitive criterion', and the only possible equilibrium under screening).

Miller and Plott attempt to address these issues by setting up controlled laboratory-style experiments, where subjects are faced with choices which allow signalling to take place, and given cash incentives in making their decisions.

The Basic Experimental Market Set Up

The Miller–Plott study is a companion paper to LMPP as discussed in chapter 4 – indeed both these authors contributed to the LMPP study. Miller and Plott (henceforth MP) constructed a signalling market experiment where the 'good' to be traded was graded either Regular (R) or Super (S). Buyers could not observe the grade of the unit. The (potential) signal which sellers could use was the number of 'quality increments' they added onto the units they sold. (These quality add-ons might be thought of as special features such as power steering or overdrive etc. in the purchase of a used car.)

The grade of the good is analogous to worker productivity in Spence's model (Super grade is equivalent to high worker productivity, Regular grade is equivalent to low worker productivity); the 'number of quality add-ons' is equivalent to the level of education; and buyers are the uninformed parties (equivalent to Spence's employers) whilst sellers are the informed party (Spence's workers).

The experiment was designed so that the cost to the seller of adding on such quality increments was greater for units which were Regular grade as compared to units that were Super grade (the 'single crossing property'). Hence a seller might be able to signal that the unit (s)he is selling is really grade Super, by adding on lots of quality increments. A seller of a Regular grade unit might try this too, but since it costs them more to add on the extra quality increments they may eventually decide it is not worth it. Hence there may be separation.

The experiments were conducted on a variety of students from Boston and California. Each experiment had (usually) six sellers and four to six buyers. The experimental markets consisted of a sequence of periods and lasted around 3 hours each. Half the sellers would be designated (by the experimenter) as sellers of Supers, and half as sellers of Regulars. (Each seller would be informed as to whether they were selling Regulars or Supers.) Each seller had two units to sell in each trading period, and they could decide for themselves how many quality increments to add on to these units. They received a pay-off from each unit traded given by

seller pay-off = price – cost.

where the price was struck in bidding between buyers and sellers (see below) and the cost of 'producing' that unit depended on the grade of the unit and how many quality increments they decided to add on to it. The marginal cost of adding quality increments to Regulars was 15 cents, and for Supers it was (usually) 2 cents. Each seller could add on these quality increments as and when they chose, subject to paying the cost for the add-ons.

Buyers could not observe the grade of the unit, but they could observe the number of quality increments. They received a pay-off from each unit traded, given by

buyer pay-off = redemption value – price,

where the redemption value (RV) was the amount paid to the buyer by the experimenter for the purchase of a unit, depending on the grade and number of quality increments. The buyer found out the grade of the unit they had bought (Regular or Super) after the deal was struck.

The RV for a Regular with no add-ons was 50 cents, and for a Super it was $2.50. Adding on quality increments raised these RVs in a non-linear fashion,[1] but Supers were always worth $2 more than Regulars. Trading was by 'double auction', conducted in public. Buyers would tender bids to buy, which specified the price they would buy at and the number of quality increments they wanted at that price (though obviously they could not specify grade). For example a buyer might bid 'B1 bids 50 at $6', meaning buyer 1 bids $6 for a unit with 50 quality increments added on. Sellers responded with offers to sell. Further bids and offers were allowed until a bid or offer was accepted. The experimenter acted as auctioneer in all this, writing the bids and offers on a blackboard.[2] At the end of each trading period buyers found out which of the sellers was actually selling Regulars and which Supers, so that all the market participants could work out how much money they had made so far. The next period of trading would then ensue, with sellers reallocated at random the role of selling either Regulars or Supers, another double auction followed and so on.

In characterizing the market outcomes, MP define an 'excess value' statistic x, given as:

$$x(q) = p(q) - RVR(q)$$

where q is the number of quality increments, p is price, and $RVR(q)$ is the buyers' redemption value for a *Regular* with q quality increments. This statistic tells us the maximum loss a buyer can face if (s)he buys a unit with a given number of quality increments q (since the worst that can happen is that the unit turns out to be of grade Regular rather than Super). If $x(q) > 0$ then buyers are paying a price which is greater than the RV they would get back from the experimenter (given the observed quality increments) if the good turned out to be a Regular. Presumably, they would only do this if they thought there was some chance the unit was a Super, since that is the only way they could make a profit on the deal. The higher is $x(q)$ then, the more confident are buyers that the unit is a Super.

This statistic is helpful in interpreting the results. Suppose a separating equilibrium held when the experiments were run. Then the more quality add-ons there are on a unit, the more confident buyers will be that that unit is a Super, and hence the higher is x. So we would expect $x(q)$ to be positively related to q. In a pooling equilibrium, by contrast, buyers read nothing into q about the grade of the unit, hence $x(q)$ would be un-correlated with q.

Results: Basic Market Set-up

To recap briefly, we want to use this market to find out if signalling occurs; if the results are in line with any of the equilibria we have looked at; if so are they pooling or separating; and if separating do they conform to the Pareto-efficient separating outcome.

MP ran experimental markets of this kind on 12 occasions. The first of these was a pilot run, the results of which were not reported. Of the 11 remaining experimental markets, eight were run using the basic market set-up outlined above (three were reserved for alternative treatments, as discussed later). The results for these eight tended to vary, but the following broad findings did emerge:

(1) *Separation occurred in all eight markets*, in the sense that by the end of the trading periods the number of quality increments added onto Supers exceeded the number for Regulars.

(2) *In six out of the eight markets*, separation appeared to be due to signalling behaviour, in that the excess value statistic was positively correlated with the number of quality add-ons (buyers were more confident the unit was Super as the number of quality add-ons increased). We shall call these 'separating-signalling' markets. Behaviour in those two markets which *failed* this test did not seem to conform to any theoretical model, and appeared inexplicable.

(3) Given the market set-up described above, Supers are worth $2 more than Regulars from the buyers point of view. Hence if 'signalling-

separation' occurs, then buyers ought *in equilibrium* to pay around $2 more for units they expect to be Supers; so the excess value statistic for units that turn out to be Supers (high observed q) ought to be close to $2, and for Regulars (low observed q) it ought to be around 0. *For three of the six 'signalling-separating' markets* this was true by the end of trading, and these markets were deemed to have reached a separating equilibrium. The dynamic pattern appeared to be one where investment in the quality add-on signal for Supers started off quite high and then fell towards equilibrium levels. For the *other* three 'signalling–separating' markets, the experiments appeared to be approaching equilibrium, but had not reached it by the end of the experiment.

(4)   In the Spence theoretical example relating to the job market, many separating equilibria were inefficient because high productivity workers over-invested in costly education ($y^* > 1$ in the notation of chapter 5). In principle the same thing can happen here, in that sellers can over-invest in the quality increments they add on to Supers. In fact MP observed that in two of the three equilibrated markets Pareto-efficient separation was achieved.

Alternative Treatments: 'High Signalling Costs'

In the basic set-up of the experiment it cost the sellers 15 cents for every quality increment they added onto Regulars, and 2 cents for Supers. All of the eight experimental markets described above conformed to this. In the remaining three experimental markets the cost of adding each quality increment to a Super was raised from 2 cents to 7 cents. This makes it more costly for sellers of Supers to signal the grade of their units by adding on quality increments. In principle, separating equilibria still exist. The question is whether the experimental markets still manage to *achieve* separation under these conditions. In fact, MP found that:

(1)   *One of the three markets* with high signalling costs appeared to converge on a pooling equilibrium. Sellers appeared to add on roughly the same number of quality increments to Regulars as to Supers, and this number was close to the efficient level in a pooling equilibrium. The price paid for Regulars and Supers was somewhat greater than would be expected in a pooling equilibrium, however.

(2)   Behaviour *in the remaining two* 'high signalling cost' experiments did not clearly conform to any equilibrium model.[3] MP speculated

that these observations might reflect problems of non-existence of equilibria as suggested by the RS screening model.

Institutional Issues

MP noticed that behaviour seemed to be affected by the 'institutional environment' in the market. The fact that buyers and sellers were in the same room and could observe each other and 'the auctioneer' had certain implications, in that it allowed information to be conveyed in other ways (e.g. 'tone of voice') apart from the quality add-on signal. Two specific issues that seemed in practise to affect behaviour were that:

(a) In certain experiments the auctioneer used coloured chalk in marking up at the end of period the agreed trades, for the last periods of trading. Trades in Regulars were circled in green chalk and Supers in red. This appeared to draw buyers attention to the fact that Supers tended to have many quality increments and Regulars had few. Public recognition of the signal was aided by this, and this appeared to assist the development of a signalling equilibrium.

(b) The double auction structure of the market appeared to introduce reputation effects in certain experiments. By permitting interaction between buyers and sellers, the double auction allows bids and offers to be made, which are not implemented (if the bid/offer is not accepted). Sellers could make offers with very large numbers of quality add-ons. These offers were unlikely to be accepted, and hence would not be implemented – but they did mark out that seller as someone who probably had Supers for sale, since a seller of Regulars was unlikely to make such an offer. Hence sellers of Supers could build up reputations in the bidding process, and these seemed to affect the final agreed price/signal outcome, in certain experiments.

Summary

MP ran experimental markets to test some of the ideas that emerge from the theoretical literature on signalling. They found that when signalling costs were low:

(i)   all the markets separated;

(ii)   in most cases the separation appeared to be due to signalling;

(iii)   in about half of these markets, the 'separating–signalling' appeared to reach an equilibrium by the final periods of trading; those that did not reach equilibrium appeared to be 'on their way' there, but had not converged by the time the experiment ended;

(iv)   of those markets that had converged, most appeared to settle on the Pareto-efficient separating equilibrium, where investment in the signal was not excessive.

When the cost of signalling was high, however, they found that:

(i)   behaviour in one market conformed in most respects to a pooling equilibrium;

(ii)   behaviour in the other two did not appear to conform to any equilibrium.

Clearly, institutions mattered (though not quite in the way predicted). The 'face-to-face' double auction set-up of the market appeared to impinge on peoples' decisions. And the apparently inexplicable behaviour in some markets provides 'food for thought' in terms of future directions for signalling models.

Further Empirical Literature on Signalling

Further experimental evidence

Brandts and Holt (1992) set out to test the *validity of refinements of signalling equilibria* – are Cho and Kreps (1987)* right in suggesting that we can use the intuitive criterion to select that signalling equilibrium which is likely to prevail in practice? They constructed an experiment where the signal could take only two values – a subject could either signal 'educated' or 'not educated', with no gradations of education level. There were only two equilibria in their experimental design (partly because the signal could only take two values), both of which involved pooling. One equilibrium passed the intuitive criterion, the other did not. In the former case, all workers signal 'educated', and the employer believes that if a worker were to switch to the signal 'not educated' then that person would be low ability. In the latter equilibrium, all workers pool on 'not educated' and the employer believes that if a worker were to switch to the signal 'educated' then that person would be low ability. The latter equilibrium is not intuitive because a low-ability worker could not possibly gain by deviating from the equilibrium in this way; he/she would be worse off by signalling 'educated', even if the employer were to believe that (s)he were high ability.

If the intuitive criterion is right, then when we run the experiment we should expect to observe only the former equilibrium (all signal 'educated'), since the alternative is supported by beliefs that are not intuitive. In fact, BH found that subjects initially played the game naively, choosing strategies that appeared superficially likely to yield attractive pay-offs. This involved (subjects designated as) high ability workers signalling 'educated', and low ability workers signalling 'not educated'.[4] This play does not conform to any equilibrium of the experimental design. Eventually, however, most of the low ability workers learnt that they were better off signalling 'educated', and play converged approximately on the 'intuitive' equilibrium where all workers signal 'educated'.

BH noted that over the adjustment path to equilibrium, (subjects designated as) employers observed that low ability workers signalled 'not educated'. These observations 'on the way' to equilibrium confirm the employers' beliefs needed to support the intuitive equilibrium, as set out above. BH set up an alternative treatment, therefore, where pay-offs were such as to cause initial naive play where high ability workers signal 'not educated' and low ability ones signal 'educated'; from there, play was observed to converge on the non-intuitive equilibrium.

BH concluded that these experiments do *not* support the 'intuitive criterion': rather, subjects start off playing the game naively, and then converged on the 'nearest' equilibrium. Observation of play over the adjustment path appeared to be used as the basis for forming beliefs in equilibrium, regardless of whether those beliefs were intuitive or not.

'Real-world' evidence

Numerous studies have tried to test the job market signalling model against real-world data. It is well-established in the empirical literature that 'more education' yields higher earnings to the individual, all else held constant. The question here is whether the returns to education arise because the individual's productivity is enhanced by education (the 'human capital' argument), or because education signals pre-existing ability, or both. Empirical investigation of this issue is fraught with difficulties and many studies have tried to disentangle the effects, with mixed results. To take a couple of examples:

(1) **Wolpin (1977)** analysed the returns to education and the educational attainment of self-employed workers as compared to employees. He argued that signalling is irrelevant to the former groups, and so education amongst these workers is likely to reflect pure human capital considerations. Using these workers as a benchmark, one can then deduce the extent to which education acts as a signal amongst employees. The results suggested that human capital effects were clearly present, but also provided mild support for the signalling hypothesis.

(2) **Riley (1979b)** argued that the unobservability of productivity was likely to be a more serious problem (and so signalling more relevant) in some *occupations* as compared to others. An analysis of lifetime earnings and education across occupations produced evidence in support of the signalling theory.

These examples are intended to illustrate how empirical studies might address the issue of whether returns to education reflect human capital or signalling effects. The literature on this is extensive, and we cannot summarize it here – for a recent survey see **Weiss (1995)**.

NOTES

1   Specifically, quality increments q added onto RV of the Regular and Super grades as follows:

$$\$.205q - \$.005q^2 \quad \text{if} \quad q \leq 20,$$

$$\$2.1 + \$.01q \quad \text{if} \quad q > 20.$$

Allowing the quality add-ons to act as a signal *and* affect buyers RV is analogous to letting education act as a signal *and* raise productivity in Spence's job market model.

2   This kind of double auction set-up to the market does not accord precisely with either the Spence signalling account (sellers move first by deciding on quality increments, buyers respond with price offers) or the RS account (buyers specify a menu of contracts on price and quality add-ons, sellers choose a contract). Instead there is possible interaction between buyers and sellers in agreeing price and quality add-ons.

3   In certain respects, behaviour in these markets accorded most closely with 'semi-pooling' equilibria of the kind briefly mentioned in chapter 5, note 10.
4   For the experiment, the terms 'worker', 'employer', 'ability', etc., were replaced by more neutral terms.

References for Part 2

Bhattacharya, Sudipto (1979), 'Imperfect Information, Dividend Policy, and the "Bird in the Hand" Fallacy', *Bell Journal of Economics*, 110, pp. 257–70.

Binmore, Ken (1992),* *Fun and Games: A Text on Game Theory* (Lexington, MA: D.C. Heath).

Brandts, Jordi and Holt, Charles (1992), 'An Experimental Test of Equilibrium Dominance in Signalling Games', *American Economic Review*, 82, pp. 1350–65.

Cho, In-Koo and Kreps, David (1987),* 'Signaling Games and Stable Equilibria', *Quarterly Journal of Economics*, 102, pp. 179–221.

Dawkins, Richard (1989), *The Selfish Gene* (Oxford: Oxford University Press).

Farrell, Joseph (1995), 'Talk is Cheap', *American Economic Review*, 85, pp. 186–90.

Gibbons, Robert (1992),* *A Primer in Game Theory* (New York: Harvester Wheatsheaf).

Kreps, David (1990),* *A Course in Microeconomic Theory* (New York: Harvester Wheatsheaf).

Leland, H. and Pyle, D. (1977), 'Information Asymmetries, Financial Structure, and Financial Intermediation', *Journal of Finance*, 32, pp. 371–88.

Mas-Colell, Andrea, Whinston, Michael and Green, Jerry (1995),* *Microeconomic Theory* (Oxford: Oxford University Press).

Milgrom, Paul and Roberts, John (1982),* 'Limit Pricing and Entry under Incomplete Information: An Equilibrium Analysis', *Econometrica*, 50, pp. 443–59.

Milgrom, Paul and Roberts, John (1986), 'Relying on the Information of Interested Parties', *Rand Journal of Economics*, 17, pp. 18–32.

Miller, Ross and Plott, Charles (1985), 'Product Quality Signalling in Experimental Markets', *Econometrica*, 53, pp 837–72.

Nelson, P. (1974), 'Advertising as Information', *Journal of Political Economy*, 82, pp. 729–54.

Riley, John (1979a),* 'Informational Equilibria', *Econometrica*, 47, pp. 331–59.

Riley, John (1979b), 'Testing the Educational Screening Hypothesis', *Journal of Political Economy*, 87 (Suppl.), pp. S227–51.

Ross, S. (1977), 'The Determination of Financial Structure: The Incentive Signalling Approach', *Bell Journal of Economics*, 8, pp. 23–40.

Rothchild, Michael and Stiglitz, Joseph (1976), 'Equilibrium in Competitive Insurance Markets: An Essay on the Economics of Imperfect Information', *Quarterly Journal of Economics*, 90, pp. 629–49.

Salop, Joanne and Salop, Steven (1976), 'Self-selection and Turnover in the Labour Market', *Quarterly Journal of Economics*, 90, pp. 619–28.

Spence, Michael (1973), 'Job Market Signalling', *Quarterly Journal of Economics*, 87, pp. 355–74.

Spence, Michael (1974), 'Competitive and Optimal Responses to Signaling: An Analysis of Efficiency and Distribution', *Journal of Economic Theory*, 8, pp. 296–332.

Weiss, A. (1995), 'Human Capital versus Signalling Explanations of Wages', *Journal of Economic Perspectives*, 9, pp. 133–54.

Wilson, Charles (1977), 'A Model of Insurance Markets with Incomplete Information', *Journal of Economic Theory*, 16, pp. 167–207.

Wolpin, Kenneth (1977), 'Education and Screening', *American Economic Review*, 67, pp. 949–58.

Part 3

Moral Hazard

This part of the book is concerned with situations where parties engage in a contract, but the actions of one party are unobservable. The moral hazard problem relates to the possibility that the latter party might 'cheat'. A 'principal–agent' framework is set up to discuss this problem. The consequences and solutions are discussed in relation to the specific case of the relationship between the shareholders and management of a firm. The former usually cannot observe the daily decisions of the latter, and hence the managers have some scope to 'cheat', i.e. pursue their own interests rather than those of shareholders.

CHAPTER 9

Moral Hazard:
Shareholder/Management Relations

So far we have analysed models where private information/hidden knowledge is present. This generated problems of precontractual opportunism, where individuals might lie prior to signing the contract. In this part of the book we turn to issues of moral hazard, where unobserved behaviour/hidden action is present. This generates problems of post-contractual opportunism, where individuals might cheat after signing the contract.

Problems of moral hazard/cheating are commonplace. A student might take notes into an exam if he believes he can get away with it – the invigilator may not notice. An Olympic runner might take drugs to heighten her performance – she may not be detected by the drug-testers. A firm or individual might fiddle a tax return – the tax authorities may not spot it. A wife may cheat on her husband if she thinks she can get away with it (and/or vice versa). A worker may take time off work claiming to be sick, when she is perfectly healthy – the employer may not find out. Another might claim unemployment benefit on the pretext that there are no jobs, when in fact there are plenty – he may go undetected by the welfare inspectors. You hire a mechanic to fix your car – seeing that you know nothing about cars he botches the job. And so on.

In this part of the book, we look at the issues raised by moral hazard problems in terms of an example relating to the shareholders and managers of a firm. In this chapter we begin by placing the manager/shareholder example in context. We set out a 'principal–agent' framework for thinking about the problem, and proceed to outline the areas where managers' and shareholders' aims might conflict. The remainder of the chapter is then devoted to a discussion of a variety of mechanisms which have been suggested to resolve the conflict.

This chapter is discursive rather than analytical. The aim is to high-light a broad set of issues in a fairly informal way, without recourse to mathematics for the most part. In the next chapter we focus on some specific issues in the manager/shareholder problem, which we analyse in depth with the aid of a formal model. The following chapter provides a guide to further theoretical literature, whilst the final chapter of this part of the book considers experimental evidence.

The Manager/Shareholder Problem

In traditional economic theory, the firm is a 'black-box'. It is simply assumed that inputs go in, outputs come out, and the over-riding prin-ciple governing all decisions in the intervening process is 'profit maximization'. For many purposes, this may be a useful working as-sumption, which yields clear, testable and potentially useful predictions about firm behaviour.

In order to achieve a deeper understanding of firm behaviour, how-ever, one must recognise that firms' decisions are made by people, and sometimes the aims of those people are not so simple. If these people are allowed some discretion they may use it to advance their own interests, leading to decisions that may be quite different to those which would maximize profit. Hence the predictions of the traditional 'profit-maximizing' theory might turn out to be wrong. As mentioned in chapter 1, one might think of 'market systems' as ones where self-interested traders interact, whereas 'hierarchies' (such as firms) are systems within which self-interested individuals interact. In this chapter we explore this latter idea.

Typically, one would expect a complex web of relationships to exist between people in a modern organization. We shall focus in this chapter on a key relationship which has long been recognized (e.g. Berle and Means, 1932), which is that between shareholders and managers. The latter *run* the firm in the sense that they make policy decisions. The former *own* the firm in the sense that they are the '*residual claimants*' and exert '*residual control*'; the shareholders claim the residual returns from the firm, and they have ultimate control to do what they wish with the firm, after all contracts are honoured.

Sole traders, partnerships, etc., aside, much of modern industry is organized on this shareholder/manager basis. It may be reasonable to assume that shareholders are interested in maximizing profits – they generally want the best return possible from their investment. But they are not the ones making the decisions. The managers make the decisions, and they may run the firm to pursue their own interests.

A pre-condition for agents within the firm to pursue their own interests is that they have some *discretion*. This discretion arises from a fundamental asymmetry of information; a manager can 'get away with' non-profit-maximizing decisions, because the shareholders cannot fully observe his/her actions. This is a classic 'moral hazard' problem of the kind outlined above.

The Principal–Agent Framework

The principal–agent framework is a stylized representation of a relationship involving decentralized decision-making, that may be applied to a wide variety of situations where people may interact under conditions of asymmetric information, and in particular moral hazard (e.g. Ross, 1973; Shavell, 1979*; Arrow, 1985; Grossman and Hart, 1983*). Broadly, the framework is as follows. One individual (designated the 'agent') acts on behalf of another (designated the 'principal') in undertaking some activity. The agent claims a return for his efforts, e.g. a fee or salary. This is the basis for the 'contract' between the two people. The reasons such a relationship may arise are many and varied, but presumably reflect the fact that there are gains from specialization, in some sense. The principal may have many such projects or activities on the go and cannot run them all, and hence delegates responsibility for each activity to an agent in this way.

The principal typically cannot (fully) observe (or at least cannot verify) the agent's *actions*. Hence there is an information asymmetry, involving 'hidden action', and the possibility of postcontractual opportunism by the agent. The contract is necessarily incomplete, since the two cannot contract on behaviour by the agent that is unobserved by the principal. The latter usually has some information to go on, however, rather than having to make decisions completely 'in the dark'. The principal is likely to observe the *outcome* of the agent's action, which allows him/her at least to make some inference about what the unobserved actions might have been. For example, if the activity or project undertaken by the agent is successful, then the principal may be able to deduce that the agent *probably* worked hard on it. The correspondence between agent's action and observed outcome is usually not deterministic (hence the word 'probably'), since the outcome may be affected by all sorts of other factors as well (e.g. luck).[1]

A central feature of this delegated decision-making problem is that the agent does not bear the full consequences of his own actions, since his decisions affect the principal as well as himself. If the agent's objectives differ from those of the principal, then the former may take advantage of the unobservability of actions to pursue his/her own ends. The problem facing the principal is then to design some form of contract such that the agent's decisions are brought as far as possible into alignment with her own wishes. The situation we have described is sometimes called an 'agency problem', and the welfare losses that may arise from it are sometimes called 'agency costs'. These costs are a form of transaction costs associated with motivation problems, as discussed in chapter 1. Not all moral hazard problems can be cast in this agency framework, but there are many situations where it is applicable.

For our purposes the shareholders are 'principals' and the management are 'agents'. For the rest of this part of the book we shall refer to any individual shareholder as 'she' and to a manager as 'he'. The goals of shareholders and managers may conflict for the following reasons (cf. Lambert and Larcker, 1985; Strong and Waterson, 1987).

Sources of Conflict

The interests of managers and shareholders may diverge, because ultimately each has different objectives and operates in a different market environment. Shareholders seek wealth in the stock market; managers seek utility in the labour market. We shall analyse market incentive effects later, but for the moment it is worth pointing out certain specific differences in objectives which may cause a manager who has some degree of discretion to run the firm in a way contrary to the objectives of shareholders.

(a)   *Perks, expense preference*: a manager may have a taste for a big office, a large number of staff, luxury company car, lavish entertainment, etc. He may claim that these things are important for his work, when in fact his expenditure on such items may be largely for his own benefit. Such spending generates utility for the manager, but it raises costs and so reduces the net pay-off to shareholders.

(b)   *Leisure preferences*: managers, like most people, are typically averse to hard work and would prefer a leisurely existence, given the chance. All other things being equal (pay etc.), they are likely to shirk, even when just a little extra effort might bring in large returns to shareholders.

(c) *Risk preferences*: shareholders typically have a diversified portfolio of assets. If shares in one firm do badly, then in a well-designed portfolio it is likely that shares in another will compensate. Managers, in contrast, tend to have much of their human capital and livelihood tied up in the one firm. Hence one would expect shareholders to be less risk averse with respect to the fortunes of any one firm in their portfolio than the managers of that firm.[2]

Differential attitudes to risk may lead to a conflict between managerial motivation and optimal risk sharing, when moral hazard is present. We shall explain this remark more fully later (and in the next chapter). A related problem is that a manager's policy of undertaking risk may also be sub-optimal from the shareholders' point of view. Suppose that in running the firm a manager has a choice of projects that he could undertake. One project may be very safe but offer only low expected returns. The other may be riskier (e.g. there may be a positive probability that the project fails so badly that the manager loses his job) but offers the prospect of much higher expected/average returns. The risk averse manager may take the former, when shareholders might have preferred the latter. If shareholders do not know that such a choice is available then they cannot enforce that preference.[3]

(d) *Time preferences*: managers may have different time preferences compared with shareholders. For example, they may be more interested in short-term rewards rather than long-term profits.

As a first approximation, therefore, we shall take it that the shareholders objectives for a firm are expected wealth maximization (which we shall call 'profit maximization', or 'maximization of shareholder value' for convenience), in line with conventional theory. Managers' objectives may deviate from this.

Mechanisms to Restore Goal Congruence

'How might this conflict of interests be resolved or minimized?' The rest of this chapter will be devoted to this question. A number of control mechanisms may be identified. We shall begin by looking at internal 'shareholder control mechanisms'. Later we turn to 'external control mechanisms'.

Shareholder control mechanisms

Is there anything that *shareholders themselves* can do in response to managerial inefficiency? One option is to sell their shares, potentially leading to a takeover bid – we discuss this idea later. For a shareholder who wishes to retain his stake with the firm, several other options are also available.

Payment by results

This is the classic response to the principal–agent problem. The idea is to motivate the agent by making him bear more fully the consequences of his own actions. The principal cannot observe the agent's actions but she can observe the outcome of those actions, and these are positively correlated. Contracting on actions is impossible, due to the unobservability problem, but contracting on outcomes is feasible and provides an (imperfect) substitute (Ross, 1973). In our case, this means that the shareholders can link pay not to *inputs* but to *outputs*, i.e. payment by results. This could be achieved by a system of bonuses, profit sharing, profit-related pay, payment by commission, giving managers shares in the company, linking pay to the company share price, etc. These mechanisms provide a manager with some incentive to maximize profits, since he will himself gain a share in profits. In the next chapter we set out a detailed model of incentive pay in a principal–agent framework.

This kind of 'payment by results' system is an imperfect substitute for contracting on managers' actions, because the two are not perfectly correlated. (Firms operate in an uncertain world, where results typically cannot be guaranteed.) The more closely are actions and results correlated, the better is 'incentive pay' as a substitute for contracting on managerial inputs. The two are perfect substitutes when actions can be directly inferred from results without error.[4]

Performance pay schemes are so common in the 'real world' as to lead one to believe that they provide an effective response to the incentive problem. Nevertheless, there are difficulties with this approach. Firstly, we have noted that managers tend to be more risk averse than shareholders, and incentive pay schemes (by their very nature) place managers in a risky situation; their pay fluctuates with the fortunes of the firm. Hence, incentive pay may induce profit maximizing behaviour by managers, but at the cost of suboptimal risk sharing between managers and shareholders. (This conflict is demonstrated formally in the next chapter.) One sophisticated response to this problem is to give managers share options, which (typically) give a manager the right to buy shares in the company at some future date, at a price agreed today. If the share price rises then the manager can exercise the option by buying the shares cheaply. But if it falls then he can simply discard the options. This kind of system retains the incentive for a manager to make profits (since this will probably raise the share price), but it may reduce the downside risk he faces if the firm happens to do badly.

Further problems arise when a manager's job involves several tasks, and the outcome of some tasks are difficult/impossible to measure and hence to reward. If the performance of some tasks is rewarded and others not, then the manager has every incentive to neglect the latter. Suppose an insurance sales manager is paid by volume of insurance policies sold. Then he may well pressurize unsophisticated customers to accept inappropriate policies, to the detriment of the firm's reputation – after all, he is not paid to sell people the 'right' policy. (See the 'equal compensation principle', in chapter 11.) Incentive schemes can likewise destroy harmony and co-operation in the corporate environment. Why should a manager help others in the management team, when he is paid by (some measure of) his *own* results?

A further problem arises in fixing appropriate performance targets over time. Suppose a manager's basic wage is fixed so as to correspond with observed historical levels of a performance, and pay incentives are introduced on top for improved performance. The manager may then deliberately hold down performance over the observation period, so that he can reap all sorts of bonuses later without having to work too hard. Say the shareholders respond by raising the performance target after a period of good results – that can make the incentive problems even worse (Weitzman, 1980). To see this, think of the old USSR, where factory managers were given performance targets set on a historical basis. If they exceeded their target, then they would be rewarded by a higher target next period! Many reacted by producing low output all the time.

Finally, the *timing* of performance targets may be problematic. If the intervals over which performance is assessed are too short, this may induce short-termist managerial decision-making; too long and the incentives are blunted (why work hard today for some potential bonus in 5 years time?). These problems are compounded if managers have several projects on the go at once, each of different duration.

Some studies (e.g. Brickley et al., 1985) have sought to demonstrate empirically the benefits of incentive schemes by showing that company stock prices increase on the announcement of the introduction of such schemes. Schleifer and Vishny (1988) note, however, that this increase is much greater for short-term incentive contracts than long-term ones. They argue that this observation might have little to do with the success of such schemes in motivating managers. It might simply be due to managers getting short-term incentive contracts when they know that good earnings are coming; the stock market recognises the pattern and stock prices rise when the scheme is announced.

Monitoring

Shareholders could choose to improve their information by investing in systems to measure managerial *inputs* into the job. They may then contract with the managers on the basis of this information (on inputs rather than outputs). Ultimately, the shareholders might use this information as grounds for dismissal of (apparently) bad managers.

There are costs involved in monitoring, of course. The best that shareholders can do is to balance these costs against the benefits which result from better information to yield an optimal level of monitoring that maximises profit (see, for example, Jensen and Meckling (1976); also see the discussion of Holmstrom's (1979)* work in chapter 11). Typically, one would expect monitoring to be incomplete at this optimum, and hence this still leaves some scope for managerial discretion.

Monitoring and dismissal of bad management may also be problematic if share-ownership is widely dispersed. Who is to bear the associated costs? The benefits of constraining managerial inefficiency are non-excludable – if one shareholder does it, all shareholders benefit. Hence there is a free-rider problem – each shareholder has the incentive to let others do the hard work. For example, it may be difficult just to persuade enough shareholders to turn up at an AGM in order to vote out an inefficient management team. If all shareholders free-ride, then the job never gets done (Stiglitz, 1985; Strong and Waterson, 1987).

Managerial re-organization

It may be possible to reorganize the management system to minimize the problem. For example, the system of supervision implicit in the management hierarchy may be open to improvement. It may be possible to rotate managers between the different jobs – that way no one can claim that there are special circumstances which affect their job and no one else.

Management systems may be designed to minimize the moral hazard problem, but as long as the fundamental asymmetry in information remains, it is hard to see how they can costlessly eliminate it. What, then, can be done about any managerial slack that remains?

'Do-it-yourself'

The 'principal–agent' problem is one where the agent acts on behalf of the principal to advance some goal. If she is dissatisfied with this, the principal could always sack the agent and 'do-it-yourself'. In our case the shareholders could run the firm. The problem with this is that the principal–agent relationship presumably developed for a reason in the first place – typically one might expect gains from the specialization of roles. The 'DIY' approach sacrifices these gains (Milgrom and Roberts, 1992, chapter 6). Further, it may be hard to implement DIY when multiple shareholders are present (e.g. each may try to free-ride by letting the others do the work of the agent).

Efficiency wages

Say there is some chance that the manager will be caught cheating, in any given period with the firm. Then one way for the firm to deter such behaviour would be to offer a premium wage (i.e. one somewhat above what he could get elsewhere), and dismiss anyone caught cheating. Unlike the 'payment by results' approach, this would be a flat wage, unrelated to observed performance. Here, the idea is to give the manager 'something to lose' – the wage premium makes it valuable to the manager to keep his job. The 'efficiency wage' fixes the premium just high enough that the manager will not want to risk dismissal through cheating (Shapiro and Stiglitz, 1984). The difficulty with this approach is that the offer of a wage premium is obviously costly, and eats into shareholders' net profits. It may be that the size of the premium necessary to deter cheating is so great that shareholders might prefer to tolerate cheating or seek another mechanism to induce efficient management.

Bonding

Say a manager posts a bond that would be forfeit if they are subsequently caught 'cheating', or if their performance is found to be inadequate in some way. Such a bond could act as a powerful incentive to deter inefficiency (Becker and Stigler, 1974). Such systems are in fact sometimes observed in reality (e.g. contractors sometimes 'post a bond' which is forfeit if they do not finish a project on time and according to specification).

One reason why explicit bonding systems are not particularly common is that in many cases the bond would have to be very substantial for it to work, and more than most people could manage on their financial resources. There are substitute mechanisms, however, which can be seen in principle to do the same job. In particular, Lazear (1979) has argued that age/wage pay scales serve the same purpose. People gain returns from long-service in a job, above and beyond those which might be warranted by the increase in their human capital. If there is some chance that they might be caught 'cheating' on the job sometime over their period of service, then dismissal means that they forfeit returns from age and seniority. The commonly observed age/wage pattern duplicates the effect of posting a bond,[5] and may serve to strengthen the efficiency wage mechanism outlined above.

External control mechanisms

Takeover threats

This mechanism revolves around the concept of the 'market for corporate control'. In this framework, management teams compete for the right to control company resources. Efficient management teams are the ones that maximize value for the shareholder, and these replace inefficient ones.

The underlying mechanism supporting this 'market' is the takeover. Say an existing management team fails to maximize shareholder value – the low profits are likely to lead to low demand for the company's shares, leading to a low share price. Realizing this, an outsider takes over the firm by buying its shares, removes the inefficient management team and replaces it with an efficient one; maximum profits are restored and the share price rises as a result. The outsider gains as the value of the shares bought rises. In fact, it may be argued that matters do not have to go so far to ensure managerial efficiency. The original management team may be deterred from inefficiency simply by the *threat* of take over.

There are, however, problems which may prevent this mechanism from achieving the desired effect. Many of these problems also revolve around issues of imperfect information.

1   Search costs: low profits may be due to a number of reasons, of which bad management is only one; the firm may have been unlucky or trading under adverse market conditions for example. Outsiders have to typically incur search (or monitoring) costs, in order to identify a suitable target for takeover. Sometimes these expenditures will be wasted – an outsider

may investigate a company only to find that it is being run efficiently. These kinds of search costs may allow inefficient management to go undetected.

2 Campaign costs: say an outsider has successfully identified a company where management fails to maximize shareholder value. Launching a takeover bid would be costly – the outsider may have to launch a publicity campaign, deal with regulatory hurdles, lay itself open to potentially damaging criticism from the management of the target firm, and so on. Suppose the inefficiently run firm is currently worth V, whereas under profit maximization it could be worth $V^* > V$. Then if $V > V^* - c$, where c are the campaign costs, the outsider still has no incentive to takeover the firm. The campaign costs provide a 'cushion' which allows some degree of managerial slack, free from threat of takeover (Yarrow, 1976).

3 Rival bids: say a takeover bid is launched. The bid may attract rivals for the target firm. Rival bidders can 'free-ride' in the sense that they need not incur the same level of search costs that the original bidder faced (the bid acts as a publicly observable signal which informs rivals of a worthwhile target). The rivals may be able to offer more for the target firm as a consequence. The original bid may fail, in which case all the expenses involved in launching the bid are wasted, from the original bidder's point of view. This kind of logic may deter the launch of a takeover bid in the first place (Stiglitz, 1985).

4 Free-riding shareholders: suppose the outside bid is launched by offering to buy shares at a price which effectively values the firm at V^0 (where $V^0 > V$). Then the outsider stands to gain from the bid if $V^* > V^0 + c$. But existing shareholders may hold onto their shares; they may, for example, reason that after takeover the firm will be worth V^*, so why accept an offer than values the firm at $V^0 < V^*$? The shareholders effectively free-ride on the bidder's attempt to remove inefficient management (Grossman and Hart, 1980*). But if enough shareholders do this then the bid fails, since the bidder does not achieve a controlling share of the firm.[6]

One way out of this free-rider problem is by compulsory acquisition of shares (Vickers and Yarrow, 1988). The idea is that once a bidding firm acquires a certain proportion of the target firm's shares, then it is allowed to purchase the remaining minority interest by compulsory purchase, at the offer price accepted by the majority. (In the UK the Takeover Code sets the critical equity stake at 90 per cent, at which point the bidder gains compulsory acquisition rights.)

5   The 'winner's curse': say a number of bidders are interested in buying the firm, but none of them know exactly its true underlying worth. They each construct an *estimate* of V^*, and then make a bid on the basis of that estimate, which they believe will allow them to make a profit from the takeover. Say the estimates of V^* are unbiased in the sense that the average estimate is about right. Then the average bidder would make a profit from the takeover. But it is not the average bidder that wins – rather it is the *highest* bidder. That highest bid is likely to be based on an *overestimate* of the value of the firm. The unfortunate winner is likely to find that the firm is worth less than expected, and so makes lower profits (perhaps losses) on the deal (e.g. see Milgrom and Roberts, 1992, chapter 15). This kind of phenomenon may make firms wary of launching a bid in the first place.

6   'Lemons' problems: it is arguable that those holding the target firm's shares know more about the firm's underlying worth than the bidder. Some existing shareholders may be managers who have intimate knowledge of the firm; others may be major institutions who have been shareholders of long standing and may be privy to superior information on the firm. They will only part with their shares if the bidder pays more than (they believe) the shares are worth. Hence the successful bidder is likely to end up with a 'lemon' (Stiglitz, 1985). If the potential bidder realises this, then he will be deterred from launching the bid in the first place.[7]

7   takeover defences: the incumbent management may act strategically to deter takeover (Stiglitz, 1985). They may lobby politicians and officials, call for the takeover to be referred for investigation by the authorities, etc. One particular defensive manoeuvre would be to introduce so called 'poison pills'. These are special securities that give the holder rights in the event of an offer for some large fraction of the firm's stock (e.g. they may give the incumbent management rights to buy shares in the target firm at low prices). Another defence might be to (threaten to) seek a 'white knight', who would rescue the target firm from the original bidder in a friendly merger, probably enjoying the advantage of lower post-merger reorganization costs. A further possibility would be for the incumbent management to collude with the original bidder in a 'greenmail' manoeuvre. The idea here is that they buy shares from the bidder at a premium price, provided he/she agrees to steer clear of the firm for some period. That way the bidder makes a 'quick buck', the inefficient management keep their jobs, and the takeover mechanism for determining corporate control is frustrated.

8   Immunity: some organizations may be perceived as immune from takeover, e.g. because of legal restrictions or because they are just 'too big' (a potential bidder might think twice before bidding for Ford say, and they may find it difficult to obtain financial backing). In these cases, incumbent management need not fear replacement through takeover. Further, (in keeping with point 7) management might actively adopt strategies that *make* them immune to takeover; for example they may put the firm in a position where any attempt at takeover results in automatic regulatory intervention.

9   'Making hay': suppose the incumbent management perceive that takeover is imminent *whatever they do*. Then there is an incentive to enjoy themselves while they can – the impending takeover *increases* the problem of wasteful/inefficient management over this period.

10   Detrimental takeovers: it is quite possible for takeovers to be *damaging* to managerial efficiency. Say, for example, that the management team of one company decides to launch a bid for another, not because the latter is inefficient but because the bidding team wishes to expand its corporate empire. Then we may end up with an inefficient management team replacing an efficient one (Vickers and Yarrow, 1988).

It is also arguable that takeovers (actual or potential) may interfere with long-term contracting. The principal and agent might have been able to alleviate moral hazard problems by contracting on a long-term basis, e.g. by establishing reputations (see below) – but the possibility of takeover may undermine these 'contracts' (see, for example, Shleifer and Vishry, 1988).

The point of this discussion is to illustrate that the takeover mechanism for ensuring managerial efficiency may be imperfect. Whether or not it does work, and if so how well, is ultimately an empirical question. Quantifying the relationship is difficult – for example, it is hard to tell what impact the *threat* of takeover has in keeping management teams 'on their toes'. Studies of the apparent impact of actual takeovers yield mixed results. Some studies (e.g. Jensen and Ruback, 1983; Jarrell et al., 1988) suggest that the mechanism is effective; others (e.g. Lev, 1983; Firth, 1980; Cowling et al., 1980; Magenheim and Mueller, 1987; Scherer, 1988) are more critical.

Lenders and bankruptcy threats

Firms typically raise money by a mixture of debt and equity. We have argued that equity-holders (i.e. shareholders) face free-rider problems in gathering information and exerting controls on managers. The presence of limited liability, however, provides debt-holders (i.e. lenders) with an incentive to control managers, since if the firm defaults they bear at least some of the cost. Stiglitz (1985) has argued that lenders are also better placed to control managers. Debt is usually much less widely dispersed than equity (e.g. often a single bank may hold all the firm's debt), hence free-rider problems are much less severe. Lenders have greater incentive to gather information on the firm and exert control. Thus, for example, we see banks running credit checks on firms, and imposing conditions on loans, which may restrict managerial discretion. Hart (1995, chapter 6) has shown how lenders can affect managerial behaviour in quite subtle ways through the terms of the loan. Ultimately, if a loan cannot be repaid, the lenders may be able to force a firm into bankruptcy, the effects of which are likely to be disastrous to the management. Once again, however, there are weaknesses with these mechanisms, as follows.

Lending controls may be ineffective: whilst it is conceivable that lenders are better placed than shareholders to 'police' managers, nevertheless they still operate under conditions of imperfect information. Monitoring and controlling loans is costly. Moreover, the objectives of lenders may diverge from those of the shareholders. Lenders are interested in ensuring that the debt will be repaid, with interest. Hence they will favour projects with low risk of failure, rather than those with the highest expected returns. In so far as lending controls serve to constrain management therefore, it may be towards reinforcing risk-averse decision-making rather than profit maximization.

Bankruptcy threats may be ineffective: looming bankruptcy may well serve to 'concentrate the minds' of management on raising profits (reducing losses). This threat is inevitably weaker in boom times than in recession, however. Furthermore, if bankruptcy is seen as inevitable regardless of managerial activity, then the management may decide to enjoy greater managerial discretion in the short run (as in argument 9 for takeovers). Some firms may be seen as immune from bankruptcy (e.g. some banks might feel that if they get into difficulties then the government will always bail them out), in which case the mechanism is ineffective (compare takeover argument 8). This point was vividly illustrated in the US Savings and Loans (S&L) crisis, where the S&L associations were insured by a federal agency and consequently took excessive risks and lost substantial sums through fraud.

Ultimately, the decision as to how much debt to take on is made (partially, at least) by management. It is arguable that if they perceive lenders as likely to constrain their activities, then they may simply choose to have low debt levels, perhaps by issuing equity instead (Vickers and Yarrow, 1988). Conversely, by taking on significant levels of debt, some managers may be perceived to be signalling a commitment *not* to engage in discretionary behaviour (Stiglitz, 1985).

Product markets

Under perfect competition, firms make normal (i.e. zero) profit in the long run. Inefficient firms could not survive in this environment. Higher costs cannot be passed onto customers in the form of higher prices, hence badly run firms would make losses and shut down in the long run. Managerial inefficiency is removed by the ferocity of competition in the product market (e.g. Winter, 1971).

Once again there are problems with this argument. Firstly, competition is unlikely to be an effective control mechanism to the extent that all firms in the industry face the same agency problem and costs (Jensen and Meckling, 1976). Secondly, the argument loses force under conditions of imperfect competition. Differentiated products may, for example, allow a firm to raise prices due to managerial inefficiency and still retain customers. Once again, the argument comes down to an empirical question 'do product markets constrain managerial behaviour?' Smirlock and Marshall (1983) provide an empirical test for product market constraints on one specific form of managerial discretion – the desire for a large staff. In a sample of US banks, they found that (all else held constant), bank employment increased with the complexity of the organization (as measured by size of assets), but not with the degree of product market concentration. This latter result supports the view that product market competition does not constrain managers' behaviour.

Managerial labour markets (reputation effects)

Fama (1980) has argued that the operation of managerial labour markets is likely to induce profit maximizing behaviour. The basic idea is that managers who wish to 'get on' have an interest in the success of the firm they work for. By contributing to the profitability of the firm they advance their own career prospects. If they do badly they may face demotion or possibly even dismissal, which is likely to be interpreted as a negative signal of their abilities by other firms and so lowers their prospects elsewhere (see chapter 3 on lay-offs and lemons). This managerial labour market mechanism largely underpins the mechanisms for advancing goal congruence discussed so far (e.g. takeovers 'worked' by threatening dismissal).

Managerial markets internal to the firm may also provide incentives for managers to monitor each other's behaviour, limiting the scope for discretion. This arises partly because the productivity of each manager often depends on that of others around him or, indeed, above and below him; hence a senior manager has an interest in promoting the efficiency of his juniors and vice versa. Junior managers have the added incentive to monitor their seniors, because they might gain by replacing or stepping over incompetent senior managers.

For this mechanism to work, it is crucial that the managerial labour market be efficient in 'pricing in' managerial behaviour into managerial pay. The problem is that it is difficult to see how this can be done in the presence of moral hazard, where that behaviour is unobserved by shareholders, and apparently good results might just reflect luck or even be due to the performance of other managers in the team. Indeed, it is arguable that managerial labour markets might create incentives that work against the interest of shareholders in certain respects.

A manager who is preoccupied with his own CV need not be doing the best job by the firm he works for. He may avoid investments that may be expected to be profitable for the firm, if they involve the risk of bad outcomes that could damage his own reputation (Holmstrom and Ricard I Costa, 1986). He may be uncooperative with colleagues and contribute little to the management team as a whole. He may waste resources (e.g. his own and others time) seeking credit where it is not due, and ensuring others get the blame for problems.

Stiglitz (1985) has argued that the concern of managers for their own reputations might induce them to 'follow the pack', i.e. run company policy in the same way as other managers in similar firms. If things go wrong, a manager can always defend himself by saying 'I only did what everybody else did'. The consequence of this is that we end up with a kind of 'herd instinct' in the way companies are run, rather than profit maximization in each firm.

Finally, the managerial labour market may influence the way in which a manager values future returns. Shareholders are typically interested in the discounted present value of the cash flows generated by (their shares in) the firm. Standard theory (see, for example, Gravelle and Rees, 1981, chapter 15) tells us that in order to maximize wealth, shareholders discount future returns at the market rate of interest. Managers may (be induced to) value future returns quite differently. In particular, they may seek short-term success in order to promote their own careers. After all, once they have promotion or a better job elsewhere, they need not be concerned about long-term adverse consequences that they leave behind. Hence managerial labour markets may act in a way which *aggravates* the conflict in interests between managers and shareholders due to their differing time preferences.

Summary

Moral hazard represents a form of postcontractual opportunism. Unobserved or 'hidden actions' lead to the possibility of cheating on a contract. Such problems are endemic to everyday life. Many moral hazard problems can be represented in terms of a 'principal–agent' framework. An important example concerns the relationship between shareholders and managers in a modern corporation.

In this chapter we discussed this relationship in informal terms. Managers' objectives may differ from those of shareholders due to the potential for managerial non-pecuniary benefits and costs; leisure preferences; differential attitudes to risk; and time preferences. Various factors, however, may serve to limit managerial discretion.

Shareholders may themselves be able to control managers by: (a) linking managerial pay to performance; (b) monitoring; (c) reorganizing management structures; (d) 'do-it-yourself'; (e) efficiency wages; (f) bonding (or age/wage scales as a substitute). Various external control mechanisms also exist in terms of: (a) takeovers; (b) constraints posed by lenders and bankruptcy threats; (c) product market constraints; (d) managerial labour markets.

These control mechanisms are closely inter-related. In each case, however, there are weaknesses and limitations which suggest that the scope for managerial discretion is unlikely to be entirely removed.

NOTES

1   If the correspondence did happen to be deterministic, then observing outcomes would be a perfect substitute for observing actions, and the moral hazard problem would disappear. (The principal could tell directly and with certainty what the agent's action had been, by inspecting the outcome.)

2   The presence of 'limited liability' acts in particular to insulate shareholders from financial disaster.

3   Note that the situation described here is actually more complex than the standard moral hazard problem, because the manager has 'hidden knowledge' about the choices facing the firm; hence there is an element of adverse

selection mixed in with the moral hazard. The key issue is still one which relates to the manager's *action* (i.e. whether he 'cheats' or not), but strictly speaking it need not matter whether those actions were *unobserved*; if the shareholders do not know the choices the manager faces then they can not tell if the actual choice made was the most profitable, whether they observed the choice or not. We shall discuss models of this kind of situation in chapter 11, point 10.

4   One entertaining and instructive example of an incentive contract is called by Rasmusen (1989) 'boiling in oil'. Say there is a certain specific outcome (or more than one) which could only arise if the manager 'cheated'. Then the principal could write a contract which specified that the manager be 'boiled in oil' if that outcome was observed (or punished in some similar way – can you think of any suitable alternatives?). Interestingly, the outcome itself could actually be quite favourable (e.g. involve high profits). As long as some feature of the outcome 'gave the game away' by showing that the manager had certainly cheated, then a 'boil in oil' clause to the contract could still be appropriate; faced with such a prospect, the manager would never cheat in the first place, and so the clause would never by invoked. Unfortunately, there seem to be certain legal impediments to such contracts. (A less colourful name for such contracts is 'forcing contracts'.)

5   Compare this argument for age/wage scales with the screening-based argument of Salop and Salop (1976) given in chapter 7. Lazear's (1979) argument is also consistent with a mandatory retirement date; the manager may well wish to continue reaping these excess wages well past the efficient date for his retirement, and must be forcibly retired to prevent this.

6   The free-rider problem arises because the benefits of removing inefficient management are non-excludable; the bidder bears the costs but cannot prevent other shareholders from sharing the benefits. Existing shareholders' hopes of a better offer may also be heightened by expectations of a rival takeover bid, of course. And speculators may be attracted into the market for the same reasons, making it more difficult for the bid to succeed.

7   This lemons problem is closely related to the 'winner's curse', and to the 'free-riding shareholders' argument. The winner's curse arises even if existing shareholders are no better informed than bidders, as long as there are several bidders. The lemons problem arises even if there is only one bidder, as long as existing shareholders are better informed than the bidder. The 'free-riding shareholders' argument was that existing shareholders will not sell at a share price that values the firm at less than V^*; this is still true in the lemons argument, but further it is argued there that bidders are less well informed about the value of V^*.

CHAPTER 10

Moral Hazard: A Principal–Agent Model

In this chapter we set out an analytical model of the kind of 'principal–agent' problem discussed in the last chapter. The literature on principal–agent problems tends to be rather technical. We present a simple illustrative example of such a model, taken from Tirole (1992). This model captures only *some* of the issues mentioned in the last chapter. But it does allow us to be precise in our treatment of those issues.

The Model

There are two people in this model – a shareholder who *owns* a firm, and a manager who *runs* it. The shareholder is the principal, and the manager is the agent. The moral hazard problem arises because the principal (shareholder) cannot observe the actions taken by the agent (manager) – in this case she cannot observe the *effort* which the manager puts into the job. The shareholder only observes the gross profit made by the firm. The shareholder provides the manager with a remuneration package in return for running the firm, and claims whatever is left from the firm's gross profit as her own.

The firm operates in a risky environment where high profits are possible but cannot be guaranteed. The shareholder is taken to be risk neutral, since she has a diversified portfolio of assets. The manager is taken to be risk averse, since his human capital is tied up in the one firm such that he is unable to diversify his risks.

This means that the shareholder wishes to maximize expected (or average) net profit, given as $E(\pi - w)$, where w is the remuneration paid

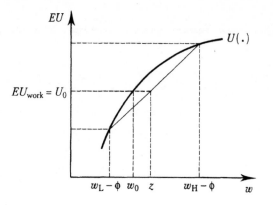

Figure 10.1   The manager's utility function (an incentive package)

to the manager, π is the *gross* profits to the firm, so $\pi - w$ is the shareholder's *net* profit, and $E(.)$ means we take the expected or average value of those net profits. The fact that the shareholder is claiming the residual of profits after paying the manager is consistent with her role as 'residual claimant' (and hence owner) of the firm. Note that the shareholder does not care about the *unpredictability* of net profits, she only wishes the expected value to be as high as possible. This is what we mean by 'risk neutral'.

The manager, on the other hand, has a utility function $U(w)$ which takes the shape indicated in figure 10.1, because he is risk averse. At this stage, the main point to note is that the manager's utility function is increasing in income *at a decreasing rate*, i.e. it is concave. This means that he prefers high wages to low wages, but the marginal utility of wages is decreasing – each extra pound adds less to utility than the last pound.

The manager seeks to maximize *expected* utility. Thus if he were offered a bet with a 50 per cent chance of winning £1 and a 50 per cent chance of losing £1, he would not take it; given the shape of the utility function, the utility gained from winning a pound is less than the utility lost from losing a pound. Such a person would require positive compensation in the form of a 'risk premium' to make him indifferent to such a bet. This is what we mean by 'risk averse' (see the appendix at the end of book).

The firm can either make high profits π_H, or low profits π_L, where $\pi_H > \pi_L$. The manager can either work hard (high effort), or he can 'shirk' (low effort) on the job. If he works hard then:

the probability the firm does well $\left(\text{makes } \pi_H\right)$ is x,

the probability the firm does badly $\left(\text{makes } \pi_L\right)$ is $\left(1-x\right)$.

If the manager 'shirks', then:

the probability the firm does well $\left(\text{makes } \pi_H\right)$ is y,

the probability the firm does badly $\left(\text{makes } \pi_L\right)$ is $\left(1-y\right)$,

where $0 < y < x < 1$. All this means is that the firm is more *likely* to make high profits (π_H) if the manager 'works' rather than 'shirks'.

The manager dislikes hard work, however. We define $\phi > 0$ as the amount of money he would have to be paid to exactly compensate him for working hard, all else held constant. This means that if the manager 'works' his utility is $U(w - \phi)$, whereas if he 'shirks' it is $U(w)$.

The manager is taken to be able to leave the firm and go to another job, if he wishes. This alternative job offers terms (wage net of work effort level) of w_0, i.e. it yields utility $U_0 = U(w_0)$. The shareholder cannot offer the manager a deal which leaves him with less utility than U_0, therefore, otherwise the manager would leave. This constraint reflects the operation of an external market for managers. (Alternatively, one might think of w_0 as income from unemployment benefit.)

At the same time, the shareholder will only wish to participate in the firm if the expected return is at least as great as that which she could get elsewhere. Specifically, we take it that the shareholder closes the firm down if expected net profit is negative. We shall generally assume that expected net profits are, in fact, non-negative but shall briefly return to this issue at the end of the chapter.

Full information benchmark solution

What would happen under the traditional conditions of full and verifiable information, i.e. where the shareholder can observe the manager's effort level (and could verify this in court)?

In this situation, the shareholder can simply decide how hard she wants the manager to work and offer him a corresponding wage, just high enough to ensure that the manager does not leave. Given that the manager is risk averse and the shareholder is risk neutral, the cheapest way of keeping the manager is for the shareholder to offer him a flat wage; no bonuses, no profit-related element etc. in the package, just a predictable income for the manager.

One way of thinking about this is as follows. Risk aversion means the manager dislikes any uncertainty in pay, and would require more money *on average* as compensation for such uncertainty he might bear (a kind of risk premium); the shareholder is interested in maximizing average net profits and so prefers to award wages which are as low as possible on average, short of losing the manager. Thus she offers a flat wage (which involves zero risk premium) to the manager.

Note well that this means we get *optimal risk sharing*, under full information: the risk averse manager bears no risk, and the risk neutral shareholder bears all the risk.

What is the flat wage level that the manager will be paid under full information? There are two cases:

Case A: the shareholder demands low effort and pays the manager a flat wage of exactly w_0, yielding utility $U_0 = U(w_0)$. This is the lowest wage she can offer before the manager decides to leave (and hence the one that gives the shareholder most profit, given low effort).[1]

Case B: the shareholder demands high effort and pays the manager a flat wage of $w_0 + \phi$. The shareholder can no longer offer a wage of only w_0 because the manager is being asked to work hard, so he will want compensation of ϕ for this otherwise he will leave. This package yields utility to the manager of[2] $U([w_0 + \phi] - \phi) = U(w_0) = U_0$.

If the shareholder insists that the manager works hard, then this leads to a higher probability of good profits, but at the cost of having to pay the manager to compensate for that hard work. If the expected gains outweigh the losses (that is if $(x - y)(\pi_H - \pi_L) > \phi$ holds true) then Case B applies, otherwise we obtain Case A.[3] We cannot say *a priori* which is the relevant solution.

Now consider what would happen under *imperfect* information if Case A applied. In this case the shareholder *wants* low effort, hence she can offer a flat wage w_0 and trust to the manager's inherent dislike of hard work to ensure that his effort level is indeed low. The solution under moral hazard is *identical* to that under full information *when the shareholder prefers low effort (Case A)*.

Imperfect information – moral hazard under Case B

For the remainder of this chapter we shall concentrate on the outcome with imperfect information in the more substantive case where the shareholder would prefer high effort if she could observe the effort level (Case B). Introducing imperfect information under these circumstances does present a problem – the shareholder could in good faith offer the manager the appropriate compensation for working hard (i.e. offer wage $w_0 + \phi$); the latter may then pocket the extra money without putting in the extra effort, and (secretly) laugh at the shareholder's naivety. If profits turn out to be high despite his low effort then that is fine, if they do not then the manager can always say 'it was not my fault, I did my best . . .' and the shareholder is none the wiser. This is the moral hazard problem, and one that is probably very familiar to most people in many different situations.[4]

Is there anything the shareholder can do in this situation? The classic solution referred to in chapter 9 is to offer a remuneration package which will *induce* the manager to work hard. There is no point linking the managers pay *directly* to his effort level, because the shareholder cannot observe this – she must link pay to something else which is commonly observable. The one thing which both the shareholder and manager can observe is the gross profits of the firm (i.e. π_L or π_H), so she could link the manager's pay package to this. This allows the manager to be offered the carrot of higher pay for higher profits as an incentive for him to work hard. That way he bears at least some of the consequences of his own actions. Such a package could be in the form of bonuses, profit-related pay or profit sharing etc. Whatever system the shareholder chooses, the end result in our model would be that the manager gets a wage (call it w_L) when poor gross profits are realized (π_L) and a wage (call it w_H) when high gross profits (π_H) are realized. Note well that there is no constraint for w_L and w_H to be the same.

The shareholder's problem can then be thought of as one of finding appropriate levels for w_H and w_L such as to maximize her expected net profit, subject to two constraints, called (respectively) the 'incentive compatibility constraint' and the 'participation constraint'. We shall deal with them in turn.

Incentive compatibility constraint

This says that w_L and w_H must be set at levels such that:

$$EU_{\text{work}} \geq EU_{\text{shirk}}.$$

The Manager's expected utility from working is at least as great as that from shirking. That way it is in the manager's own interest to work hard, i.e. his incentives are 'compatible' with the desires of the shareholder. Note that the greater the value of w_H above w_L the greater the incentive to the manager to work hard, and so the higher is EU_{work} relative to EU_{shirk}.[5] Formal expressions for EU_{work} and for EU_{shirk} are given in the appendix to this chapter.

Participation constraint

This constraint says that w_L and w_H must be set such that

$$EU_{work} \geq U_0.$$

That is, the expected utility from staying with the firm and working hard must be at least as great as the utility he would get from going to another job elsewhere. That way we ensure that it is in the manager's interests to stay with (i.e. 'participate' in) the firm. This constraint reflects the operation of the external market for managers.

Solution for net profit maximization

We have written these constraints as weak inequalities (i.e. we use the '$\geq$' sign), since any value for EU_{work} which is at least as great as U_0 is necessary for the manager to 'participate', and any value for EU_{work} at least as great as EU_{shirk} is necessary for him to work hard (see note 5). If the shareholder sets w_L high and w_H at astronomical levels, for example, then both constraints will probably be satisfied. But such a policy will not maximize the shareholder's expected net profit. In fact, maximization of expected net profits subject to these two constraints dictates that the shareholder sets w_L and w_H at levels such that both constraints are *binding* (i.e. they hold with equality):

$$EU_{work} = EU_{shirk} = U_0.$$

The driving force behind this solution is that the shareholder wants to set wages as low as possible on average, to leave herself the maximum expected net profit. Hence she offers the manager wages that are only *just enough* to ensure that he stays (participation) and that he works hard (incentive compatibility). To show that *both constraints are binding* at a solution, consider what would happen in the alternative cases:

(1)   Suppose that only the participation constraint was binding ($EU_{work} = U_0$). This means that the shareholder's expected net profits are effectively constrained only by the offer of w_H and w_L such that the manager chooses to stay. But we have already seen that expected net

profit maximization under such circumstances yields a solution where $w_H = w_L = w_0 + \phi$, and that is not consistent with incentive compatibility since the offer of a flat wage offers no incentive to motivate the manager. Hence this case cannot be a solution.

(2)   Suppose that only the incentive compatibility constraint was binding ($EU_{work} = EU_{shirk}$). This means that the shareholder's expected net profits are constrained only by the offer of w_H and w_L such that the manager is motivated. But then the shareholder could always lower w_L (say). The difference between w_L and w_H would still be sufficient to motivate the manager, and the shareholder would leave more profit for herself. Hence this case cannot be a solution either.

Features of the solution

1   Risk sharing is sub-optimal. In order to find wages such that $EU_{work} = EU_{shirk} = U_0$ we *must have* $w_H > w_L$, and so the risk averse manager ends up facing some uncertainty over his wages. Under full information the risk neutral shareholder bore all the risk. Under imperfect information, however, uncertainty over the wage is necessary to motivate the risk averse manager (i.e. to satisfy incentive compatibility).

2   The manager is exactly as well off in expected utility terms under imperfect and full information. This is because the participation constraint is binding in both cases, hence the manager gets expected utility equivalent to U_0 in both cases.

3   The shareholder is worse off under imperfect information. To see this, note that the manager faces uncertain wages ($w_H > w_L$), but still gets the same expected utility $EU_{work} = U_0$. The manager must therefore receive some compensation via a higher average wage for the uncertainty he faces, to leave him as well off as he had been with a certain wage, given that he is risk averse.

The expected wage payment under imperfect information (with hard work) is

$$xw_H + (1 - x)w_L.$$

The wage with hard work under full information is $w_0 + \phi$. The above argument then establishes that

$$xw_H + (1 - x)w_L > w_0 + \phi,$$

where the difference between the left- and the right-hand sides gives the risk premium that the manager requires to exactly compensate him for the uncertainty he faces in his wages. The appendix to this chapter gives a diagrammatic exposition of this point.

Since the risk neutral shareholder pays more wages on average under imperfect information in order to motivate the manager, so we can conclude that the expected profits left over for the shareholder are on average lower, that is $E(\pi - w)$ is lower than under full information. Hence the shareholder is worse off.

4 The full information solution Pareto-dominates the imperfect information solution. This is because the manager is no better off (result **2**), but the shareholder is worse off than under full information (result **3**).

The welfare loss due to imperfect information arises because risk bearing is not optimally shared between the shareholder and the manager. At a solution it turns out that the whole of this loss falls on the shareholder because the contract she can offer is constrained by the external market for managers.

Alternative solutions (under Case B)

We have shown above that if the shareholder prefers high effort under full information, then she must accept a cut in expected profits in order to induce high effort under imperfect information. Call the latter level of expected net profits Π_{work}. She has two alternatives to this. Firstly she could tolerate slacking, yielding expected net profits Π_{shirk}, or she could shut the firm down, yielding expected profits of zero.

It is conceivable that the shareholder might prefer to tolerate slacking under imperfect information rather than induce hard work (i.e. it is possible for $\Pi_{work} < \Pi_{shirk}$), even though she preferred high effort under full information.[6] This is because *inducing* high effort is costly to the shareholder, as we have seen, since she has to pay the manager a risk premium. That premium could be so great as to make the incentive scheme not worthwhile.

Finally, it is even possible that the shareholder decides to close the firm down altogether (a power she has as 'residual controller'/owner of the firm). Say under full information the firm makes positive expected net profits when the manager works hard, but negative expected net profits when he shirks. Further, take it that the incentive package to induce hard work under imperfect information is so costly (in terms of the risk premium) that it ends up yielding negative expected net profits also. Then we have $\Pi_{work} < 0$, $\Pi_{shirk} < 0$, and the shareholder prefers to close the firm down and earn 0 under imperfect information, where she would have kept it running and made a profit under full information. This 'shut down' option in a sense reflects the operation of a market for the services of the principal; just as the manager may not work for the firm if the expected utility there is less than elsewhere, so the principal may do the same.

The manager ends up equally well off under any solution – he always end up with utility U_0 (e.g. if the shareholder shuts down, then he goes to another firm and still gets U_0). But if Case B applies the shareholder is always worse off compared to the full information outcome; if she induces hard work then she must pay a risk premium; if she tolerates slacking then she bears the welfare loss due to sub-optimal effort, and if she shuts the firm down she loses all profit from the firm.

The imperfect information outcome is therefore Pareto-inefficient in each of these solutions compared to the outcome under full information, given Case B. It is important to note, however, that whichever imperfect information solution actually obtains, that outcome is Pareto-efficient *given the presence of imperfect information* in the market. No benign authority acting under similar information constraints could make either party better off without making the other party worse off. To see this, take the case where the principal prefers the incentive contract solution ($w_H > w_L$) to tolerating shirking or closing down. The welfare loss in this case is minimized; the loss is due to the risk averse manager facing uncertain wages, and the spread of wages in the solution contract is the *minimum possible*, consistent with inducing high effort. We cannot reduce the risk sharing problem any further. Finally, note that if the principal opted for shutdown or slacking instead of incentive pay, then she does so because she *prefers* that outcome; out of all the possible outcomes under imperfect information she chooses her most preferred.

The role of attitudes to risk

Our analysis hinges on the fact that the manager is risk averse, whereas the shareholder is risk neutral. If the manager were also risk neutral, then it would not matter who bears the risk. The shareholder could throw as much risk as she liked on the manager as part of an incentive scheme, and there would be no loss from suboptimal risk sharing. The sort of remuneration package described above ($w_H > w_L$) would be no more costly on average than payment of a flat wage, and hence the shareholder's expected net profits need not suffer. This point is again demonstrated diagrammatically in the appendix to this chapter.

Summary

In this chapter we investigate the consequences of moral hazard in a relatively simple situation. A shareholder owns a firm, and delegates responsibility to a manager for running it. The former is taken to be risk neutral since she can diversify her risks, the latter is risk averse since he has his livelihood heavily tied up in the one firm. The firm's profits depend partly on luck, and partly on the manager's effort level.

Under full information the shareholder can dictate whether she wants the manager to work hard or not. The shareholder may find it more profitable to dictate high effort, but the converse is also possible. If the former holds, then the shareholder must pay the manager a wage that compensates him for his hard work. Whether the shareholder prefers high effort or low effort, the risk sharing outcome is always optimal under full information, i.e. the risk neutral shareholder bears all the risk, and the risk averse manager bears none.

Under imperfect information the shareholder cannot observe (or at least cannot verify in a court of law) the manager's effort level. If the shareholder *wanted* low effort, then this would not matter. The same outcome emerges under imperfect information as under full information.

If the shareholder wanted the manager to work hard however, then with imperfect information she would have to offer some inducement i.e. she must make it 'worth the manager's while'. To provide the manager with the right incentives, the shareholder can pay him more when the firm gets high profits. That way the manager's interests are aligned with the shareholder's towards working for high profits.

Unfortunately, such a deal inevitably means that the manager shoulders some of the risk. In order to compensate for this risk, the shareholder must pay the manager more *on average*. This compensation leaves the manager exactly as well off in expected utility terms as he was under full information. But it eats into the shareholder's expected net profits, leaving her clearly worse-off. The welfare loss arises because of suboptimal risk sharing, and it is the shareholder who bears this loss.

Alternatively, the shareholder may find that it is so costly to induce the manager to work hard under imperfect information, that she would rather give up the attempt, and let the manager 'shirk' for the standard flat wage (w_0). The manager is still as well off as before but imperfect information leads to losses for the shareholder due to sub-optimal effort. Finally, the shareholder may prefer to shut the firm down under imperfect information, yielding net profit of zero, when she would have kept the firm running with positive expected net profit under full information.

Whatever happens, if the shareholder prefers high effort with full information then the imperfect information outcome is Pareto-dominated by the full information outcome. The consequences of moral hazard are either that the shareholder suffers from having to compensate the manager for bearing risk; or she has to tolerate shirking when she would prefer the manager to work hard; or she shuts the firm down and makes nothing.

NOTES

1   The offer of w_0 leaves the manager exactly indifferent between staying or going. We break this 'tie' by employing the convention that at a point of indifference the manager stays.

2   The term $[w_0 + \phi]$ is his wage payment, and from this we deduct ϕ for the money value of disutility of hard work, leaving us with $w_0 = w_0 + \phi - \phi$.

3   People often assume the shareholder will always want the manager to work hard (perhaps they like to see the manager suffer!). The reason this may not be true is that the shareholder has to *pay* for the hard work, and it is not always worth it.

4   Game theorists might like to know that our analysis of imperfect information can be thought of as identifying subgame perfect solutions to a two-stage game (stage 1 the shareholder offers the manager a contract; stage 2 the manager decides to accept or reject, and if he accepts he decides how hard to work: this then determines the probability of a good outcome). The use of subgame perfection as a solution concept implies that agents (managers) cannot make empty threats about what they would do in stage 2, to influence the outcome in stage 1 (see Kreps, 1990*).

5   When $EU_{work} = EU_{shirk}$ the manager is indifferent between working and shirking. In the event of such a 'tie', we employ the convention that the manager will work hard. A similar point applies to the participation constraint that follows, i.e. when $EU_{work} = U_0$ we take it that the manager stays (see note 1).

6   The exact formulae are:

$$\Pi_{work} = x(\pi_H - w_H) + (1 - x)(\pi_L - w_L)$$
$$\Pi_{skirk} = y\pi_H + (1 - y)\pi_L - w_0.$$

Appendix: The Incentive Pay Package

The incentive pay package gives those values of w_H and w_L that maximize net profits for the shareholder, in the case where she wants the manager to work hard under imperfect information. Expected utility to the manager from 'working' and from 'shirking' are given as:

$$EU_{work} = xU(w_H - \phi) + (1 - x)U(w_L - \phi) \qquad (A1)$$

$$EU_{shirk} = yU(w_H) + (1 - y)U(w_L). \qquad (A2)$$

Net profit maximization in this case is achieved where the shareholder sets w_H and w_L such that these expressions exactly satisfy the following:

$$EU_{work} = EU_{shirk} \quad \text{(incentive compatibility)}$$
$$EU_{work} = U_0 \quad \text{(participation)}.$$

We wish to show here that the expected wage payment that arises in the solution to this problem is higher than that which would arise under full information, that is:

$$xw_H + (1 - x)w_L > w_0 + \phi. \qquad (A3)$$

To see this, consider figure 10.1 which depicts an illustrative solution for the incentive pay package. The vertical axis gives the manager's expected utility, and the horizontal axis gives his wage *net of the money cost of high effort*. We deduct the cash amount ϕ because as far as the manager is concerned this merely compensates him for the hard work he is putting in. After deducting ϕ, the (hard working) manager under full information gets $[w_0 + \phi] - \phi = w_0$, and under imperfect information he gets $w_L - \phi$ if profits are low and $w_H - \phi$ if they are high. At a solution, these quantities are such that $EU_{work} = U_0$.

Now note the point z on the horizontal axis of figure 10.1. This point is found by drawing a horizontal line from EU_{work} until it intersects the straight line between $U(w_L - \phi)$ and $U(w_H - \phi)$ on the diagram and then going directly down to the horizontal axis. In algebraic terms, z is given as a weighted average of $(w_L - \phi)$ and $(w_H - \phi)$, that is:

$$z = x(w_H - \phi) + (1 - x)(w_L - \phi). \qquad (A4)$$

If we multiply out the bracketed terms, cancel out where appropriate, and collect terms we get:

$$z = xw_H + (1 - x)w_L - \phi. \tag{A5}$$

The next step is to note from the diagram that

$$z > w_0 \tag{A6}$$

(this follows from the concave shape of the utility function, which reflects the manager's aversion to risk).

So, if we add ϕ to both sides it follows that:

$$z + \phi > w_0 + \phi. \tag{A7}$$

But if we add ϕ to z we see from equation (A5):

$$z + \phi = xw_H + (1 - x)w_L$$

hence expression (A7) is equivalent to saying:

$$xw_H + (1 - x)w_L > w_0 + \phi \tag{A8}$$

which is the result given in the main text.

Finally, note what would happen *if the manager were risk neutral*. His utility function would then be a straight line, rather than the concave shape in figure 10.1. We would then find that $z = w_0$ (contrary to (A6) above). Following through the same steps as before, we find that the expected wage payments in this case would be the same under full as they are under imperfect information. The manager could, in this case, be motivated at no extra cost to the shareholder, because he requires no compensation for bearing risk.

CHAPTER 11

Further Literature on Moral Hazard and Agency Theory

In this chapter we discuss generalizations of the formal theory on moral hazard in an agency context. The emphasis of this chapter is on the theoretical modelling considerations that arise when we extend the basic framework in these directions. In some cases these raise new issues that have not been considered so far; others connect back to the fairly informal discussion of shareholder–manager problems in chapter 9; and many relate to applications of the principal–agent framework beyond the shareholder–manager example.

Point 1   Constraints on the Incentive Contract

One obvious difficulty that has not been considered so far is that incentive pay packages might run into constraints on the contract that may be offered, such as a wage floor (**Tirole, 1988**). Such a floor might reflect the operation of a minimum wage policy or some legal minimum level of pay; it might reflect a subsistence level of income that the agent requires to stay alive; or it may arise because the principal cannot offer a wage less than zero.

Suppose that (within the context of the model set out in chapter 10) w_0 represents an *absolute minimum* wage. The principal is then constrained to offer a wage package with $w_H > w_L \geq w_0$ (if she wishes to motivate the agent). The agent may *choose* to work hard when faced by this package, but that is a voluntary choice on his part; he could still shirk if he wishes. Shirking would yield utility rankings of the various outcomes as $U(w_H) > U(w_L) \geq U(w_0)$. His expected utility would then be a weighted average of

$U(w_H)$ and $U(w_L)$, and this strictly *exceeds* $U(w_0)$. When the wage floor is binding (the principal would like to offer a wage package where wages may dip below w_0, but she cannot) then this implies that *the participation constraint is not binding*: the agent gets $EU > U_0$. The agent enjoys an *economic rent* as a consequence – he gets a deal from the principal that yields greater expected utility than he could get elsewhere.

Point 2 Multiple Effort Levels

In real-world situations there are likely to be gradations of effort level that the agent can decide on, rather than just 'working' versus 'shirking'. In the most general case, effort might be a continuous variable taking any value between some lower and upper limits (perhaps 0 and ∞ respectively). References which generalize the model in this way are too numerous to mention[1] (**Kreps, 1990,** gives an outline, for example). These more general models confirm the insights yielded by our simple model of chapter 10. Two further insights that we would wish to highlight from the more general models are that:

(a) It is possible for *both* effort and risk-sharing to be at sub-optimal (i.e. not first best) levels under moral hazard. Where there are many effort levels to choose from, then the principal might trade off the risk-premium involved in getting motivation right against the losses from allowing some degree of sub-optimality in effort.

(b) It is possible for effort to be *too high* under moral hazard. Normally we tend to think of the agent slacking on the job when hidden action is present, but Kreps (1990)* gives a nice numerical example where the optimal incentive package in equilibrium causes the agent to work too hard, as compared to the first best full information outcome. The idea is that a *fully informed* principal may prefer the agent to exert medium effort levels (e.g. because high effort levels require substantial compensation). An *imperfectly informed* principal may, however, find it cheaper to induce *high* effort (via an incentive package) relative to the increased expected profits, than to induce medium effort or allow slacking. Such a situation might arise, for example, because the probable outcomes are such that high effort virtually *guarantees* high profits so that the agent requires near zero risk premium, whereas inducing medium effort may require a substantial risk premium.

Point 3   Multiple Profit Levels:
The Form of Incentive Pay Contracts

The issue here is about the relationship between pay and performance that is specified in the agent's contract, when moral hazard is present. In the model of chapter 10 there were just two states of the world (low gross profits and high gross profits) so the incentive pay contract needed only to specify w_L and w_H. More generally, there are likely to be many possible performance outcomes (e.g. profits may vary from terrible to poor to OK to good to excellent, etc.). What, then, can we say about the likely impact of higher performance on agent's pay in an optimally designed (i.e. profit maximizing) contract? The surprising answer is 'not very much'.

One might, for example, expect to be able to say that, in an optimal contract 'the better the performance, the more the agent gets paid', or at least that his pay does not fall. That sounds reasonable enough. Unfortunately, as **Grossman and Hart (1983)*** show, we cannot even say that – it is quite possible for wages to *decrease* with improved performance, over some ranges. To illustrate this, consider the following situation. Say the agent can 'work' or 'shirk' and expected (or average) net profits are higher if the agent is induced to 'work'. Further assume that there is a specific gross profit outcome $\Pi 1$ that is only ever likely to be observed if the agent 'shirked'. In order to discourage the agent from shirking, the principal is likely to offer very low wages ('boil them in oil'? – see chapter 9) if that level of profits $\Pi 1$ is observed – *even if that particular level of profits happened to be quite high*. The threat to 'boil the agent in oil' if that outcome is observed ensures that the agent will never shirk. Thus we can get relatively high (and possibly increasing) wages over most profit ranges, but a dramatic fall towards the 'boil in oil' level when $\Pi 1$ is observed. The optimal wage contract is not monotonically increasing in observed performance.

The obvious question that follows is to ask 'under what conditions is the optimal incentive package likely to stipulate higher pay for higher performance?' The answer to this question turns out to be rather technical (Grossman and Hart, 1983*) but roughly speaking two conditions are involved:[2]

(a)   'The monotone likelihood ratio property' holds. This basically says that the chances of observing high profits as compared to low profits tends to increase as effort increases.

(b)   The 'concavity of the distribution function property' holds. This says in essence that the marginal impact of effort on performance tends to be lower when effort levels are high.

If these properties hold, then the standard principal–agent model predicts that rewards *will* increase with performance. From a theoretical point of view the possibility that they do *not* hold (so that pay may fall with performance over some ranges) is intriguing, but it is also problematic for at least two reasons. Firstly, it means that the *predictive* content of the model is weak. We argued earlier (see chapter 5 on signalling) that theories which say 'anything is possible' are not particularly useful; a good theory ought to yield clear (and falsifiable) predictions, and in this respect the principal–agent model does not. The second problem is that in the 'real world', incentive contracts *do* usually give higher pay for higher performance; this model does not seem to be able to come up with a good explanation for this (simply saying that 'in the real world the above two conditions usually hold' does not seem a very satisfactory answer).

Further literature in the area has tried to develop the principal–agent model in order to provide a deeper understanding of the forms of incentive contracts we observe in reality. Consider first of all the following sorts of contracts: commission sales, piece rates and crop shares (where tenant farmers rent land from a landlord and keep a share of their crops for themselves). Contrast these with sales bonus systems (where salesmen get rewards for reaching specified targets). In all these systems, the agent's reward increases with his performance. In the former types of systems, however, not only are the agents' rewards positively related to performance, but the relationship is *linear* of the form:

$$\text{wage} = \alpha + \beta \cdot \text{performance.} \tag{11.1}$$

To take the case of commission sales, we measure performance by revenue from sales volume. If the salesman makes no sales, his performance is zero, and he just gets a 'basic pay' of $\alpha \geq 0$. As his sales increase, so rewards increase at the rate $\beta \geq 0$; e.g. if $\beta = 0.1$ then he gets 10 cents for every extra \$1 of sales.

Holmstrom and Milgrom (1987)[*] attempted to explain why in the 'real world' incentive schemes often involve pay that not only increases with performance, but increases in this linear fashion. They set up and analyse a multi-period principal–agent model, and show that whilst linear incentive schemes may not be optimal, they often produce solutions that are '*close to*' optimal. They showed that *optimal* rules are often highly complex, and sensitive to the precise specification of the model; *linear* schemes are by contrast *robust*, i.e. they work well (if not optimally) in most environments. This robustness derived from the fact that linear schemes apply equal incentive pressure at all points – no matter what your sales are so far, one more sale will get you the same extra bit of commission income. And linear schemes also have the great practical advantage of being easy to administer and to understand.

This might explain the popularity of such schemes. Why then do we also observe systems such as bonus schemes, which involve pay hikes at certain performance thresholds and hence are apparently highly non-linear? Such systems apply very uneven incentive pressure – once a salesman has reached a specific target, there is little incentive to make the next few sales. Holmstrom and Milgrom's analysis suggests, however, that such schemes can *resemble* linear packages to the extent that (a) the period over which targets are specified are made sufficiently short, so that the agent does not go for extended lengths of time with little incentive pressure, and (b) the salesman can act strategically over the timing of sales, so that if a particular sale would gain them little reward *now* then they can defer it (say) to a period when it does reap a reward.

Point 4   The Value of Extra Information

We have assumed in our discussion so far that the only information that the principal has to go on (in assessing the agent's effort level) is some measure of performance such as the gross profits of the firm. In the 'real world', the principal may not be so completely 'in the dark'. The shareholders of a firm may have a variety of other sources of information – some of them internal to the firm, such as detailed information obtained from auditors and perhaps contained in company accounts, others external such as information on the performance of other similar firms, or perhaps on the 'state of the economy' as a whole. It may be possible to incorporate such information into the incentive contract in a way that lowers the agency costs (**Holmstrom, 1979*; Shavell, 1979***).

To extend our example of chapter 10, we shall consider a case where information is costlessly available on the general state of the economy in terms of whether 'good times' prevail, or 'bad times'. If the agent 'works' then the chances of the firm doing well in the good times is x_g, and in the bad times it is x_b, where $x_g > x_b$. Similarly, we have $y_g > y_b$ if the agent shirks. This means that the firm is *more likely* to do well in 'good times' than 'bad times', given the effort level of the agent (as usual, we have $x_g > y_g$ and $x_b > y_b$).

This information could be incorporated into the pay package by offering wages in 'good times' of w^g_L if the firm does badly, and w^g_H if the firm does well. These are calculated to (just) satisfy the participation and incentive compatibility constraint set out in chapter 10, *evaluated using x_g and y_g*. Similarly, wages in 'bad times' of w^b_L and w^b_H are offered, which satisfy these constraints evaluated using x_b and y_b. Thus the reward for high profits in good times may be less than that offered in bad times in this extended contract, to reflect the fact that it is harder for the agent to produce good profits when the economy as a whole is in a downturn.

'Fine-tuning' the pay package in this way lowers the average wage paid by the principal to the agent to a level closer to that paid under full information, by reducing the risk premium paid to the agent; the agent no longer bears any risk for that part of the variability in the firms returns which is due to the general state of the economy (and so is outside his control). The agency costs are reduced, since the principal is now better off whilst the agent is no worse off in expected utility terms. Hence the extra information (on the state of the economy) has value here in terms of the reduction in agency costs.

One way of thinking about this is that it is 'as if' the principal faces a standard problem of statistical inference; she observes the firm's profits and must infer from this the agent's action. Extra information (such as data on the state of the economy) is valuable in so far as it allows her to draw *more accurate* inferences about the action from observation of the outcome.[3]

We can illustrate how this works to reduce agency costs, by taking an extreme case where the *only* source of 'bad luck' or 'good luck' facing the firm lies in the variation in the state of the economy – so that once the principal observes this information and the firm's gross profits then she can infer *exactly* whether or not the agent worked hard. Observation of these two variables becomes an exact substitute for observing the agents' effort directly, and the principal has (in effect) full information – she can offer the agent a flat wage (flat in the sense that it does not vary with profits, it depends only on how hard the agent worked) relieving him of all risk-bearing, and hence requiring zero risk premium.

To go to the other extreme, now consider a case where $x_g = x_b$ and $y_g = y_b$, specifically excluded from the above. Here the principal is unable to draw more accurate inferences about the agent's behaviour with this information than without it; if she tried using this information in the pay package she would end up offering the same pay deal in both good and bad times, hence the average wage would be unchanged. Agency costs are not reduced, and the extra information has no value in this context. In Holmstrom's terminology, the observed profits would be a 'sufficient statistic', in that data on the 'state of the economy' adds no information of value in setting the pay package to motivate effort than that already contained in the profits data.

So far, we have assumed that the information available on the state of the economy is free. We can now elaborate on the example by introducing a *price* on obtaining that information. For example, the principal may have to set up a costly accounting system to produce information internally in the organization. When would the principal pay the price for the information? If the information is of no value, then the principal would clearly *not* pay to acquire it. In general, where there is such a price, then the principal would be willing to buy the information when its value in terms of $E(\pi - w)$ is at least as great as its price.

Point 5   Optimal Incentive Intensity

From now on we shall assume that the incentive package is in effect linear, in tune with the arguments of point 3 above. The linear package is of the form given by equation (11.1), where β can be thought of as a measure of 'incentive intensity' embedded the contract. The idea here is that the higher is β, the more steeply rewards increase with performance, and hence the greater (or more intense) the incentive faced by the agent to strive towards high performance. What factors affect the level of β which the principal should offer to get the highest net profits from the agent's activities (i.e. what determines the 'optimal incentive intensity')?

First of all, we shall take it that the environment in which the principal and agent operate is such that (i) expected gross profits increase with effort at a decreasing rate (i.e. 'concavity of the distribution function', see above) and (ii) the marginal cost to the agent of supplying effort is positive and increasing in effort. Assumption (i) says that as effort increases it gets harder to squeeze out further gains in expected gross profit; assumption (ii) says that if the agent works a 12-hour day it is more costly (requires greater compensation) to supply an extra hour than if he worked a 4-hour day. Under these assumptions it can be shown (see, for example, **Milgrom and Roberts, 1992, chapter 7** for a derivation) that the optimal incentive intensity will be higher (all else being equal):

(a)   *The more responsive is the agent's effort to the financial incentives* (i.e. the lower the rate at which marginal effort costs rise with effort level). It is not worth offering large financial inducements for little increase in effort.

(b) *The greater the impact of effort on gross profits*. There is little point inducing the agent into great efforts, if the impact of those efforts on the firm's profits are negligible.

(c) *The less risk averse is the agent*. We have seen that a remuneration package which induces effort results in the principal paying a higher wage on average, in order to compensate the agent for the resulting risk that he bears. The more averse is the agent to that risk, the greater the compensation needed. The principal must 'balance' the benefits from higher agent effort due to the incentive scheme, against the costs of the higher average wage as compensation for agent risk bearing. The optimal 'balance' shifts in favour of lower incentive rewards, the more risk averse the agent happens to be.

(d) *The lower the precision with which agents' effort is assessed*. We showed in point 4 above how extra information could be used to alleviate the agency problem by allowing the principal to (in a sense) infer more precisely the agent's effort. We also made the point that where the extra information allowed exact inference of the agent's effort, then the agency problem would disappear and the optimal incentive was zero ($\beta = 0$ and the agent receives a flat wage). This is a benchmark case of 'perfect precision' in assessing agent's effort. As the information gets poorer and so assessment of the agent's effort becomes less precise, so the optimal incentive intensity (β) increases.

Point 6   Equal Compensation of Diverse Activities

Say an agent undertakes many different activities for the principal, and has to allocate his effort between these activities. Often there is no adequate single summary measure of performance across these activities. A good example which the author knows something about would be the university lecturer who has to divide his effort between teaching and research. The same sort of issue arises in most jobs, however, since people usually have a number of different task and responsibilities – a manager might run different branches of a firm for example or have responsibilities for different sections of the firm's activities. How is an agent with diverse activities to be motivated in terms of appropriate incentive packages?

The agent is ultimately interested in the marginal return he gets on effort across the different activities. If one activity yields higher returns on effort than another, he will devote all his effort to the former. If working on one branch of the firm makes more money than another branch, then to maximize his return net of effort costs the manager works on the high performance branch. In order to get an agent to devote effort to *both* activities, his marginal return on effort must be rewarded equally across the two activities. This is what **Milgrom and Roberts (1992)** call the 'Equal Compensation Principle'.

In practice, it can be extremely difficult to design incentive packages which satisfy this principle, not least because performance is often very difficult to measure in certain spheres. If the principal gets the incentives wrong then she may severely distort the agent's behaviour, by motivating him to entirely neglect certain aspects of his work. In such circumstances, the principal might be better off abandoning the incentive package altogether.

It is easy to think of examples where problems of this kind arise. In the UK, there are widespread press reports of the mis-selling of pensions, insurance, mortgages and other financial products. Part of the problem would appear to be that the sales representatives are rewarded by sales volume, and hence they use high pressure selling techniques. They get no reward for devoting effort to assessing whether the *customer* is better off with one product or another, or none at all. Hence they neglect this issue, the firm and industry reputation suffers, and large-scale legal wrangles over compensation may follow – but the sales representatives' behaviour is rational given the offered incentives.

Returning to the university lecturer example, it is often argued that research performance is easier to assess than teaching performance, and in the past rewards (promotions, salary etc.) have tended to be based on the former. As a result, teaching may suffer. Students may have their own stories to tell on this.

Point 7   Multiple Agents

In many real-world situations the principal might have to deal with several agents. An owner might have several managers; an employer might supervise several workers; a school headteacher usually has many teachers underneath her to deal with, etc. In this section we look at two related questions that arise in this context; firstly we consider whether the principal can reduce agency costs by incorporating an element of *comparative* performance into the incentive package, and secondly we examine the role played by the principal when dealing with a *team* of agents.

On the first point, **Lazear and Rosen (1981)** and **Green and Stokey (1983)** – henceforth LR–GS – analyse a model incorporating multiple (risk averse) agents, where each agent's performance depends partly on their own effort, partly on a 'luck-factor' that affects *all* the agents, and partly on their own individual luck. These 'luck-factors' are in effect random variables, the former being common to all agents (e.g. the general trading conditions in the market), and the latter being specific to individuals (e.g. whether you happen to strike lucky with a lucrative deal, say, even though general trading conditions might be bad). The (risk neutral) principal only observes the performance of the agents. She could offer each agent an incentive contract of the kind discussed in chapter 10, where each agent's pay depends only on his performance. LR–GS note, however, that in the 'real world', rewards are often based also on *relative performance* – e.g. an employer might rank the performance of his workers and reward the best performer with higher pay or promotion, say. Such a reward structure is called a 'tournament'. In what context are such tournaments likely to yield better results than separate incentive contracts?

LR–GS show that the answer to this question depends on the relative variability attached to the common versus the individual-specific luck-factors affecting performance. If the individual-specific luck-factor has a lower variance than the common luck-factor, then the tournament is better; vice versa, and the separate contracts are better.

The intuition for this is that if agent's performance varies greatly with general trading conditions (and individual-specific luck matters little) then the independent contracts would subject agent's pay to substantial volatility that is outside their own control; their pay would rise and fall with the market, and they would require a substantial risk premium to compensate them for these fluctuations. A tournament substantially alleviates this problem since it is relative performance that matters. The absolute performance of each agent fluctuates with the market but relative performance is likely to be more stable, and hence rewards based on a tournament largely filter out this market based volatility in agents' pay. The tournament throws less risk on the agents, and hence reduces the agency costs by lowering the risk premium necessary to keep them.

By contrast, if market conditions matter little in affecting performance, but individual luck matters a lot, then the tournament has the opposite effect. The tournament leads to agent A's pay depending partly on the performance (and therefore the *luck* of agent B) and vice versa. Where each agent's luck factor is highly variable, then the tournament throws *extra* variability into A's pay package that is outside his control – why should he lose out, just because B struck lucky? Hence the tournament leads to increased risk premia in each agent's pay package (and raises agency costs), relative to the independent contracts.[4]

We now turn to the second issue mentioned earlier, concerning the role of the principal when faced by a *team* of agents who work together. Consider a situation where agents act in a team, in the sense that their *joint* efforts affect performance; the contribution of any one agent may be affected by the efforts of others. In such circumstances Alchian and Demsetz (1972) argued that the role of the principal/owner was to act as a monitor of agents' behaviour (see chapter 1, note 4). **Holmstrom (1982)*** developed a formal model of this kind of situation which demonstrated that the principal could play quite another role from that envisaged by Alchian and Demsetz.

Say the behaviour of individual agents in the team is privately observed, but the overall performance (team output) is commonly observable. The output from joint performance may be certain (i.e. not subject to random forces). A moral hazard problem still arises in that each member of the team has an incentive to free-ride since it is individually rational to sit back and let others take the strain. An incentive package may be used to try to motivate the team. The key issue that Holmstrom highlighted, however, is that *group incentives are not credible*, in the absence of a principal. The point is that introducing group incentives means that penalties must be imposed if performance is poor, such that the team members do not receive all the output; the principal gets the excess, and this acts as a punishment to the team of agents and hence a deterrent to shirking. In equilibrium, the agents respond by not shirking, such that the penalty need never be enforced – the mere threat of it can solve the moral hazard problem.

If no principal were present, then there would be no way of attaining this outcome, since the threat of punishment would not be credible. To see this, say the team could produce a Pareto-efficient outcome of 100 units if they all worked hard, but free-riding leads to slacking and they produce only 50 units. The optimal penalty for slacking might be that they must destroy some or all of these units – but once they have produced those units they have no incentive to actually carry out the penalty *themselves*. The penalty is not credible, and the team know it: hence we end up at a Pareto-inefficient outcome with 50 units. If a principal were present, however, then she could credibly carry out the penalty by walking off with some or all of the units produced – hence faced with a credible threat the team would not slack in the first place but rather produce the 100 and then be able to keep them.[5]

Point 8 Moral Hazard over Time

Up to now we have been concerned with 'one-shot' games where principals and agents interact once and then the game is over. A wealth of literature has now developed which attempts to model *enduring* relationships, i.e. when the principal–agent game is played again and again between the same players. This literature concentrates on the notion that some or all of the efficiency losses that may arise in the one period analysis may be ameliorated when the game is repeated over time.

Radner (1985)* set out a principal–agent model where the game was played out an infinite number of times. One of the most basic conclusions to emerge from this analysis (and other similar studies) is that there are many equilibria that may be identified in this context. One obvious equilibrium is that the solution to the one-period model be repeated in every period for ever; if the principal offers the same (one-period equilibrium) contract in every period, then the agent can do no better than take his (one-period equilibrium) action in every period, and vice versa – hence both players are playing best responses to each others strategies and we have a Nash equilibrium. In a repeated context, however, there are other equilibria also; for example, long-term contracts may be feasible, where the principal and agent contract on a stream of future payments with the possibility of punishment for 'cheating' built into the contract in the form of reduced payments after observation of a series of bad outcomes. The ability to assess performance over a *sequence* of periods allows the principal to assess the agents' behaviour more accurately (the latter cannot claim they were unlucky *forever*). And the promise of future payments (rewards for good performance, punishment for bad) may be made credible by the establishment of a 'reputation'.

A key influence which affects the kinds of equilibria that may be obtained under repeated moral hazard lies in the discount parameter(s) of the principal and the agent. If the players are very impatient (discount future returns heavily) then the more efficient outcomes may be unsustainable – for example, the threat of future punishment for cheating may not deter the agent from cheating, if he does not value future returns very highly. Call the discount parameter r: then if $r = 1$ the players are 'perfectly patient', i.e. they value returns tomorrow equally to returns today; if $0 < r < 1$ they are impatient in that returns tomorrow are valued less highly than today, and the further is r from 1 the more impatient they are.

Radner demonstrated the following specific results:

(a) There are equilibria in the infinitely repeated game which remove some of the efficiency losses associated with the one-period equilibrium, even with impatient players ($r < 1$). That is, principal and agent can be better off in an enduring relationship.

(b) For perfectly patient players ($r = 1$), the first best full information solution can be achieved as an equilibrium of the repeated imperfect information game. Some intuition for this result is given below.

(c) The equilibria described above can be implemented by a 'review strategy' as follows. The principal offers contracts which involve payment of wages that are part of the first-best contract (say), and reviews performance over a number of periods. If cumulative performance is below some threshold then she would punish the agent over a penalty phase by paying the lower wages that are associated with the one-period equilibrium. The agent responds to the threat of punishment by not cheating. This kind of review strategy is a form of long-term contract, which specifies payments to the agent now and in the future in terms of observed performance over several periods.

With this kind of 'review strategy' in place, it is possible to give some intuition for result (b) above. The idea behind this result is that (with an infinite time horizon) the principal can observe performance over such lengthy time intervals that she can assess the underlying agent's behaviour with virtually pinpoint accuracy, such that the principal is effectively full informed about that behaviour (i.e. with enough repetitions of the game it is 'as if' she has full information); and with no discounting (i.e. $r = 1$) any penalties for misbehaviour she might impose at the end of this sequence of observations are just as painful to the agent as if she had punished him today.

An interesting alternative perspective is provided by **Fudenberg, Holmstrom and Milgrom (1990)*** – henceforth FHM – who argue that the benefits of enduring agency relationships may in fact be achievable by a series of *short-term contracts*, under certain conditions; complex long-term game playing in terms of 'review strategies', retaliation, etc., may be unnecessary. We shall focus on a key condition here, which concerns access to credit markets.[6] Models of the kind suggested by Radner ignore the possibility of saving and borrowing over time in the credit markets. To see the importance of this, imagine a situation where a patient ($r = 1$) agent can save and borrow in a way that exactly smooths his income over time. It would not matter if he had a bad month (say) in terms of lower income, because he would just borrow a bit to make up the shortfall; likewise if he had a good month he would put a bit by for the future. Thus by dealing in the credit market in an inter-temporal context, the agent can shield himself from income fluctuations, making him effectively risk neutral in his dealings with the principal, in a way that is impossible in the one-period model. And with an effectively risk neutral agent, there are no agency costs – the agent takes on as much risk as necessary to motivate him, without demanding any risk premium. Thus, a series of short-term contracts may be sufficient to exploit the efficiency gains from the long-term agency relationship.

Point 9   Ex-Post Renegotiation

The credibility of performance-related pay schemes can be destroyed by the potential for ex post renegotiation. The literature on this issue is surveyed by **Dewatripont and Maskin (1990)**, who give the following example. A teacher tries to motivate her pupils to work hard by setting them an exam, to be taken on Tuesday. Say the pupils study on Monday. Then come Tuesday, both teacher and pupils have an incentive to cancel the exam – the purpose of it was to motivate the pupils and that has been done, so why incur the costs to both sides of sitting the paper, marking the scripts etc.? The reason this kind of 'renegotiation' causes damage, however, is that if the students are able to anticipate the cancellation, then they would not bother to study in the first place, and hence the exercise fails in its original purpose. The exam lacks credibility.

The same thing can happen in our shareholder/manager example. Say we elaborate on the story of chapter 10 very slightly, so that the sequence is as follows:

Stage 1:   the principal designs the contract.

Stage 2:   the agent takes his unobserved action (effort level).

Stage 3:   the outcome (π) is observed.

Say the contract in Stage 1 was designated to motivate the agent as discussed earlier, where the agent gets w_L if π_L is observed and w_H if π_H is observed. Then between Stages 2 and 3 there is scope to renegotiate the contract in a way agreeable to both parties.

With the original contract, the principal's expected payment to the agent (for the latter to work hard in Stage 2) is $xw_H + (1 - x)w_L$ (which we showed was strictly greater than the full information payment of $w_0 + \phi$). Between Stage 2 and Stage 3, the principal and agent could agree a new contract offering $w_0 + \phi + \Delta$ for certain, where Δ is positive but very small such that the following holds

$$xw_H + \left(1 - x\right)w_L > w_0 + \phi + \Delta > w_0 + \phi.$$

The principal would prefer the new contract to the original one (since expected wage payments are lower, from the first inequality). The agent would also prefer the new contract. To see this, note that the original contract yielded expected utility $EU_{work} = U(w_0)$ in equilibrium. The new contract yields utility $U(w_0 + \phi + \Delta - \phi) = U(w_0 + \Delta)$ since the payment of ϕ just compensates for the disutility of hard work, to leave the agent with payment $w_0 + \Delta$ in net terms. Now $U(w_0 + \Delta) > [EU_{work} = U(w_0)]$ and the agent clearly prefers the new contract, as does the principal.

The scope for mutually agreeable renegotiation between Stage 2 and 3 arises because the benefits from the original performance-pay package of motivating the agent are in the past, but the losses from sub-optimal risk sharing are still present; the action has been taken but the outcome is still uncertain. The renegotiated contract therefore restores all risk back to the risk neutral principal.

The courts are hardly likely to insist that the original contract be honoured in this situation, since both parties agree to the renegotiation. But, just as in the teacher–pupil example, the possibility of such renegotiation does damage by destroying the credibility of the original incentive package. At Stage 2 the agent can (and in equilibrium will) anticipate the renegotiation that will occur between Stages 2 and 3 and so will not bother to work hard. Motivation fails because the parties know that at the end of the day the incentive contract will be torn up anyway.

As Dewatripont and Maskin note, there may be ways of avoiding these renegotiation problems. The parties may be able to precommit themselves in some way to abide by the original contract. They may, for example, deliberately introduce rigidities which make it difficult/costly to change the contract at a later date. One possibility would be to write clauses in the contract which forfeit money to some outsider, if the contract were to be renegotiated. (This is similar to Holmstrom's (1982)* argument cited in section (7) about the role of the principal in motivating teams.) Introducing a cost to renegotiation could bind the parties to the original agreement.

Point 10   Mixing Moral Hazard and Adverse Selection: Hybrid Models

So far, we have kept the study of moral hazard and adverse selection problems largely separate in order to distinguish as clearly as possible between them, and to isolate the specific issues raised by each problem. In many real-life situations, however, both problems may be present, often interacting in quite complex ways.

Consider the case of an author (the principal) who deals with a publishing group (the agent) to market her book. (A rock and roll band negotiating a recording contract, or an inventor dealing with some organization to market her product, are also examples.) The author may not have much idea of the sales potential of the book, while the publishing group may be much better informed (hence the private information). The publishers may also require motivation to promote the book properly (hence the hidden action). What kind of contracting system is most likely to cope best with these asymmetric information problems?

Say the author sells the copyright to the publishers: then the latter have motivation to promote it properly (since they receive all the sales revenue), overcoming the moral hazard problem. The problem is that the presence of adverse selection means that the author is unlikely to get a good price for it: the publishers will only buy it at a price below what it is worth.

Say a 'royalty system' was used instead, whereby the author gets a royalty for every unit sold. That way the author shares in the returns if the book is a runaway success – but the publishers have less incentive to promote it properly, since they get a smaller cut of the return from each sale.

One theme of the literature in this area is that the principal may be best off structuring her offer in a way that *extracts* (some part of) the hidden knowledge from the agent. This may be possible by offering a *contingent contract* (**Sappington, 1991**). The author could ask the publishers to forecast sales, and then make the incentives of the contract depend on the forecast. If they forecast high sales, then the author gets a large lump sum payment plus low royalties per unit; if they forecast low sales, she gets a small lump sum but large royalties per unit. With this kind of contingent contract the publishers have an incentive to be truthful in their forecast – since if, for example, they believed sales were likely to be high then they would prefer a contract with low royalties to the author.[7]

A topical case in point that mixes moral hazard and adverse selection in this way is the example of a regulator of a private firm such as a utility for example (Baron, 1989*). The regulator (principal) tends to have poorer information than the firm (the agent) about its potential profits; she also usually cannot fully observe the actions of the firm. The regulator has the problem of setting up controls on the firm in order to maximize some measure of social welfare. In setting up a set of controls, she may then ask the firm for forecasts of profits and make the controls contingent on the forecast. The contingent contract might, for example, specify a price for the product and a level of lump sum subsidy/tax for every level of profits the firm might forecast, much like the author/publisher case cited above.

Summary

In this chapter we have sketched a number of ways in which the simple principal–agent model of chapter 10 might be elaborated. These extensions allowed for:

(1) constraints on the contract, and the possibility of economic rents accruing to the manager;

(2) multiple effort levels, and the possibility of moral hazard leading to excess effort compared to the first best outcome;

(3) multiple profit levels, and the implications for the form of the incentive contract (in theory rewards can decrease with performance; in practise they often increase linearly);

(4) the value of extra information (how additional information can be incorporated into the contract to reduce agency costs);

(5) the determination of the optimal intensity of incentives;

(6) the problems of motivating agents who undertake diverse activities as part of their job, and the consequences of getting motivation wrong;

(7) the motivation of multiple agents, including a comparison of the performance of tournaments versus independent contracts in this context, and a re-examination of the role of the principal when faced by a team of agents;

(8) multi-period models where the moral hazard/principal–agent game is repeated, and the possibility of reducing agency costs in this context either via long-term contracts or a sequence of short-term contracts;

(9) ex post renegotiation of the contract;

(10) and models that mix moral hazard and adverse selection, and the attractions of contingent contracts in this context.

Over the course of the discussion we have cited various applications of the agency model, by way of examples of different settings where a particular extension of the model might become relevant. These included: the motivation of university lecturers to do teaching and research; the motivation of management teams; the author who deals with a publishing company to promote her book; and the regulator of a privatized firm. These are just a few cases in point. The principal–agent framework is rich and flexible enough to cover all sorts of issues that affect the daily lives of most people.

NOTES

1   There are technical problems that arise in solving the continuous effort case, however. In essence, continuous effort means there are an infinite number of incentive compatibility constraints that must be satisfied, such that the desired effort level is the one chosen by the agent in favour of the infinite number of alternative effort levels. This is virtually impossible to solve analytically. One way around this is to use the 'first-order approach', whereby the incentive compatibility constraints are replaced by a condition which says that the desired effort level satisfies a first-order condition for a maximum, from the agent's point of view. The difficulty with this is that first-order conditions are neither necessary nor sufficient for a global maximum in this context; hence the approach is only valid under rather strong assumptions (see Kreps, 1990*, for details).

2   More formally, condition (a) is that

$$\frac{p\left(\text{high } \pi \text{ given high effort}\right)}{p\left(\text{high } \pi \text{ given low effort}\right)} \geq \frac{p\left(\text{low } \pi \text{ given high effort}\right)}{p\left(\text{low } \pi \text{ given low effort}\right)}.$$

Condition (b) basically says that if we plot expected profit against effort level (the latter on the horizontal axis) then the plot should appear concave, i.e. have the same shape as the utility function in figure 10.1.

3   We say '*as if*' in the above because strictly speaking what is really going on is that the principal is using the extra information to tailor the incentive package in a way that motivates the agent more efficiently. The principal does not *need* to make inferences of the kind suggested in the 'as if' story, because the principal is assumed to *know* what the agent *would do* in the situation he faces, even if she cannot observe his behaviour.

4   Note that these results are related to Holmstrom's (1979)* analysis of informativeness, as discussed in point 4. Here the principal has, in a sense, extra information with which to assess the behaviour of agent i in that she observes the performance of agent j as well as that of i (and vice versa). The tournament is a rather crude (but potentially effective) way of incorporating the information on performance of j into the contract with i, and vice versa.

5   In the language of game theory, we are invoking subgame perfection here: without a principal, the subgame perfect equilibrium is to slack and share the 50 units output, with one it is to work and share 100 units.

6   For completeness, we should perhaps note that the conditions are specifically that: (1) the agent and principal have equal access to credit markets, as explained in the text that follows; (2) all public information can be used in contracting; (3) recontracting takes place with common knowledge about technology and preferences; and (4) that the expected utility frontier associated with efficient trades given the moral hazard is downward sloping.

7   By asking for a sales forecast, the author is effectively requesting an announcement from the publishers of their private information – and the incentives in the contingent contract are designed such that the publishers have an incentive to be truthful. An alternative and perhaps more direct way of extracting the private information would be simply to offer the publishers a choice between a contract with low lump sum payment and high royalties, versus one with large lump sum and low royalties. The publishers then reveal their private information via the choice they make. The former approach is termed by Baron (1989)* as the 'revelation formulation' of the problem, the latter the 'delegation formulation'.

For the record, the contract for this book involved straightforward royalties, with no lump sum. Could it be that the publishers expect only modest sales?

CHAPTER 12

Moral Hazard: Experimental Evidence

In this chapter we outline and discuss some laboratory experiments on moral hazard problems. The discussion is based on a series of papers by DeJong, Forsythe, Lundholm and Uecker (1985), DeJong, Forsythe and Lundholm (1985), DeJong, Forsythe and Uecker (1985, 1988), and DeJong, Forsythe, Schatzberg and Uecker (1993), focusing primarily on the paper cited first, henceforth called DFLU (the discussants' comments on this paper by Young (1985) are also worthy of interest). Like LMPP on lemons, and MP on signalling, these experiments by DFLU do not *exactly* fit the theoretical model we have discussed, but they do capture the essence of the underlying moral hazard problem. The basic framework is one where subjects in the experiment take the role of either principal or of agent; a principal can hire an agent to perform some service, at some agreed price. The principal faces uncertainty over some potential financial loss, and the quality of service provided by the agent affects the *chances* of avoiding that loss. The principal cannot observe the quality of service, but she can observe the financial loss (which she has to bear). Neither can she deduce with certainty what the quality of service was from observing the outcome, since better quality service only raises the *chances* of avoiding the loss (it does not guarantee a good outcome). From the agent's point of view, providing good quality services is costly.

DFLU do not investigate the impact of 'performance pay' packages on the outcome, nor do they analyse the role of risk preferences (they assume all players are risk neutral). They introduced *several* principals and *several* agents into each experiment, and considered the effects of the following on the experimental market outcome:

(a) *Multi-period effects (reputation)*. DFLU allow several periods of trading to take place in each experiment, wherein the subjects can form reputations.

(b) *Post-observation investigation.* In some treatments, DFLU allowed (subjects in the role of) principals who had suffered unfavourable financial outcomes to pay a fee which allowed them to determine exactly what the quality of service supplied by the agent had been. The outcome of the investigation was publicly disclosed (all traders in the experiment were informed whether or not that agent had 'cheated').

(c) *Liability rules.* In further treatments, the investigation fee was backed up by a liability rule. In these cases, if a principal discovered (on payment of the investigation fee) that the quality of service fell below a pre-specified minimum standard set by the experimenter, then the agent became liable for the financial losses. In some of these treatments, the outcome of investigation was privately disclosed (i.e. only the principal involved in the transaction was informed), in others it was publicly disclosed.

The Experimental Markets

The experiments were run using students from the University of Iowa as subjects.[1] Each market experiment took 2½–3 hours to run and involved a sequence of trading periods (subjects were told the experiment would last up to 3 hours; they did not know exactly when the experiment would end). The subjects were given cash incentives, with payments at the end of the experiment ranging from $10 to $25.

Each market consisted of three subjects who were given the (identical) role of agents, plus four subjects who were given the (identical) role of principals. In each trading period, principals were given an endowment of $1.30 and agents an endowment of $0.50. Transactions were by sealed offer auction, as follows. To begin a trading period, agents submitted an offer to each principal specifying a price for an offered quality level of service. Principals would then choose which agent (if any) they wished to deal with. The 'match' between principals and agents was made public, but the nature of the offer was not. The agent would then tell the experimenter the quality of service he would *actually deliver* – hence he could 'cheat' by, say, *offering* high quality service but *delivering* low quality. After the agents specified delivered quality, the principals faced a gamble on a financial loss of $0.80. The better the quality of service specified by the agent, the lower the chances to the principal of suffering this loss. The gamble was carried out (the experimenter would

Table 12.1 DFLU experimental market parameters

Principal			Agent	Total	
Level of service q	Probability of loss[a] $P(q)$	Expected loss $P(q)l$ ($)	Cost of service $c(q)$ ($)	Expected cost[b] ($)	Expected surplus[c] ($)
No purchase	1	0.80	0	0.80	1.00
1	0.8	0.64	0.08	0.72	1.08
3[d]	0.5	0.40	0.20	0.60	1.20
5	0.1	0.08	0.65	0.73	1.07

Similar experiments were run in DFL (1985), with slightly different parameters to those described above.

[a] The loss involved is $0.80 throughout.

[b] Total expected cost calculated as $P(q)l + c(q)$.

[c] Total expected surplus is principal's expected return + agent's expected return

$$= (\$1.30 - price - P(q)l) + (\$0.50 + price - c(q))$$
$$= \$1.80 - \text{total expected loss.}$$

[d] The total expected surplus is maximized at quality level 3. The parameters above were used in all seven markets. The investigation fee (where applicable) was $0.32.

use some random device to determine whether the principal suffered the loss or not, according to the specified probability) and the agent and principal were informed of the outcome. They each calculated their profits from the trading period, and the next trading period would begin and take exactly the same form as the previous one. At the end of the experimental market, subjects were paid their total winnings in cash.

The parameters for the market experiments are given in table 12.1. The agent could offer/deliver quality level 1, 3 or 5, and this affected the probability of loss (in the gamble) as indicated in the table. The higher the quality delivered, the greater the cost to the agent (so delivery of quality 1 cost the agent 8 cents, delivery of a 5 cost 65 cents, for example). With these market parameters, quality level 3 maximized subjects' surplus through trade (i.e., it made the most money, in expected terms, out of the experiment).

Seven separate experimental markets were carried out. The first two were 'base runs', using the parameters in table 12.1 with no special treatments. In the next two the principal was allowed to pay a fee of $0.32 to identify the quality of service that had been supplied, in the event of a loss. Markets 5 and 6 retained 'identification for a fee', and further introduced a liability rule, whereby if the agent was found upon investigation to have delivered quality of less than the minimum standard (set by the experimenter at level 3), then the agent had to cover the $0.80 loss. The outcome of the investigation was *publicly announced* in markets 3, 4, 5 and 6. In the seventh and final market, the same treatments were applied as for markets 5 and 6, except that the results of the investigation were *privately disclosed* to the principal directly affected.

Theoretical Predictions: Benchmark Cases

Full information

With full information, principals could observe (and verify if needs be to outsiders) the quality of service delivered by the agent. DFLU assume they are risk neutral, in which case they would aim to maximize their expected net profit $E(\pi)$, which in each trading period is given as

$$E(\pi) = \$1.30 - price - P(q) \cdot l \tag{12.1}$$

where $1.30 is their endowment at start of period, q is the contracted quality level of service, $P(q)$ is the probability that the principal suffers the financial loss (given the contracted quality), l is the size of the money loss, and *price* is the price paid by the principal to the agent for the service.

DFLU argue that, in theory, if (risk neutral) agents price their services competitively[2] then one would expect them to earn zero profits, so that

$$price = c(q)$$

where $c(q)$ is the cost to the agent of supplying quality level q. Substituting back into (12.1) for the *price* gives a principal's expected return as

$$E(\pi) = \$1.30 - c(q) - P(q) \cdot l.$$

Examination of table 12.1 shows that this quantity is maximized when the level of q is 3.[3] This is also the level of quality that maximizes the total surplus from trade to both principal and agent. Hence we would expect under full information for trade to be conducted at quality level 3 for all units, at *price* = $c(q = 3)$ = $0.20. The principal would never pay a fee to identify q, since quality of service would be freely observable under full information anyway.

One-period moral hazard model[4]

In the absence of 'fee identification' and liability rules, agents always deliver the lowest quality ($q = 1$) to minimize their costs, given that principals cannot observe q. In competitive markets with zero expected profit in supply, we find *price* = $c(q = 1)$ = \$0.08. This price is the minimum required for the agent to participate in the market. In general, pricing such that the agents' expected profit is zero acts as a *participation constraint* in the same way as the shareholder could not provide a wage package that yielded utility below U_0 to the manager in the previous chapter.

Allowing 'fee identification' does not alter this outcome, since in a one-period model there is no point in the principal invoking this option; fee identification is costly and (on its own) it does not change the outcome of the transaction since the principal still has to bear the financial loss. (Technically, paying the fee to identify quality is a dominated strategy).

Introducing the liability rule to back up the identification fee does change matters. Here, the principal can transfer the loss onto the agent if the latter is found to deliver sub-standard quality (i.e. q of less than 3), hence the principal potentially has *something to gain* by investigation (and the agent potentially has something to lose by delivering low quality). DFLU show that in this case the market has a *mixed strategy* competitive equilibrium. Define ρ = probability of (principal) investigating, α = probability of (agent) delivering sub-standard quality ($q = 1$). Then DFLU show that in equilibrium the following holds (those interested in a derivation are directed to the appendix to this chapter):

price = \$0.20, $\alpha = 0.4$ and $\rho = 0.19$.

The idea here is that in equilibrium the principal *may* investigate but she may not; and the agent *may* respond by supplying service that is up to standard, but he may 'cheat'. The mixed strategy equilibrium is rather like taking penalties in soccer. The penalty-taker may sometimes aim to the goalkeeper's left, and sometimes to his right; and the keeper (simultaneously) may sometimes dive left, sometimes right. The point is that the principal and agent/penalty-taker and goal-keeper *keep each other guessing*. (The appendix at the end of the book discusses this example at greater length.)

Multi-period models – reputation effects

In a multi-period context there are numerous possible equilibria, consistent with a wide variety of outcomes. As a result, sharp theoretical predictions about behaviour are not available. (See chapter 11 for a discussion of some of the theory on multi-period models). DFLU put forward the following three *hypotheses* which, if confirmed in the experiments, would provide strong support for the presence of reputation effects:[5]

(a)   'There is a positive and non-negligible frequency of investigations, when investigation is allowed but no liability rule is present.' There is no point in paying the fee in a one-period model (in the absence of a liability rule), hence the only rational reason for doing so here would be through some dynamic effect such as a desire to learn the agent's concern for his reputation (e.g. 'I will not deal with that agent again, he is a cheat').

(b)   'The frequency of low quality deliveries is lower when investigation is present than when it is absent (no liability rule in both cases).' If the introduction of investigation causes agents to deliver better quality service (even when they are not liable for deliver of shoddy service), that suggests that they are concerned for their reputation.

(c)   'The frequency of investigations and of low quality deliveries is higher under private as opposed to public disclosure of the outcome of the investigation.' Public disclosure of the supply of shoddy service is more damaging to an agent's reputation than private disclosure. Hence, if agents are concerned for their reputation, they will deliver better quality goods when disclosure is public. Under private disclosure, principals interested in learning agents' reputations must also investigate more often, since they cannot free ride on information provided by other principals' investigations.

Results

The results of running the experiments are given in table 12.2. As each experimental market progressed, subjects choices are likely to reflect (a) dynamic effects such as reputation effects derived from previous decisions, and (b) learning effects, whereby subjects gain experience of the

Table 12.2   DFLU results

Market set-up	Market	Frequency of $q = 1$ delivery α	Frequency of investigation ρ	price[b]	Efficiency[c]
'No investigation,	1	0.53 (0.41)	–	0.33 (0.32)	0.54 (0.53)
no liability'	2	0.68 (0.90)	–	0.26 (0.20)	0.51 (0.43)
Average	1 + 2	**0.61** (0.68)		**0.29** (0.26)	**0.53** (0.48)
'Investigation[a]	3	0.47 (0.88)	0.11 (0)	0.28 (0.23)	0.55 (0.43)
only'	4	0.20 (0.37)	0.06 (0.07)	0.39 (0.31)	0.64 (0.67)
Average	3 + 4	**0.39** (0.61)	**0.09** (0.04)	**0.31** (0.27)	**0.59** (0.55)
'Investigation[a]	5	0.04 (0.13)	0.49 (0.17)	0.46 (0.35)	0.38 (0.58)
and liability'	6	0.03 (0.05)	0.19 (0)	0.32 (0.23)	0.73 (0.97)
Average	5 + 6	**0.04** (0.09)	**0.32** (0.09)	**0.39** (0.29)	**0.55** (0.76)
'Investigation and liability' (private disclosure)	7	**0.20** (0.15)	**0.61** (0.75)	**0.33** (0.33)	**0.26** (0.16)

Figures are averages over the experimental market. (Figures in brackets are averages over the last five periods of the experimental market.)
[a] Disclosure of the outcome of the investigation was public.
[b] Price statistics are approximate (based on data reconstructed from figures in DFLU).
[c] Efficiency calculated using formula in the text.
Averages given in bold type.

experimental laboratory situation and of the decisions they have to make. It is difficult to disentangle these, therefore DFLU present results both for the choices made in each experimental market over *all* trading periods, and over the *last five periods* (the latter are given in brackets in table 12.2). We shall concentrate on the figures for the full duration of each market, and on the average figures for markets 1 and 2, 3 and 4, etc.

In all markets, some deliveries of quality level 5 were made, though DFLU argued that these seemed to be 'outliers'. There is no obvious reason for agents to deliver $q = 5$, in that trading surplus is maximised at $q = 3$;[6] and in the markets where liability rules are present delivery of type 3 is enough to ensure that the agent is safe from liability.

The results in the 'base markets' with no investigation and no liability show that whilst the majority of times agents tended to deliver low quality service, nevertheless around 30–40 per cent of the time they delivered better service. These results are closer to the benchmark predictions of the one-period moral hazard model than the full information model, in that there was clear evidence of cheating, i.e. delivering quality lower than is jointly optimal and (often) lower than was offered[7] because quality is unobservable. The results are, however, still a long way from the benchmark prediction of $\alpha = 1$ (all units delivered are minimum quality). In market 2, behaviour appears to approach that level by the end of trading, but in market 1 it tends to move away. The average price of deliveries was around $0.30, tending to be higher in market 1 (where the delivered quality was higher) than in market 2. There is a tendency in these (and virtually all other) experimental markets for prices to fall towards the end of trading. These observed prices are inconsistent with the predicted price from the one-period moral hazard model (of $0.08) and are even greater than the cost of producing quality level 3 service ($0.20). These findings may reflect reputation effects. The presence of clear profits to agents does, however, challenge DFLU's assumption (in their theory) of competitive price setting.[8] The results suggest that agents were able to exploit principals to a degree, particularly in early trading when the latter perhaps lacked experience.

In markets 3 and 4 where investigation was allowed (with public disclosure), we find a sharp drop in the frequency of delivery of low quality service (over the full duration of the experiment).[9] These observations confirm hypothesis (b), supporting the view that reputation effects are at work. We also find a non-trivial frequency of investigation in 3 and 4 (approximately one loss in every ten was investigated) supporting hypothesis (a) in favour of reputation effects. Prices were not markedly higher in markets 3 and 4 than in markets 1 and 2, despite the improved quality of delivered units, though they are still substantially above the cost of producing even quality level 3.

In markets 5 and 6, where a liability rule was used to back up costly investigation, deliveries of $q = 1$ were almost completely eliminated ($\alpha \simeq 0$). The drop in frequency of low quality deliveries in markets 5 and 6 as compared to markets 1 and 2, and also compared to 3 and 4, was statistically significant. There is also an increase in the frequency of investigations, rising from around one in ten in markets 3 and 4, to 3 in 10 in markets 5 and 6.[10] The observations of $\alpha \simeq 0$ and $\rho \simeq 0.3$ in markets 5 and 6 (with liability rules) are at odds with the theoretical benchmark prediction from the one period moral hazard model of $\alpha = 0.4$ and $\rho = 0.19$ (perhaps because of reputation effects). Average prices were substantially higher in these markets than in markets 1–4, consistent with the substantial improvement in quality of service delivered. Observed prices once again generate clear profits to agents, though the

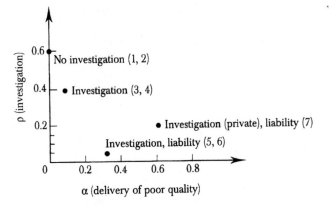

Figure 12.1   Results for the experimental markets

general tendency for prices to fall towards the end of trading was particularly marked in these experiments (and in experiment 6 prices approached the cost of delivering quality level 3).

In market 7 with costly investigation and a liability rule, disclosure of the outcome of investigation was made private (rather than public in markets 5 and 6). The result is an increase in the frequency of delivery of low quality service *and* of investigation of losses (both effects are statistically significant using data for all trading periods). These results support hypothesis (c) in favour of the presence of reputation effects.

Figure 12.1 illustrates some of these results. We see the frequency of investigation (ρ) increase and the delivery of poor quality (α) decrease with the introduction of (a) investigation and (b) liability, under public disclosure of investigation results. It also shows the pick-up in investigation and low quality deliveries when disclosure is private.

Efficiency

Clearly, the most successful markets in terms of eliminating cheating are 5 and 6, where costly investigation is backed up by a liability rule and disclosure is public. That does not mean that these markets are necessarily the most efficient, however, since in these markets the payment of an investigation fee reduces the surplus from trade. DFLU calculate an index of efficiency to measure and compare performance across markets. This index is calculated as the average (per period) trading surplus actually extracted by the subjects in a market, relative to the maximum expected surplus per period that the subjects could have realized:

$$\text{efficiency index} = \frac{\text{average realized trading surplus per period}}{\text{maximum potential expected surplus per period}}.$$

In essence, this statistic tells us how much money subjects made out of the experimenter, relative to what they could have made. Figures for this index are given in table 12.2. They show that in terms of *efficiency* there is little to choose between markets 1 and 2, 3 and 4, and 5 and 6. The latter appear more efficient in the last five periods, but that partly reflects the (costly) build-up of reputations in previous periods; over the full duration of the markets, there is no substantial difference between 5 and 6 and the previous markets. One very strong result however is that market 7 is clearly less efficient than markets 1–6; private disclosure is a rather poor market institution in terms of extracting trading surplus for the subjects.

Summary and Conclusions

DFLU's analysis of moral hazard problems in an experimental context suggests the following broad conclusions:

(i)   There is evidence of 'cheating' in the sense that, with quality unobserved, the frequency of deliveries of quality below the efficient level (and below that offered) was substantial.

(ii)   There is evidence of reputation-building over several periods of trade. Specific evidence across the different market set-ups confirms hypotheses (a)–(c) in support of reputation effects.

(iii)   Where the market set-up was one of 'no investigation–no liability rule', the frequency of delivery of 'above minimum quality' was substantial, contradicting the predictions of the one-period moral hazard model. It would seem natural to attribute this observation to reputation effects, providing further support for (ii) above. If this interpretation is correct, then reputation effects appear to have the power to reduce the level of 'cheating' behaviour, but they do not eliminate it altogether (markets 1 and 2).

(iv)   Strengthening reputation effects via an option to investigate (and publicly reveal) the cause of a financial loss appears to reduce cheating still further (markets 3 and 4).

(v)   Further introducing a liability rule served to virtually eliminate 'cheating', as long as disclosure of the outcome of investigation remained public (markets 5 and 6).

(vi)   'Investigation plus liability rule' was rather less successful in reducing cheating when disclosure was private (market 7).

(vii)   No market institution was particularly successful when performance was measured by an efficiency index. Allowing (publicly disclosed) investigation and introducing liability rules reduced cheating, but the welfare benefits from this were largely offset by the cost of investigation. The least efficient performance was in the market where 'investigation plus liability' was allowed but the results of investigation were privately disclosed.

DFLU analysed a number of further features of their experimental markets; interested readers are directed to their original paper. From our point of view their results illustrate the moral hazard problem in an experimental context, and gives us some feel for the impact of various measures to reduce the problem.

NOTES

1   Interestingly, DFU (1988) conducted equivalent experiments on a pool of *professional businessmen*, and found that the average performance of businessmen was not statistically different from that of students.

2   It is, of course, debatable whether the presence of three agents and four principals is sufficient to ensure competitive pricing. At the same time, DFLU do not explore the game-theoretic implications of having several principals and several agents, as noted in Young (1985). In further work, DeJong, Forsythe, Schatzberg, and Uecker (1993) investigate the effects of explicit opportunities for *collusion* amongst agents on delivered quality in experimental markets when moral hazard is present.

3   The expected return under these circumstances, as given by the formula in the text, is 0.5, 0.58, 0.70, and 0.57 for 'no purchase', $q = 1$, $q = 3$, and $q = 5$ respectively.

4   DFLU call this the 'lemons model'; to avoid any confusion with Akerlof's lemons, we re-term it the 'moral hazard model'. In this model, agents compete for orders from principals, and competitive pricing ensures that

agents receive a price just high enough to induce them to stay in the market, whilst the principals extract all the surplus from trade. DFLU also present an alternative model (termed by DFLU as the 'ripoff model') where the reverse happens; principals compete for services, and competitive pricing ensures that principals receive service just high enough to induce them to stay in the market, whilst the agents extract all the surplus from the trade (in the absence of investigation and liability clauses this means that agents charge a price equal to cost of providing quality level 3, and deliver just enough 3s such that principals make zero expected profit).

5   Note that the experimental subjects did not know exactly when trading would end. Hence, the backward induction arguments which point to replication of the one-period model predictions in each period do not apply (these arguments are loosely discussed in DFL).

6   One might argue that agents deliver type 5 to enhance their reputation and gain a better price in later periods. The point is, however, that in view of the lower overall trading surplus associated with $q = 5$ (see table 12.1) one would not expect principals to be prepared to pay prices for these deliveries that were high enough to make it worth the agent's while to build such a reputation.

7   DFLU's paper contains information on quality offered versus quality delivered, and on the prices charged. Broadly speaking, their results suggest that within each experiment, agents did receive higher prices for the *offer* of higher quality – and that some agents clearly 'cheated' in the sense of offering high quality and attracting high prices, but in the event delivering low quality.

8   The results are actually somewhat closer to the so called 'rip-off model' mentioned in n. 4 above than the 'one-period moral hazard model' (our terminology). In the former, competitive pricing favours the agents who extract all the surplus whilst principals make an expected return of nothing. In the latter, competitive pricing favours the principal who makes all the profit and the agent makes nothing. The results show that the reality lay somewhere between these extremes. These observations support Young's (1985) argument that the competitive theory fails adequately to capture the strategic choices facing multiple principals and agents (see note 2 above).

DFL (1985) present some further empirical results based on similar 'no investigation/no liability' experiments to those in markets 1 and 2 presented in DFLU, except slightly different parameters to those given in table 12.1 were used.

9   This difference between markets 1 and 2 versus 3 and 4 over all market trading periods was statistically significant; the difference for the last five periods is much smaller, however, and was not statistically significant.

10   This increase was statistically significant, in the data for all trading periods. A much smaller increase is observed in the data for the last five periods, which was not significant.

Appendix

The Mixed Strategy Competitive Equilibrium with Liability Rule

Mixed strategy equilibria are discussed in the appendix at the end of the book. To compute such an equilibrium, the trick is to: (i) find α such that the principal is indifferent as to how often to investigate, and (ii) find ρ such that the agent is indifferent as to how often he delivers substandard service. If we can find α and ρ to satisfy both (i) and (ii) and be consistent, we have a mixed strategy equilibrium. To pursue the penalty-taking analogy, it is equivalent to determining the probability with which the goalkeeper dives left such that the kicker is indifferent whether he kicks the ball right or left, and then calculating the probability the kicker kicks the ball left such that the goalkeeper is indifferent whether to dive right or left.

The principal

Say, the principal trades with an agent, and a financial loss occurs. She must decide whether to investigate the loss or not. The expected loss if she *does not* investigate is;

$$\text{loss}\left(\text{no investigate}\right) = l. \tag{A1}$$

The expected loss if she *does* investigate is:

$$\text{loss}\left(\text{investigate}\right) = \left(1 - \alpha\right)\left(l + F\right) + \alpha F, \tag{A2}$$

where F is the investigation fee. The investigation reveals substandard service with probability α; hence (A2) tells us that if service is substandard the principal loses the fee F (whilst the loss l is paid by the agent), if it is *not* then she pays the fee F *and* bears the loss l.

For the principal to be *indifferent* between investigation and non-investigation, we set (A1) equal to (A2)

$$l = \left(1 - \alpha\right)\left(1 + F\right) + \alpha F \tag{A3}$$

solving for α gives:

$$\alpha = F/l$$

With the experimental parameters $F = \$.32$, and $l = \$0.80$, this gives $\alpha = 0.4$, as indicated in the main text.

The agent

He chooses between supplying substandard goods ($q = 1$) or goods that meet the minimum standard ($q = 3$). Note that there is no point supplying $q = 5$, since this just involves the agent in extra costs. The expected cost of supplying substandard service ($q = 1$) is:

$$\text{cost (substandard)} = c_1\big[(1 - P_1) + P_1(1 - \rho)\big] + P_1\rho(c_1 + l) \qquad \text{(A4)}$$

$$= c_1 + P_1 l\rho, \qquad \text{(A5)}$$

where $c_1 = c(q = 1)$ is the agent's cost of 'producing' quality level 1 and $P_1 = P(q = 1)$ is the probability of a loss occurring given $q = 1$. By supplying ($q = 1$) service, the agent incurs a direct cost of c_1, but there is also a further possibility of a liability claim on the agent. If there is no financial loss (which happens with probability $(1 - P_1)$) then there is no claim; even if there is a loss (which happens with probability P_1) the principal may decide not to investigate (probability $(1 - \rho)$), in which case there is no claim once again. Hence the first term in (A4) shows that in either of these cases the agent pays no more than c_1. If a loss occurs and the principal investigates, however, then the agent will pay c_1 *and* bear the loss l as a result of the liability rule; this outcome is reflected in the second term in (A4). Equation (A5) may be obtained by cancelling terms in (A4).

The expected cost to the agent if he supplies services of quality $q = 3$ is given as:

$$\text{cost (standard)} = c_3 \qquad \text{(A6)}$$

where $c_3 = c(q = 3)$ is just the cost of 'producing' quality level 3. There is no prospect of a liability claim here, since the agent has met the minimum standard.

For the agent to be indifferent between supplying $q = 1$ and $q = 3$, we set (A5) equal to (A6):

$$c_1 + P_1(l)\rho = c_3$$

which solves to yield:

$$\rho = (c_3 - c_1)/P_1 l. \tag{A7}$$

With the experimental values for c_3, c_1, P_1, and l, this gives $\rho = 0.19$, as indicated in the main text.

Competitive prices

Under competitive pricing the agent makes zero return from supply, hence we have

price = agent's expected costs = c_3 = 0.20

as indicated in the main text.

(Note that by construction from (ii) above the expected cost of supplying q_1 is the same as the cost of supplying q_3. Hence, whether the agent actually supplies $q = 1$ or $q = 3$, his expected cost is the same, i.e. it is c_3.)

References for Part 3

Arrow, K. (1985), 'The Economics of Agency', in J. Pratt and R. Zeckhauser (eds), *Principals and Agents: The Structure of Business* (Cambridge, MA: Harvard Business School Press).

Baron, D. (1989),* 'Design of Regulatory Mechanisms and Institutions', ch. 24, vol. 2 of R. Schmalensee and R. Willig (eds), *Handbook of Industrial Organisation* (Amsterdam: North-Holland).

Becker, G. and Stigler, G. (1974), 'Law Enforcement, Malfeasance and Compensation of Enforcers', *Journal of Legal Studies*, 3, pp. 1–18.

Berle, A. and Means, G. (1932), *The Modern Corporation and Private Property* (New York: Commerce Clearing House).

Brickley, J., Bhagat, S. and Lease, R. (1985), 'The Impact of Long-range Managerial Compensation Plans on Shareholder Wealth', *Journal of Accounting and Economics*, 7, pp. 115–30.

Cowling, K., Stoneman, P., Cubbin, J., Hall, G., Domberger, S. and Dutton P. (1980), *Mergers and Economic Performance* (Cambridge: Cambridge University Press).

DeJong, D., Forsythe, R. and Lundholm R. (1985), 'Ripoffs, Lemons and Reputation Formation in Agency Relationships: A Laboratory Market Study', *Journal of Finance*, 50, pp. 809–20.

DeJong, D., Forsythe, R. and Uecker, W. (1985), 'The Methodology of Laboratory Markets and its Implications for Agency Research in Accounting and Auditing', *Journal of Accounting Research*, 23, pp. 753–93.

DeJong, D., Forsythe, R. and Uecker, W. (1988), 'A Note on the Use of Businessmen as Subjects in Sealed Bid Offer Markets', *Journal of Economic Behaviour and Organisation*, 9, pp. 87–100.

DeJong, D., Forsythe, R., Lundholm, R. and Uecker, W. (1985), 'A Laboratory Investigation of the Moral Hazard Problem in an Agency Relationship', *Journal of Accounting Research*, 23 (Suppl.), pp. 81–120.

DeJong, D., Forsythe, R., Schatzberg, J. and Uecker, W. (1993), 'Collusion and Product Quality: A Laboratory Investigation', discussion paper, University of Iowa, Department of Accounting.

Dewatripont, M. and Maskin, E. (1990), 'Contract Renegotiation in Models of Asymmetric Information', *European Economic Review*, 34, pp. 311–21.

Fama, E. (1980), 'Agency Problems and the Theory of the Firm', *Journal of Political Economy*, 88, pp. 288–307.

Firth, M. (1980), 'Takeovers, Shareholder Returns, and the Theory of the Firm', *Quarterly Journal of Economics*, 94, pp. 235–60.

Fudenberg, D., Holmstrom, B. and Milgrom, P. (1990),* 'Short Term Contracts and Long Term Agency Relationships', *Journal of Economic Theory*, 51, pp. 1–31.

Gravelle, H. and Rees, R. (1981), *Microeconomics* (New York: Longman).

Green, J. and Stokey, N. (1983), 'A Comparison of Tournaments and Contracts', *Journal of Political Economy*, 91, pp. 349–64.

Grossman, S. and Hart, O. (1980),* 'Takeover Bids, the Free Rider Problem, and the Theory of the Corporation', *Bell Journal of Economics*, 11, pp. 42–64.

Grossman, S. and Hart, O. (1983),* 'An Analysis of the Principal–Agent Problem', *Econometrica*, 51, pp. 7–45.

Hart, O. (1995), *Firms, Contracts and Financial Structure*, Clarendon Lectures in Economics (Oxford: Oxford University Press).

Holmstrom, B. (1979),* 'Moral Hazard and Observability', *Bell Journal of Economics*, 10, pp. 74–91.

Holmstrom, B. (1982),* 'Moral Hazard in Teams', *Bell Journal of Economics*, 13, pp. 324–40.

Holmstrom, B. and Ricard I Costa, J. (1986), 'Managerial Incentives and Capital Management', *Quarterly Journal of Economics*, 101, pp. 835–60.

Holmstrom, B. and Milgrom, P. (1987),* 'Aggregation and Linearity in the Provision of Intertemporal Incentives', *Econometrica*, 55, pp. 303–28.

Jarrell, G., Brickley, J. and Nether, J. (1988), 'The Market for Corporate Control: The Empirical Evidence Since 1980', *Journal of Economic Perspectives*, 2, pp. 49–68.

Jensen, M. and Meckling, W. (1976), 'Theory of the Firm: Managerial Behaviour, Agency Costs and Ownership Structure', *Journal of Financial Economics*, 3, pp. 305–60.

Jensen, M. and Ruback, R. (1983), 'The Market for Corporate Control: The Scientific Evidence', *Journal of Financial Economics*, 11, pp. 5–50.

Kreps, David (1990),* *A Course in Microeconomic Theory* (New Yrok: Harvester-Wheatsheaf).

Lambert, R. and Larker, D. (1985), 'Executive Compensation, Corporate Decision Making and Shareholder Wealth: A Review of the Evidence', *Midland Corporate Finance Journal*, 2, pp. 6–22.

Lazear, E. (1979), 'Why is there Mandatory Retirement?', *Journal of Political Economy*, 87, pp. 1261–84.

Lazear, E. and Rosen, S. (1981), 'Rank-order Tournaments as Optimum Labour Contracts', *Journal of Political Economy*, 89, pp. 841–64.

Lev, B. (1983), 'Observations on the Merger Phenomenon and a Review of the Evidence', *Midland Corporate Finance Journal*, 1, pp. 6–16.

Magenheim, E. and Mueller, D. (1987), 'On Measuring the Effects of Mergers on

Acquiring Firm Shareholders', in Coffee, J. et al. (eds), *Knights, Raiders, and Targets* (New York: Oxford University Press).

Milgrom, P. and Roberts, J. (1992), *Economics, Organisation and Management* (Englewood Cliffs, NJ: Prentice Hall International).

Radner, R. (1985),* 'Repeated Principal–Agent Games with Discounting', *Econometrica*, 53, pp. 1173–98.

Rasmusen, E. (1989), *Games and Information* (Oxford: Blackwell).

Ross, S. (1973), 'The Economic Theory of Agency: The Principal's Problem', *American Economic Review*, 63, pp. 134–9.

Sappington, D. (1991), 'Incentives in Principal–Agent Relationships', *Journal of Economic Perspectives*, 5, pp. 45–66.

Scherer, F.M. (1988), 'Corporate Takeovers: The Efficiency Arguments', *Journal of Economic Perspectives*, 2, pp. 69–82.

Shapiro, C. and Stiglitz, J. (1984), 'Equilibrium Unemployment as a Worker Discipline Device', *American Economic Review*, 74, pp. 433–44.

Shavell, S. (1979),* 'Risk Sharing and Incentives in the Principal and Agent Relationship', *Bell Journal of Economics*, 10, pp. 55–73.

Shleifer, A. and Vishny, R. (1988), 'Value Maximisation and the Acquisition Process', *Journal of Economic Perspectives*, 2, pp. 7–20.

Smirlock, M. and Marshall, W. (1983), 'Monopoly Power and Expense Preference Behaviour: Theory and Evidence to the Contrary', *Bell Journal of Economics*, 14, pp. 166–78.

Stiglitz, J. (1985), 'Credit Markets and the Control of Capital', *Journal of Money Credit and Banking*, 17, pp. 133–52.

Strong, N. and Waterson, M. (1987), 'Principals, Agents, and Information', in R. Clarke and T. McGuiness (eds), *The Economics of the Firm* (Oxford: Blackwell).

Tirole, J. (1988), *The Theory of Industrial Organisation* (Cambridge MA: MIT Press).

Vickers, J. and Yarrow, G. (1988), *Privatisation: An Economic Analysis* (Cambridge MA: MIT Press).

Weitzman, M. (1980), 'The Ratchet Principle and Economic Incentives', *Bell Journal of Economics*, 11, pp. 302–8.

Winter, S. (1971), 'Satisficing, Selection, and the Innovating Remnant', *Quarterly Journal of Economics*, 85, pp. 237–61.

Yarrow, G. (1976), 'On the Predictions of Managerial Theories of the Firm', *Journal of Industrial Economics*, 24, pp. 267–79.

Young, S.M. (1985), 'Discussion of a Laboratory Investigation of the Moral Hazard Problem in an Agency Relationship', *Journal of Accounting Research*, 23 (Suppl.), pp. 121–3.

Part 4

Mechanism Design: Applications to Bargaining and Auctions

Many different sorts of economic systems or 'mechanisms' exist for handling transactions of various kinds. This part of the book considers the question of how to design an 'optimal' mechanism to deal with some specified form of transaction, when problems of private information and unobservability are present. We first outline a method for analysing such questions, based on the 'revelation principle'; we then illustrate this method using a simple bargaining example. The following chapters apply the idea to the question of auction design, and consider how well 'real-world' designs such as English and Dutch auctions deal with problems of private information.

CHAPTER 13

Mechanism Design and the Revelation Principle: A Bargaining Example

In chapter 1 we discussed the design of economic systems in relation to problems of imperfect information. Two broad classes of system were identified – market systems where traders respond to price signals, and hierarchical systems where economic decisions are directed by authority. Within each class, different sorts of market and organizational models may be identified. Each system or 'mechanism' may have advantages and disadvantages as a way of carrying out any given form of transaction.

The literature on mechanism design relates to this kind of issue, particularly in relation to problems of private information and unobservability. The questions raised might be of the form: 'how best to design a used car market to minimize inefficiencies due to adverse selection problems?', 'how to design recruitment mechanisms to minimise the welfare losses that may arise due to inefficient signalling', and so on.

There are both positive and normative aspects to the economics litera-ture on these issues. On the positive side, the argument made by econo-mists in the Coase-tradition is that economic structures will themselves evolve in a way that minimizes inefficiencies – those mechanisms we observe in reality will tend to be the ones that are best suited to dealing with a particular transaction. On the normative side, the literature seeks to recommend the best mechanism design for dealing with some transaction.

The crucial question that arises is then 'how are we to *identify* the best feasible mechanism design?' for dealing with some transaction. This is no trivial task. A major difficulty that arises is that there are typically virtually unlimited numbers of ways of conceivably handling some par-ticular transaction. How are we to compare them all? In this chapter we introduce a method which allows us to overcome this kind of difficulty, with respect to transactions in the presence of private information. This technique rests on a key idea called 'the revelation principle'. The next section outlines this principle, and gives an informal 'proof' of it. The following section outlines how it may be used as part of a general method to identify mechanism designs that are optimal given the presence of information constraints. After that we give a concrete numerical application and illustration of this method in relation to a simple bargaining problem. In the remaining chapters of this part of the book we consider the case of auction design in this context.

The Revelation Principle

We call a system for handling some form of transaction a *mechanism*. A case in point which we shall refer to here would be an income tax system. Such mechanisms typically place the people involved in a strategic situation (e.g. 'how much income should I declare on my tax form?'). It would seem sensible to expect that an equilibrium will tend to emerge as the outcome of play, in such a strategic situation.[1] Where private information is present, one key point of strategy concerns the issue of whether to play truthfully or not ('should I under-declare my income', for example). Different mechanisms place people in different strategic situations; in some mechanisms the equilibrium might involve lying, in others it might involve truth-telling. For example, in some tax systems one can imagine an equilibrium where the tax rates are low enough, and the probability and penalty for being caught evading tax high enough, that people tend to truthfully declare their income; in other systems, the equilibrium may be such that high tax rates are needed because people evade, because the taxes are so high. . . .

Some terminology will be helpful at this stage. Call any mechanism where people may be induced to be dishonest (lie/cheat) in equilibrium a 'non-truth-telling' (or NTT) mechanism. By contrast, call any mechanism where people are induced to be honest in equilibrium a 'truth-telling' (or TT) mechanism. The **revelation principle** states that 'Any equilibrium outcome for a potential transaction under any non-truth-telling mechanism can be replicated by the equilibrium outcome of some truth-telling mechanism.'

This is such a simple idea that it can be hard to grasp. It says, by way of illustration, that we can reproduce the equilibrium of a tax system where people may choose to lie, with the equilibrium of another tax system where they choose to be honest. The validity of the revelation principle can be proven formally (see, for example, Myerson, 1979*). We shall attempt merely to sketch an informal proof here, to back up our statement of this principle. The argument runs as follows.

Suppose there are two players in a game, each potentially having private information. They could transact under some NTT mechanism; that is, they play a game which involves either/both of them potentially misrepresenting their information in equilibrium. For example, a taxpayer may name a false income level in his tax return to his tax authority. The equilibrium results in some tax payment.

To show that the revelation principle is valid, we need to demonstrate that some TT mechanism could achieve the same equilibrium outcome. For this purpose, imagine that some mediator who was commonly known to be entirely honest was present. Consider an alternative to the NTT mechanism above, where the mediator went to each player separately and asked them confidentially for their private information, and then calculated and played out best-response strategies for the original (NTT) mechanism on behalf of each player.[2] The mediator might say to each player 'tell me your private information, and then I can work out and play the best strategy on your behalf'. Faced with this situation each player would have no incentive to lie to the mediator, since if they mislead him then that may cause him to play the wrong strategy on their behalf; lying could only cause hurt to themselves. Put another way, if any individual could gain by lying to the mediator in the new mechanism, then they could expect to gain by lying to themselves in the original NTT mechanism, which is absurd. Hence we conclude that they tell the mediator the truth.

The situation faced by each player is rather like the one faced by a defendant talking to his lawyer. Say the defendant placed complete trust in the integrity of his lawyer, and that lawyer needed certain information from him in order to be able to make out the best possible defence in court. Then the defendant has nothing to gain from lying to his lawyer, since that would only imperil his own case. It is also rather like the businesswoman telling her accountant the truth so that the accountant can work out the best tax dodges.

To continue with the argument, the only decision that the original players have to make in the new mechanism is 'what to tell the mediator', and we have established that they have an incentive to be truthful. The (correctly informed) mediator then proceeds to do on each player's behalf what that player would have done for himself – that is, the mediator plays out the same best-response strategies the players would have played, and so reaches the same equilibrium as that in the original mechanism.

Think about this. We have constructed a new mechanism where the original players have an incentive to be truthful, and reached the same equilibrium outcome as that which was reached in the non-truth-telling mechanism. The new mechanism may therefore be declared a truth-telling mechanism and it yields an equilibrium that replicates the equilibrium of the original non-truth-telling mechanism. The same argument holds for any NTT mechanism we might consider. This is exactly what the revelation principle asserted.

One criticism of all this is that the whole story relies on some wondrous character who has complete integrity and is totally honest – the mediator. Where are such fine people to be found? and without them, does not the whole story break down? This criticism misses the point. We do not wish to argue that the above story describes commonly observed real-world behaviour. What we have done is merely to construct a (very sketchy) logical proof of the revelation principle – we have shown that there is some conceivable mechanism where the players would want to tell the truth and which would yield the same equilibrium as the original one where they lied.

A second criticism is 'so what?' 'Say this so-called revelation principle is true – what possible use has it got?' The point of the next section is to answer this by showing how the revelation principle may be used to assist in 'mechanism design'.

A method for mechanism design using the revelation principle

We argued earlier that it may be possible to compare the performance of alternative specified mechanism designs, but that it seemed rather difficult to establish whether any given design is in any sense optimal; there might be another design that we had not considered which is better than all the ones we have examined. The following method uses the revelation principle to get around this problem. The technique is:

Step (1)   Restrict attention to cases where the players have the incentive to be (and therefore are) truthful in equilibrium. That is, we impose constraints on the solution such that the players would not want to lie.

Step (2)   Find the 'best' feasible equilibrium given these truth-telling constraints. Quite how we define 'best' depends on the objectives of the designer – it might, for example, mean maximizing some social welfare function.

Step (3)   Apply the revelation principle. Since any equilibrium of an NTT mechanism can be replicated by the equilibrium of a TT one, we can conclude that no NTT mechanism could yield a better outcome that that found in Step (2). We could, if we wished, proceed to analyse observed 'real world' (and most likely NTT) mechanisms to see if they do as well as that in Step (2). (We will not find any that do better.)

To make these ideas more concrete, we now present a numerical example relating to a bargaining problem. This example is taken from Myerson (1991).

Mechanism Design: A Bargaining Example

Bargaining problems arise in many spheres of economics. Employers bargain with workers over pay and conditions; countries bargain over international trading arrangements; firms bargain with suppliers over supply contracts, and so on. Consequently, a large literature on bargaining has developed. One important theme of this literature concerns problems of imperfect information, particularly in relation to the 'strength' of each party's bargaining position. Most readers will be familiar with a situation where one or more parties tries to give the impression of 'strength' to get a better deal (personal relationships are beset by such problems – by pretending you do not care for the other person, you might be able to get him/her to run around after you). An important theorem in economics states that in certain specified situations, imperfect information will inevitably result in welfare losses in equilibrium (see later). In the following we give an example which illustrates the problem, and design a mechanism which minimizes the welfare losses, using the technique set out above.

The example involves a buyer and a seller bargaining over the sale of a single good. Both are risk neutral. There is a one-time opportunity to trade – if they fail to trade, then the good stays with the seller. The seller might value the good quite highly, or he might not care much for it. If he values it highly, that puts him in a 'strong' bargaining position, in the sense that he genuinely would not accept a low price for the good – he would rather keep it. If he cared little for the good, on the other hand, then that puts him in a 'weak' bargaining position – he could try bluffing by pretending he would reject a low price but in truth he would part with the good for very little. The seller knows how much he values the good, but the buyer does not – the seller's valuation is private information (for short, we say that the seller's valuation is private).

Table 13.1   Full information equilibrium

	Strong buyer ($V = 20$)	Weak buyer ($V = 100$)
Strong seller ($V = 80$)	(0, *)	(1, 80 to 100)
Weak seller ($V = 0$)	(1, 0 to 20)	(1, 0 to 100)
Overall probability of trade = 0.75		

Tables 13.1–13.5 list pairs in the form: probability of trade, price of good. An asterisk (*) indicates no price, since no trade occurs. V is the trader's valuation of the good.

The buyer is in a symmetrical position. She might value the good highly, in which case that puts her in a weak bargaining position, since she would be willing to pay a high price for the good. Or she might put a low value on the good, in which case she would be in a strong position in that she would only pay a low price for it. The buyer's valuation is also private.

To put some numbers on the situation, say a 'strong seller' values the good $80, and a 'weak' one values it at $0. The buyer knows these are the only two possible seller valuations, but she does not know whether the seller she faces is weak or strong. A strong buyer values the good at $20, and a weak one values it at $100. The seller knows these are the only two possible buyer valuations, but does not know whether the buyer he faces is weak or strong. We also assume for simplicity that the probability of the seller being strong is $^1/_2$, the probability of the buyer being strong is $^1/_2$, and both of them know this. Neither player can control their own valuations (e.g. a buyer cannot choose to value the good at $20 in order to strengthen her bargaining position).

Trade under full information

The mechanism design problem might then be to find a way of organizing the bargaining in such a way as to realize maximum gains from trade. To analyse this problem, consider first of all what would happen under full information, where both traders knew each others valuations. The various possible outcomes are set out in table 13.1. If a strong seller plays a strong buyer then there are no gains from trade (the good yields most utility staying with the seller), hence the probability of trade is zero. In all other cases, trade is mutually beneficial as long as the price is (strictly) in the range indicated. For example if a strong seller plays a weak buyer, then with a price >80 the seller gains, and with a price <100 the buyer gains. The price in these cases cannot be exactly determined. Say they decide to 'split the difference', then the price would be 90 in this case, 50 if they are both weak, and 10 if the seller is weak and the buyer strong. The total probability of trade is 0.75, since there are four equally likely combinations of buyer and seller, and they always trade except in the one case where the seller and buyer are both strong.

'Split the difference' under imperfect information

Now consider what happens under imperfect information. To begin to analyse this, say the buyer and seller play under a 'split the difference' mechanism design of the kind mentioned above. That is, the seller and buyer simultaneously say how much they value the good, and as long as the buyer's named valuation is higher than the seller's then they trade at a price exactly halfway between the named valuations. Further assume that the seller can only name a value of either 0 or 80, since anything else would obviously be a lie (remember, the buyer knows that there are only two types of sellers, the weak or the strong type); similarly the buyer can only say '20' or '100', since anything else would obviously be a lie (and the seller knows this).

The first question is 'would either/both players lie or tell the truth' under this mechanism. Consider a weak seller, whose true valuation was 0. He could say he values the good at '0', or he could lie by saying '80'. Imagine for the moment that the buyer was always truthful. If the weak seller says his valuation in '0', then he would expect to make $10 \times \frac{1}{2} + $50 \times \frac{1}{2} = 30, since the chances of the buyer being weak (in which case the price is 50) is a half, and the chances of the buyer being strong (in which case the price is 10) is also a half. If the weak seller lied by saying '80', then he would expect to make $90 \times \frac{1}{2} = 45, which is more than $30, hence the (risk neutral) weak seller has an incentive to lie. We can conclude from this that truth-telling is not an equilibrium of this mechanism design, since even if all buyers tell the truth then weak sellers (at least) have an incentive to lie.

If truth-telling is not an equilibrium then what is? In fact there are three Nash equilibria, which are listed in tables 13.2–13.4. In the first, the seller is truthful, but the buyer always claims to be 'strong', yielding an outcome of 'non-trade' whenever a (genuinely) strong seller is present, and trading at a price of $\frac{1}{2}(20 - 0) = 10$ whenever a (genuinely) weak seller is present.[3] The second equilibrium is the mirror image of the first;

Table 13.2   Split the difference equilibrium (a)

	Strong buyer (V = 20)	Weak buyer (V = 100)
Strong seller (V = 80)	(0, *)	(0, *)
Weak seller (V = 0)	(1, 10)	(1, 10)

Overall probability of trade = 0.5

Table 13.3   Split the difference equilibrium (b)

	Strong buyer (V = 20)	Weak buyer (V = 100)
Strong seller (V = 80)	(0, *)	(1, 90)
Weak seller (V = 0)	(0, *)	(1, 90)

Overall probability of trade = 0.5

Table 13.4   Split the difference equilibrium (c)

	Strong buyer (V = 20)	Weak buyer (V = 100)
Strong seller (V = 80)	(0, *)	(0.4, 90)
Weak seller (V = 0)	(0.4, 10)	(0.64, 50)

Overall probability of trade = 0.36

here the buyers always tell the truth and the sellers always declare that they are strong. The result is that trade never takes place if the buyer is strong, and it always takes place if the buyer is weak, at a price of 90.

Neither of these equilibria look very appealing from a welfare point of view. In both equilibria, the overall probability of trade is 0.5 (in the first case this is the probability that the seller is weak, in the second it is the probability that the buyer is weak) compared to 0.75 under full information. Furthermore, where trade does take place the deals seem rather inequitable. In the first equilibrium the price of 10 is rather low and favours the buyer, in the second the price of 90 is rather high and favours

Table 13.5   A general trading mechanism

	'Strong' buyer ($V = 20$)	'Weak' buyer ($V = 100$)
'Strong' seller ($V = 80$)	$(0, *)$	$(q, 100 - y)$
'Weak' seller ($V = 0$)	(q, y)	$(1, 50)$

the seller. Note the irony – 'split the difference' sounds fair, but it can produce very unfair equilibria.

The last equilibrium under 'split the difference' is more equitable (table 13.4). Here weak buyers and weak sellers lie with probability 0.6 (and tell the truth with probability 0.4); strong buyers and strong sellers tell the truth.[4] The problem here, however, is that so few of the potentially beneficial trades are realized; the overall probability of trade is just 0.36[5] which compares very unfavourably with the full information solution of trade with probability 0.75.

Optimal mechanism design: applying the revelation principle

Is there an alternative design to the 'split the difference' trading mechanism which realizes more of the gains from trade in equilibrium, under imperfect information? To answer this question we use the revelation principle. To proceed with this, we must first find a 'truth-telling mechanism'. We shall take it that this mechanism has the general form indicated in table 13.5. The traders name a valuation. There is no trade when a 'strong' buyer meets a 'strong' seller (i.e., they claim to be 'strong'); trade with probability 1 at a price of 50 when a 'weak' seller meets a 'weak' buyer; trade with probability q at price y when a 'weak' seller meets a 'strong' buyer; and trade with probability q at price $100 - y$ when a 'weak' buyer meets a 'strong' seller.[6] This trading mechanism treats buyers and sellers symmetrically; that is, it is *equitable*. If both buyers and sellers are genuinely weak, then the price of 50 divides the trading surplus equally between the two. The case where the seller has the bargaining advantage is symmetrical to that where the buyer does.[7]

Strictly speaking, we do not need to make these assumptions (e.g. the direct mechanism could allow for asymmetric treatment of buyers and sellers), but we shall do so to keep the analysis simple. We now need to find those values of q and y which induce truth-telling.

Step 1 Set out the truth-telling constraints. There are two sets of these: the first set of constraints ensures participation in the sense that the traders prefer to (truthfully) bargain rather than to walk away from the negotiating table, and the second set ensures that each type of trader will want to tell the truth. These are called participation constraints and incentive compatibility constraints, respectively (just as in the principal–agent model of chapter 10).

In our numerical example, *the participation constraint* is simply:

$$y \leq 20. \tag{13.1}$$

If this condition did *not* hold, then a strong seller would have an incentive to walk away rather than participate (truthfully) in the mechanism, since participation would only result in a risk of trading with a weak buyer at a price less than the strong seller's valuation ($100 - y < 80$ when $y > 20$). A strong buyer is in a symmetrical position and also requires condition (13.1) to participate.[8] As regards *weak* sellers or buyers, they could always (truthfully) participate as long as prices are non-negative (so that $y \geq 0$), which we assume is always the case.

The *incentive compatibility constraints* in this example also turn out to be simple. Consider a weak seller. If he tells the truth he makes:

TRUTHFUL PAYOFF $\frac{1}{2}qy + \frac{1}{2}50$

and if he lies he gets:

UNTRUTHFUL PAYOFF $\frac{1}{2}q(100 - y)$

(where once again we do not have to worry about the buyer lying since in the equilibrium buyers will tell the truth by construction). Hence the weak seller has no incentive to lie as long as:[9]

$$\frac{1}{2}qy + 25 \geq \frac{1}{2}q(100 - y)$$

which reduces to the incentive compatibility constraint for a weak seller of:

$$q \leq 25/(50 - y). \tag{13.2}$$

We can do a similar analysis for a strong seller, and it turns out that the participation constraint (13.1) is enough to ensure that he would never want to lie. Intuitively it is hard to imagine a strong type ever wanting to pretend to be weak since this merely gives unnecessary ground in the negotiations.

The analysis for buyers is symmetrical, and yields the same incentive compatibility constraint (13.2). Hence we can conclude that as long as the participation constraint (13.1) and incentive compatibility constraint (13.2) hold, then both types of buyer and seller will participate in the mechanism, and tell the truth.

Step 2   Next we must find that mechanism design which yields the 'best' truth-telling equilibrium. For our purposes we shall define 'best' as meaning 'that which yields the highest probability of realizing mutually beneficial trades'. The chances of a weak buyer and weak seller trading are fixed beforehand at 1. Hence in practice this means finding that equilibrium with the highest value of q. Looking at constraints (13.1) and (13.2) this is computationally trivial. The highest possible q for given y is

$$q = 25/(50 - y), \tag{13.3}$$

i.e. where the incentive compatibility constraint is binding. Clearly, q is increasing in y in this equation, hence to get the highest possible q overall, we set y at its highest value subject to constraint (13.1), that is

set $y = 20$, yielding

$$q = (5/6).$$

This completes Step 2. The solution is a game of the general form of table 13.5, with $q = (5/6)$ and $y = 20$. It is important to understand that the equilibrium of this mechanism is one where people tell the truth (i.e. it is in their own self interest to do so). And this mechanism is specifically designed to achieve the highest probability of mutually beneficial trade, i.e. it has the highest q.[10] The total probability of trade in this mechanism is then

$$\tfrac{1}{4} \times q + \tfrac{1}{4} \times q + \tfrac{1}{4} \times 1 = 2/3$$

which may be compared to the outcome under full information, where trade occurred with probability 0.75.

Step 3   The revelation principle tells us that the best outcome we can obtain (if our aim is to maximize q) is that outcome derived in Step 2. No conceivable mechanism design will do better, whether it induces truth-telling or not.

The consequences of private information in this context are that we simply cannot realize all gains from trade, since the equilibrium in Step

2 involved $q < 1$. This outcome is no accident; it illustrates a quite general theorem derived by Myerson and Satterthwaite (1983)* and alluded to in our introduction to bargaining problems. The theorem holds for a general class of bilateral trading problems, where the seller and buyer have private valuations of the good. Suppose that gains from trade are possible (in that the buyer may value the good more highly than the seller) but not certain (in that the seller may value the good more highly than the buyer);[11] then the theorem states that there is no mechanism design which satisfies all the participation and incentive compatibility constraint *and* exploits all potential gains from trade. Thus the consequence of imperfect information in this context is that there is no way of organizing trade in a way that ensures that the object gets traded whenever the buyer values it more than the seller.

To understand this in terms of our example, consider what could happen if we ignored the truth-telling constraints that dictated $q < 1$ and just let the traders bargain freely, e.g. with $y = 20$. The costs of satisfying the truth-telling constraints do not just 'go away'; rather we end up with positive incentives to lie (e.g. a weak seller would find it too tempting to pretend to be strong in order to pick up the $(100 - y) = 80$ payoff in the event that he meets a weak buyer). And we have already seen what happens when traders lie – the earlier split-the-difference mechanism induced dishonesty, and yielded considerably lower probabilities of trade in equilibrium than those under the truth-telling mechanism above.

You may feel uncomfortable with the mechanism designed in Step 2 (these are good reasons for such discomfort – see the discussion of further literature at the end of this chapter). We could in principle take the analysis a stage further, by analysing observed real world mechanisms until we found one that yielded the same equilibrium (as suggested in Step 3 of the general method). Unfortunately, our numerical example is a bit too artificial for us to be able to fruitfully pursue this idea here. In the next chapter we shall look at this avenue more closely in relation to the question of auction design.

Summary

This chapter is about designing mechanisms for transactions under imperfect information. It would seem fairly straightforward to be able to compare and rank the performance of various specified mechanisms on certain criteria such as Pareto-efficiency. The more difficult question which we have posed and have attempted to answer here is 'how can we identify the performance of some mechanism as "optimal"?' A methodology for answering this kind of question was outlined, based on the revelation principle. This principle says that the equilibrium of any transaction mechanism where transacters might (want to) lie can be replicated by the equilibrium of another mechanism where they (want to) tell the truth.

The methodology for mechanism design involved the following steps. Firstly, we set out the constraints that must be satisfied such that all traders have an incentive to participate in the mechanism, and to tell the truth. Secondly, we find the best feasible equilibrium subject to these constraints. The revelation principle then implies that no alternative mechanism can be found that can improve on that equilibrium. We could, if we wished, then search for some specific 'real-world' mechanism that yielded that 'best' feasible equilibrium.

This technique was illustrated in relation to a numerical problem of bargaining between buyers and sellers potentially trading under imperfect information about each others valuations of a good. Under full information all gains from trade were realized. Under imperfect information, an apparently 'natural' and 'fair' mechanism design called 'split the difference' was shown to give traders positive incentives to lie, and yielded equilibria that were often very unfair, and realized only a small fraction of the potentially beneficial trades.

The general method outlined above was applied to this situation. The results of this exercise was a mechanism design that maximized the chances of mutually beneficial trade. This mechanism was by construction *equitable* in the treatment of buyers and sellers, and clearly realized more of the potential gains from trade than the 'split the difference' design. The 'optimal' mechanism still did not realize *all* the potential gains from trade, however, and hence was Pareto-inferior to trade under full information. This feature of the solution was no accident, since it has been shown that there are always unrealized gains from trade in the kinds of situations modelled here, due to the presence of imperfect information. The optimal mechanism design served to minimize this problem.

Further Literature

Point I   Mechanism design: implementation problems

We set out in this chapter a method for finding an optimal mechanism design, based on the revelation principle. Consider a situation where we have used this method to find an NTT mechanism design that has a (lying/cheating) equilibrium which replicates the equilibrium of the best truth-telling mechanism design (Step 3 of the methodology). The question then arises 'Will people play the NTT mechanism design in the desired way?' If people play in some other way, then our attempts at mechanism design will be frustrated. There are two obvious reasons for thinking that things might go wrong:

(i)   The NTT mechanism design may have *multiple equilibria*. If so, then people may well play the 'wrong' equilibrium, yielding outcomes which we might find undesirable.

(ii)   People may make mistakes. The NTT mechanism may have a unique equilibrium (the one which we are aiming for) but people may fail to make the right decisions, e.g. because reaching that equilibrium may involve complex strategic calculations. If so, then once again we may end up with an undesirable outcome.

One response to these problems (see **Kreps, 1990***, for example) is to seek an NTT mechanism that implements the desired outcome through the play of *dominant strategies*. People are much less likely to 'go wrong' in that context because each person's best strategy is independent of what other people do.

It may, of course, be the case that there is *no mechanism* that implements the original desired outcome in dominant strategies. Thus, we may have to settle for a poorer outcome, if we want to be more confident that people will play in the desired way.

We can find *the best outcome that may be implemented in dominant strategies* by constraining the TT mechanism to induce truth-telling in dominant strategies. We then look for a NTT mechanism that yields the same dominant strategy outcome. Once we have found such a mechanism we can conclude that no other mechanism yields a better outcome in dominant strategies. This follows from the *revelation principle in dominant strategy mechanisms*, which is an extension of the 'ordinary' revelation principle – it says that whatever can be achieved as a dominant strategy outcome of an NTT mechanism can also be achieved as a dominant strategy outcome of a TT mechanism.

Point 2   Bargaining: agreeing the mechanism

The above analysis of bargaining assumes that there is some scope to choose a bargaining mechanism, and that all the traders agree to it. It may be, for example, that the traders get together in a pre-bargaining stage (in the corridors, for example) to agree on the mechanism whereby bargaining will take place. They work out the best trading mechanism between them there (say, the one in matrix 5 with $y = 20$, and $q = 5/6$). When the mechanism is in place they then enter the bargaining room and bargaining proper begins, with traders naming their types (weak or strong) and arranging prices and trades as dictated by the mechanism.

As **Myerson (1991)** makes clear, this story is naive, because the traders are likely to start playing games in the corridor at the pre-bargaining stage. If a seller proposes a certain mechanism (say), then the buyer is likely to make inferences as to whether that seller is 'weak' or 'strong'. Knowing this, the seller may deliberately propose a certain mechanism which could make the buyer think he was strong. Similarly, say the buyer accepts or makes a counter-proposal – then the seller is likely to read into this the likely type of buyer (and the buyer knows it).

Two issues emerge as a result. First, once the pre-bargaining game is over, the buyers and sellers may each have a pretty clear idea of the other's type (weak or strong), and so the bargaining game itself will be different. Secondly, with all this game playing going on at the pre-bargaining stage, what hope is there that they will actually come up with an 'optimal' plan like that derived in the main text?

The presence of a mediator may assist the trading parties to agree such a mechanism. The proposal for the mechanism could come from the mediator, who might then persuade the parties to agree to it on the basis that it is (a) Pareto-efficient and (b) maximizes the realisation of potential gains from trade. Even in the presence of a mediator, however, the parties still have an incentive to (possibly falsely) communicate strength by rejecting proposed mechanisms that favour weak types.

Perhaps the most likely mechanism to emerge from such negotiations is one of the general form described in matrix 5, but with $y = 0$ and $q = 0.5$. Such a mechanism still satisfies the truth-telling constraints set out in the main text, and it is also Pareto-efficient given the presence of imperfect information in the market (see note 10). With $y = 0$, strong buyers and sellers get their highest expected payoffs (e.g., a strong seller gets a price of 100 when he meets a weak buyer, which is the maximum a weak buyer would pay). And since both buyers and sellers are likely to want to *convey the impression* that they are strong (whether true or not) in the pre-bargaining negotiations, so this is a mechanism that both are likely to accept. Given that both weak and strong types agree to this mechanism, so the fact that a trader agrees to it is uninformative, and hence after agreeing this mechanism each trader will be none the wiser about the other types when they walk into the bargaining room proper.

Point 3   Bargaining: precommitment problems

Say the traders manage somehow to agree a mechanism such as that described in the main text ($y = 20$, $q = 5/6$). Then they are likely to run into commitment problems in actually implementing it. Such problems are well recognized in the literature (see, for example, **Milgrom and Roberts, 1992**, chapter 5, for a discussion). One such problem runs as follows. Say after agreeing the mechanism the seller (truthfully) declares himself as 'weak' (valuation = 0) and the buyer as 'strong' (valuation = 20). Then the mechanism dictates that (if they trade) the price should be 20. But what is to stop the buyer from unilaterally tearing up the agreement at that point and saying 'the good is worthless to you, so I am not paying you more than 1 for it – take it or leave it'. If the traders cannot credibly *precommit* to abide by the mechanism before they reveal their type (weak or strong) then the agreement on the mechanism is worthless. The (weak) seller in this example would know that a strong buyer would renege on the agreement, and so that seller has the same old incentives to lie (say 'strong') as before, and our fancy mechanism has got us nowhere.

A second problem of precommitment runs as follows. Say that the traders have managed to overcome the first problem somehow, such that they *abide by the price* dictated by the mechanism. The mechanism further dictates that, for our weak seller/strong buyer, trade will only take place with probability $q = 5/6$. Thus once they have declared their types, the traders must find some random device such as rolling a die – if the die shows up with any number 1–5 then they trade, but if it is 6 then they must walk away without trading.

Now most people would find it frustrating to find that they cannot trade just because a die shows 6, even though the seller is openly saying that he is willing to accept a price for the good that the buyer is saying he is willing to pay. Moreover (if the mechanism is working properly), they both know that the other is being completely truthful. The clear temptation once again is to (in this case mutually) tear up the agreement, and trade anyway. But if the traders know that this will happen then the same old incentives to lie in the first place reappear, and the fancy mechanism breaks down. Once again the traders need a credible means to precommit to not trading when the die shows 6, before stating their types. Readers might recognize this kind of problem as the same one of 'ex post renegotiation' mentioned in chapter 11, point (9).

Can you think of any credible precommitments to avoid these problems? (hint, see chapter 11, point (7), for some ideas).

Point 4   Bargaining over time

The example in the main text involves a one-time opportunity to trade – either the buyer and seller succeed in trading or they fail. It may be argued that if there is any chance of mutual benefit in the trade, then if they fail once they might manage to trade effectively later. Incorporating time into economic models leads to many varied and complex possibilities, as we saw in the discussion of principal–agent models (chapter 11, point (8)). However, it is interesting to note that in this context the time dimension could actually make the bargaining problem more intractable and the welfare losses even greater. These losses arise not through failure to trade, but through delay of trade. **Myerson (1991)** gives the following example: suppose the traders discount future income at a rate of 10 per cent per period. The bargaining goes on in open-ended fashion with an opening offer-price from the seller of 90 and an opening bid-price from the buyer of 10. Now if the buyer is strong he would never accept the seller's offer, and similarly if the seller is strong he would never accept the buyer's bid. The weak types might concede to the other's demand, but not necessarily straightaway – a weak buyer might wait awhile to see if the seller caves in first, and vice versa. Thus they have an incentive to stick to their named price until at some point in time one gives in and settles at the other's price. In the equilibrium that Myerson constructs, the chances of any one trader conceding at some given point in time are very small, such that if both types are weak we could expect a wait of 15.4 years before trade takes place, or 24.5 years if only one of them is weak. Discounting the expected returns from trade back to the present yields a very low present value. It is equivalent in our one-time bargaining game of trade with a probability of 0.36 if both types are weak, and 0.22 if only one type is weak – considerably worse than the outcome of our one-time mechanism described in the main text.

Point 5   Bargaining: traders' valuations

The characterization of buyers and sellers in the example as either 'strong' or 'weak' is obviously rather extreme. The central point (noted in the main text), however, is that as long as valuations are private and the highest possible valuation that can be held by the seller is greater than the lowest possible valuation that can be held by the buyer, then we know by the Myerson–Satterthwaite theorem that it is impossible to construct a mechanism that will exploit all potential gains from trade. **Myerson and Satterthwaite (1983)*** do, in fact, give an alternative example to that cited here, where buyers and sellers valuations were both drawn from a uniform distribution with a minimum valuation of zero and a maximum of one. In line with their theorem, no trading mechanism could exploit all gains from trade. They showed in that context, however, that no alternative mechanism could improve on the 'split the difference' design.

NOTES

1   We refer here and throughout this part of the book specifically to *Nash* equilibrium, where players play mutual best responses.

2   Such a mechanism is known in the literature as a direct mechanism, since it involves the players directly telling a mediator their private information.

3   To see that this is an equilibrium, note that a strong seller always keeps the good and hence gets a payoff of 80 from telling the truth, and would only get 10 (the price of the good) if he lied; a weak seller gets 10 from telling the truth, and 0 if he lies (he keeps the good which is worthless to him). A weak buyer makes $\frac{1}{2}(20 - 10) = 5$ if she lies or if she tells the truth, and a strong buyer makes $\frac{1}{2}(100 - 10) = 45$ if she lies or tells the truth. Hence the sellers would lose and the buyers cannot gain by any change of strategy, and we have an equilibrium.

4   To see that this is a equilibrium, note that all potential traders are indifferent here between lying and telling the truth. For example, a weak seller gets expected returns from truth-telling of $10 \times 0.8 + 50 \times 0.2 = 18$, and from lying of $90 \times 0.2 = 18$. It does not matter whether he lies, tells the truth, or plays a mixed strategy where he lies with some probability; the expected returns are always the same. Hence he cannot gain by deviating from the strategy of lying with probability 0.6. A similar argument holds for all the other potential traders – and since none of them can gain by deviating we have a Nash equilibrium.

5   If a strong buyer meets a weak seller, the former tells the truth but the latter only does so with probability 0.4, and if he lies the deal falls through; hence the chances that the two will trade are only 40 per cent, where under full information they would always trade. Similarly if a weak seller meets a strong buyer. If a weak seller meets a weak buyer, then the chances of them both claiming to be strong is $0.6 \times 0.6 = 0.36$; hence at least one of them claims to be weak (and so trade takes place) with probability 0.64. The

overall chances of trade taking place are therefore $0.25 \times 0.4 + 0.25 \times 0.4 + 0.25 \times 0.64 = 0.36$ (we take into account in this calculation that the chances of a particular combination of buyer and seller types meeting are always 0.25).

6   That is, the traders use some random device to determine whether they trade or not in these circumstances. For example, if $q = {}^{1}/_{2}$, then they might trade if the roll of a die comes up with even numbers, and not trade if it comes up with odd numbers. See more on this in the 'further literature'.

7   In the latter case the price of y ensures that the buyer makes $(20 - y)$ and the seller makes y from trade, in the former case the seller makes $(100 - y) - 80 = (20 - y)$ and the buyer makes $100 - (100 - y) = y$.

8   In the event of a tie (i.e. a point of indifference, e.g. where $y = 20$) we assume that traders choose to participate.

9   We break the case of a tie by assuming people tell the truth.

10 Myerson (1991) shows that equation (13.3) is necessary and sufficient for *ex post* Pareto-efficiency given the presence of imperfect information. There are, of course, many mechanism designs that satisfy (13.3) – the one identified in the text is that Pareto efficient design which yields the highest q. The full information equilibrium Pareto-dominates all the imperfect information ones, of course.

11 The latter possibility (no gains from trade) occurred in our numerical example when a strong seller met a strong buyer. In all other cases, gains from trade exist.

CHAPTER 14

Auction Design: Theory

Auctions are a popular way of organizing and completing certain kinds of transactions. They are an ancient form of trading mechanism, which may be traced back to Roman times and earlier. Nowadays they are common in the sale of such diverse goods as antiques, fine art, second hand furniture, houses, livestock, land, government bonds, bankrupt assets, etc. and in the awarding of contracts (e.g. for building a road, or running a service). Despite the apparent diversity, there are important features that are shared in these examples. Firstly, the units being traded are potentially quite valuable, and secondly each unit is unique and may command an individual price. Livestock vary, so a different price may be appropriate for each animal; similarly for antiques or fine art etc. Auctions are well suited to such situations.

Auctions may take various different forms. For example, they may be of a kind where potential buyers have to submit sealed bids to an auctioneer; the highest bid wins, and the winning bidder pays the bid price for the good. An alternative design would be an 'open cry' or English auction, where bidders collect in a room and communicate successively higher bids (e.g. via a shout or maybe just a nod). Potential bidders drop out of the bidding as the price rises until only one bidder is left, and that person wins the good at a price given by their highest bid.

This chapter considers the organization of auctions as a mechanism design problem. Auctions can be seen as games played under imperfect information. Information problems arises in that, for example, each bidder typically does not know how much other bidders are prepared to pay for the good (and neither does the original owner). Bids for the good are usually decided on in a strategic way, hence it is a game. The issues involved in analysing auctions are actually related to the bargaining problem outlined in the previous chapter. The main differences between the two are that in the auction environment (a) the seller is usually taken to be *precommitted* to sell (at least for prices above some reserve price level), and (b) there are typically *many* potential buyers bidding for the good.

The different kinds of auctions alluded to above generally place bidders in different strategic situations, and consequently affect the decisions they make and the final outcome that is likely to be observed from the auction. The literature on auction theory developed from the seminal work of Vickrey (1961). In this chapter we draw on that literature to set out theoretical predictions on auction behaviour. We compare the expected prices that are predicted to emerge from various auction settings, and assess whether the final allocation of the good is likely to be Pareto-efficient. Finally we consider the design of 'optimal auctions', using the techniques for mechanism design outlined in the previous chapter. The next chapter considers experimental evidence on auction behaviour.

The Auction Environment

Consider a situation where the owner of a single indivisible object puts that good up for sale by auction. Suppose for simplicity that there is no resale market – the winner of the auction keeps (or 'consumes') the good. There are a fixed number of bidders. The auction is characterized by *independent private valuations*. That is, valuations are private in that each bidder knows what the good is worth (its value) to him, but does not know what it is worth to other bidders. Further, these valuations are taken to be independent in that each bidder's valuation is unrelated to others' valuations. Thus for example, a bidder who values the good highly cannot infer from this that others are likely to value it highly too (formally, bidders' valuations are privately observed independent random draws from a known prior distribution). The situation faced by bidders is implicitly taken to be *symmetric* in that all bidders in the auction face the same strategic decisions, knowing their own valuation but not others' valuations. Bidders are taken to act independently in making their bids (no collusion).

The seller is taken for simplicity to be risk neutral and to value the good at zero. Thus she would be willing to put the good up for auction as long as the expected price was positive. We assume that she cannot place a 'reserve price' on the good (or that the reserve price is zero).

In the 'guide to further literature' at the end of this chapter, we look at the consequences of relaxing many of the above assumptions. Before we proceed further, however, it is important to draw a distinction between the above 'independent private values' setting of the auction environment, from an alternative known as 'common value auctions'. In common value auctions the value of the good is *the same* to all bidders, but it may be *uncertain*. For example, say bidders are bidding for the rights to drill an offshore oil field – the value of that oil field (in terms of the profit to be made from extracting and selling the oil) is not known for sure at the time that the bids are made. Whatever that value turns out to be, however, it is likely to be (roughly) the same for all the bidders. By contrast, the private value auction analysed here might be for some work of art (say). Different bidders might have a different appreciation of the piece, and hence be prepared to pay different amounts of money for it (note that we assume for simplicity that they cannot resell it).

Common value auctions raise different theoretical issues, and cannot be analysed in terms of the framework used here (we would need at least another chapter to look at these!). In the real world, auctions tend to involve an element of *both* common and private values – that is, bidders' valuations are often uncertain, they vary (privately) across bidders, and they tend to be correlated rather than independent. In the 'further literature' we discuss the implications of this, but for the main body of this chapter we concentrate on the pure 'independent private values' case.

Four Auction Designs

English ('open cry') auctions: this familiar auction design was described in the introduction. It is also known as an 'ascending-bid auction', because it involves rival bidders successively upping the price, until no one is prepared to bid any more.

Dutch auctions: here the auctioneer starts with a high price and lowers it until someone decides to bid, by agreeing to buy the good at the named price. This design is also known as a 'descending-bid auction', for obvious reasons.

First price sealed bid (FPSB) auctions: this auction design was also described in the introduction, and involves bidders submitting bids in sealed envelopes. The highest bid wins, paying the bid price for the good.

Second price sealed bid (SPSB) auctions: this is a rather unfamiliar auction design, but one which turns out to be useful from the point of view of understanding auction theory. It was first suggested by Vickrey (1961) and hence is sometimes known as a 'Vickrey auction'. The design involves bidders submitting sealed bids, with the highest bidder winning *but only paying a price equal to the second highest bid*.

Theoretical Predictions: English and SPSB Auctions

Imagine a bidder in an English auction. As the price is bid up he has to decide whether to outbid his rivals or to withdraw. If a rival bids some amount below our bidder's valuation then it is in his interest to outbid the rival, since he still has something to gain from winning the auction. If rival bidders take the bidding *above* his valuation, however, then it is in his interests to withdraw. One can think of the bidder has having a maximum or ceiling bid in his mind, that maximum being his valuation of the good. It is a dominant strategy for the bidder to bid up to that maximum, i.e. this is his best strategy *whatever* his rivals decide to do.[1]

Now imagine a bidder in a SPSB auction, where he must submit his bid in a sealed envelope. Because the winner only pays the second highest bid in this SPSB auction, it is once again in his interests to write down the maximum he is willing to pay for the good, and again that maximum is given as his valuation of the good. If he wins the auction then the chances are that the second highest bid will be less than his valuation, and so he makes a profit or surplus. If he bids less than his valuation then he risks not getting the good at a price acceptable to him, and if he bids more then he risks paying more for the good than it is worth to him. Once again, bidding his valuation is a dominant strategy[2] (note 1 also applies here).

This analysis suggests that whilst English and SPSB auctions appear outwardly different, the underlying considerations are actually the same. The auctions are strategically equivalent, or 'isomorphic'.[3] In both cases, bidders' incentives are to 'reveal the truth'. In the SPSB auction this is most obvious because each bidder's dominant strategy is to write down their valuation of the good in a sealed envelope. In English auctions they just keep bidding up to their valuation.

The (Nash) equilibrium that arises from all bidders playing their dominant strategy (of truth-telling) in these auction designs has the following properties:

(a)   The winning (highest) bid comes from the bidder who values the good most highly, and hence the allocation is Pareto-efficient. The person who gets the good is the person who gets the most pleasure from it. (To see that this is efficient, say that the good had gone instead to someone with a lower valuation – then further mutually beneficial trade between that person and the bidder with the highest valuation would be possible.)

(b)   The price paid for the good will be the second highest bid. Since all bidders tell the truth, the second highest bid is equal to the second highest valuation (SHV) across all the bidders. Thus we can determine the equilibrium price as $p = \text{SHV}$.

In the SPSB auction these results follow directly from everyone playing their dominant strategy of writing down their valuation in the sealed envelope, with the highest bidder winning and paying the second highest bid. In the English auction, result (a) arises because the bidder with the highest valuation is the last person to drop out of the bidding, and result (b) arises because the person with the second highest valuation is the penultimate bidder to drop out, and he drives the bidding up to his valuation of the good.[4]

Theoretical Predictions: Dutch and FPSB Auctions

Now imagine a bidder in a Dutch auction. The bidder could decide *before the auction began* on the price at which to bid for the good. If the auction price does in fact fall to that level then he can step in with his bid and get the good; if someone else steps in to bid before him (and therefore bids more than his bid price) then he does not get the good. How exactly does he decide on his bid price? This is a difficult decision. The lower the bid the lower the chances of winning, but the greater the profit (or 'surplus') the bidder makes if he does win.

Now compare this with the situation faced by a bidder in a FPSB auction. The bidder must make an identical decision to that in the Dutch auction of choosing a price to bid for the good (in the FPSB auction he writes the bid price down and puts it in an envelope). The strategic issues involved in choosing the bid price are also the same, i.e. the lower the bid price the lower the chance of winning but the greater the surplus if he does win. The Dutch and FPSB auctions are therefore also strategically equivalent or 'isomorphic', at least in theory. The auction designs are outwardly different, but these differences are (in theory) superficial.

Thus we have collapsed the original four auction designs down to just two: (Dutch = FPSB) versus (English = SPSB). These two differ from each other in that in the former bidders decide on a bid price for the good, and in the latter they decide on a *maximum* or ceiling bid for the good. Whether or not people actually *behave* in the same way when playing Dutch or FPSB auctions and playing English or SPSB auctions, is an empirical question which we shall consider in the next chapter on auction experiments.

The main theoretical issue which remains to be resolved concerns exactly how bidders will behave in Dutch/FPSB auctions. They must pitch the bid in a way that trades off the probability of winning against the surplus from winning. There is no dominant strategy in this context, since the optimal bid that a bidder might put in (i.e., that which is best for him) typically depends on the bids of other bidders.

In the absence of a dominant strategy, the best we can do by way of deriving theoretical predictions is to look for (Nash) equilibria of the auction game. To illustrate how this might be done without delving too far into algebra, we make a few assumptions. Firstly we take it (initially) that there are two risk neutral bidders, labelled 1 and 2. Secondly we assume that their valuations of the good are drawn from a uniform distribution with values scaled between 0 and 1, as depicted in figure 14.1.[5] This says that the minimum value that a bidder might place on the good is zero (in which case it is worthless to that person), the maximum value he might place is 1, and any valuation in-between is equally likely. Each bidder knows his own valuation, he knows that his rival's valuation is drawn from the same distribution, but he does not know exactly what his rival's valuation is. The valuations are taken to be independent draws from this distribution, as mentioned earlier.

Bidder 1 has expected return $E(R)_1$ from the bid, given as:

$$E(R)_1 = (V_1 - b_1)q(b_1 \geq b_2) \tag{14.1}$$

where he gets the good with probability q, in which case he receives a surplus of $V_1 - b_1$ (he fails to get the good with probability $(1 - q)$, in which case he receives nothing). We write the probability as $q(b_1 \geq b_2)$ in equation (1) to make it clear that the probability of making the winning bid (and hence getting the good) is given as the chances that his bid is as least as great as the other person's (in the event of a tie $(b_1 = b_2)$ we assume that bidder 1 gets the good).

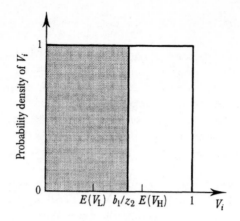

Figure 14.1　The distribution of bidders' valuations

Let us take it for the moment that both bidders have a bidding strategy where they decide on their bids as some constant fraction of their valuation:

$$b_i = z_i V_i \tag{14.2}$$

where $0 < z_i \leq 1$. We shall return later to justify this. Now the probability that bidder 1 gets the good is $q(b_1 \geq z_2 V_2)$ since $b_2 = z_2 V_2$. This may be rewritten as $q(b_1/z_2 \geq V_2)$. Return to figure 14.1 and note the point marked (b_1/z_2) on it. The second bidder's valuation V_2 is a random draw from this distribution, so the probability V_2 is no greater than (b_1/z_2) is given by the shaded area to the left of (b_1/z_2). This area is given as[6]

$$\left[\text{horizontal distance up to } (b_1/z_2)\right] \times \text{vertical distance}$$
$$= (b_1/z_2) \times 1$$
$$= (b_1/z_2)$$

so we conclude from this reasoning that $q(b_1 \geq b_2) = (b_1/z_2)$. Thus equation (14.1) now becomes

$$E(R)_1 = (V_1 - b_1)(b_1/z_2). \tag{14.3}$$

To find that bid b_1 which maximizes this expected return, we calculate the first-order condition:[7]

$$\frac{dE(R)_1}{db_1} = (V_1 - 2b_1)/z_2 = 0 \tag{14.4}$$

which solves to yield the optimal bid as:

$$b_1 = \frac{1}{2}V_1. \qquad (14.5)$$

This says that the bidder maximizes his expected return by placing a bid which is exactly half his valuation of the good – e.g. if it is worth 2/3 to him, then he bids 1/3. The second bidder faces a symmetrical problem, and hence his optimal bid will also be half his valuation $b_2 = \frac{1}{2}V_2$. Now note that in this kind of bidding strategy, the bid is indeed a constant fraction of the valuation, and hence the assumption made earlier and contained in equation (14.2) does actually hold true ($z_i = \frac{1}{2}$, true for both bidders).

The bidding strategies where both bidders bid half their valuations are therefore optimal for each bidder, given the other bidder's strategy; that is, they are mutual best responses, and hence are Nash equilibrium strategies.[8]

The analysis may be generalized to the case of N bidders, where N may take on any positive integer value. Without delving into the algebra, we simply note that this yields a bidding strategy for bidder i as:

$$b_i = \frac{N-1}{N}V_i. \qquad (14.6)$$

When $N = 1$, that is there is just one bidder, then this equation says (quite sensibly) that that bidder simply bids the minimum amount that the seller would accept, which in our example is a price of zero. When $N = 2$, equation (14.6) reduces to the solution in equation (14.5), saying bidders bid half their valuations; if $N = 3$ then bidders bid 2/3 of their valuation; if $N = 4$ they bid 3/4 of their valuation, and so on. As N increases, each bidder bids a higher fraction of their valuation, and as N tends to infinity so bidding tends towards the full valuation.

There are two main points to note from this analysis:

(a) The highest bid always comes from the person with the highest valuation of the good (because the higher is V, the higher is b_i in equation (14.6)), and so the outcome is Pareto-efficient, as was the case for the English/SPSB auction.

(b) The price paid is given as the highest bid, which in turn is given as $V_H(N-1)/N$ where N is the number of bidders and V_H is the highest valuation.

These conclusions are subject to the following qualifications.

(i) The outcome depends on play of 'best responses' which are not dominant strategies. Given the scope for miscalculating your rival's strategy, and the complexity involved in working out your best response to it, one might expect the predicted outcome to be more 'fragile' than in the English/SPSB auction. On occasion people might overbid yielding a higher price, say, or sometimes the person with the highest valuation might underbid and perhaps not get the good.

(ii) The results depend on some of the simplifying assumptions. In particular, both bidders were taken to be risk neutral. We show in the discussion of 'further literature' at the end of the chapter that if the bidder with the highest valuation is less risk averse than his rival(s), then it is quite possible that their optimal bidding strategies may result in a rival getting the good. Thus, differential attitudes to risk can result in inefficient outcomes in Dutch/FPSB auctions. If the winning bidder is risk averse, he would also pay a higher bid-price than if he was risk neutral (he bids more to reduce the risk of not getting the good).

Finally, it is perhaps worth noting that as long as N is finite, equation (14.6) says that bidders understate their valuations – their equilibrium bids are 'lies' in the sense that they systematically bid less than the good is worth to them. In fact, we can show that 'truth-telling' cannot be an equilibrium of these kinds of auction. To see this consider what would happen if bidder 2 actually did 'tell the truth' by bidding his full valuation, in the two-bidder auction. Then bidder 1 would have expected return:

$$\left(V_1 - b_1\right)q\left(b_1 \geq V_2\right) = \left(V_1 - b_1\right)b_1$$

which is maximized where $b_1 = \frac{1}{2}V_1$. Hence even if bidder 2 told the truth, bidder 1 would not; the best response to truth-telling is to lie, thus truth-telling cannot be a Nash equilibrium of this auction. This point will be of relevance when we come to consider 'optimal auctions', where we look at truth-telling in relation to the revelation principle.

Expected Revenue Equivalence

Consider these auctions from the seller's point of view. She is likely to prefer to sell her good in that auction design which is most likely to give her the higher price. We know that English/SPSB auctions deliver an actual price equal to the second highest valuation (SHV), and Dutch/FPSB auctions deliver a price equal to $V_H(N - 1)/N$. The seller does not, however, usually know beforehand what these valuations are. Hence she must compare the *expected* prices in the two auctions. Have we any reason to think that the SHV might on *average* be more than $V_H(N - 1)/N$, or vice versa?

In fact the answer to this, and one of the most fundamental results in auction theory (due to Vickrey, 1961), is that they are likely to be the same. That is, the two types of auction deliver equivalent expected revenue to the seller. To see this, we shall continue with the example begun in the previous section where bidders' valuations are independent random draws from a uniform distribution.

In order to calculate expected prices, we need to think about the likely valuations that bidders in the auction place on the good. Consider first the case of two bidders; what are the expected values of two independent random draws form the uniform distribution in figure 14.1? To answer this question, say we knew that the bidder with the higher valuation of the good valued it at V_H. Then the lower valuation V_L must come from a point in the distribution to the left of V_H. Since any value for V_L between 0 and V_H is equally likely, we can deduce that on average V_L will lie exactly halfway between O and V_H. Conversely, say we did not know V_H, but we knew the lower valuation was some amount V_L. Then the higher valuation must lie between V_L and 1, with any valuation in between being equally likely. The average or expected value of V_H will than be exactly halfway between V_L and 1.

Putting these observations together, we can deduce that the expected values of the highest and the lowest of 2 draws from this distribution will divide up the horizontal distance 0 to 1 into three equal segments as depicted in the diagram, and so $E(V_L) = 1/3$ and $E(V_H) = 2/3$. In an English/SPSB auction, the expected price is the expected value of the SHV, that is $E(p) = E(V_L) = 1/3$. In a Dutch/FPSB auction the expected price is half the expected value of the highest valuation, that is $E(p) = \frac{1}{2}E(V_H) = 1/2 \times 2/3 = 1/3$. Thus the expected prices are the same.

The same argument works if there are more bidders, except that rather than having two expected valuations which divide the interval up into three segments, we now have N expected valuations which divide the interval up into $(N + 1)$ segments. The expected value of the highest valuation is then $E(V_H) = N/(N + 1)$, analogous to $E(V_H) = 2/3$ in the two bidder case. Given the bidding strategy in a Dutch/FPSB auction written down in equation (14.6), the expected price in that case is:

$$E(p) = \left(\frac{N-1}{N}\right) E(V_{\mathrm{H}}) = \left(\frac{N-1}{N}\right)\left(\frac{N}{N+1}\right) = \frac{N-1}{N+1}.$$

In an English/SPSB auction the expected price is the expected value of the second highest valuation, which is simply $(N-1)/(N+1)$; that is, it is one segment down from the highest valuation. Thus in an English/SPSB auction the expected price is:

$$E(p) = E(\mathrm{SHV}) = \frac{N-1}{N+1}.$$

Again both auctions deliver the same expected price. As the number of bidders increases, that expected price rises. In the limit as N tends to infinity so the expected price in both auctions tends to the maximum valuation possible in the distribution, which is 1.

Our explanation of this 'expected revenue equivalence' has relied on a number of assumptions, particularly that the bidders' valuations are drawn from the uniform distribution depicted in figure 14.1. The equivalence result holds much more generally, however, even if the distribution is not uniform.[9] It is arguable that our prediction for expected revenue in the English/SPSB case is likely to be more robust than in the Dutch/FPSB case, since the former is founded on the play of dominant strategies whereas the latter is not.

Optimal Auctions from the Seller's Viewpoint: Applying the Revelation Principle

So far we have compared English/SPSB and Dutch/FPSB auctions in terms of the efficiency of the outcomes, and the expected prices. What about alternatives to both these types of auction designs? Both types turned out to be efficient, hence there is nothing to be gained in that department by looking at alternative auction designs. There may, however, be some different design which yields a higher *expected price* than all the auction designs analysed so far. The (risk neutral) seller is effectively in a monopoly position in the supply of the object in question. She is also usually the person that chooses the auction design. Hence she will want to use that auction design which maximizes the expected price for the good.

The revelation principle can be used to show that the auction designs considered above are, in fact, optimal from the seller's point of view, under quite general conditions. A full derivation and outline of the relevant conditions is beyond the scope of this book (see Mas Colell et al., 1995). However, we shall *illustrate* the result with reference to a rather limited class of auctions. In the 'Further Literature' section of this chapter we shall also discuss situations under which the auction designs considered above may *not* be optimal.

Consider again the case of two bidders whose valuations are drawn from the uniform distribution of figure 14.1. We shall restrict attention to that *class of auction designs* where the highest bidder wins and pays a price p which is given as some fraction β of his bid:

$$p = \beta b \tag{14.7}$$

where $0 \le \beta \le 1$. Note that if $\beta = 1$ then the winner pays his bid, and we are back in the Dutch/FPSB environment.

This class of auctions includes FPSB as a special case. But it does not, for example, allow us to make the price paid depend on other peoples' bids, which is want happens in SPSB. That kind of generalization would be too technical for our purposes.

Sticking with equation (14.7) therefore, we ask whether there is any auction design which involves some specified value of β, which is likely to yield more expected revenue to the seller than using $\beta = 1$ as in the Dutch/FPSB design.

Applying the revelation principle, we look first for auction designs in which truth-telling is an equilibrium. This involves introducing participation and incentive compatibility constraint, as in chapter 13. The participation constraints here are that both (risk neutral) bidders do not expect to make losses from participating in the auction. If they tell the truth (as they shall in the truth-telling equilibrium) then this means:[10]

$$\left(V_i - \beta V_i\right)q\left(V_i > V_j\right) \ge 0 \tag{14.8}$$

which is trivially satisfied by having $\beta \le 1$.

The incentive compatibility constraints are that the expected returns to each bidder are maximised when they bid their valuation ($dE(R)/db_i = 0$ when $b_i = V_i$). That way they have an incentive to tell the truth. To satisfy this, we shall first assume that bidder 2 does indeed tell the truth by bidding $b_2 = V_2$, and then work out bidder 1's best response to this. With $b_2 = V_2$ we have

$$E(R)_1 = \left(V_1 - \beta b_1\right)q\left(b_1 \ge V_2\right)$$

where $q(b_1 \geq V_2) = b_1$ by the same argument used earlier in the analysis of Dutch/FPSB auctions.[11] Thus $E(R)_1 = (V_1 - \beta b_1)b_1$. To maximize this, take:

$$\frac{dE(R)_1}{db_1} = V_1 - 2\beta b_1 = 0 \qquad (14.9)$$

and so $b_1 = V_1/2\beta$.

We want to find β such that bidder 1 tells the truth by bidding $b_1 = V_1$. From equation (14.9) we find that this is only true if $\beta = \frac{1}{2}$. In an auction design where the winner pays a price equal to half his bid, therefore, bidder 1's best response is to tell the truth when bidder 2 tells the truth. Given that bidder 2's situation is symmetrical, his best response is also to tell the truth when bidder 1 tells the truth. Hence when $\beta = \frac{1}{2}$ truth-telling is a mutual best response, and so a Nash equilibrium. Equation (14.9) suggests[12] that if $\beta > \frac{1}{2}$ then people will understate their valuations ($b_1 < V_1$), and that was in fact the equilibrium outcome of the FPSB auction (people bid half their valuation). If $\beta < \frac{1}{2}$ then it suggests that bidders will overstate their valuations ($b_1 > V_1$). The equilibrium of the auction with $\beta = \frac{1}{2}$ is efficient in that the bidder who values the good most highly wins, by putting in the highest bid. The actual price paid is half the highest bid = valuation. The expected price is half the expected value of the highest valuation, that is:

$$E(p) = \frac{1}{2}E(V_H) = \frac{1}{2} \times 2/3 = 1/3$$

which is the same as the expected price of the Dutch/FPSB (and indeed of the English/SPSB auctions), in the two bidder case.

We are interested in this section in finding the 'optimal auction' design from the point of view of the seller, i.e. that design which delivers the highest expected price. Within the class of auctions where the price paid is some fraction of the winning bid ($p = \beta b$), we have found that the only design which yields truth-telling is where $\beta = \frac{1}{2}$. Since there is only one such design we can conclude that the equilibrium of that design must also be the best (in terms of expected p) in which truth-telling applies. The revelation principle then implies that this best truth-telling equilibrium is at least as good as any equilibrium of any other design in this class ($p = \beta b$, $\beta \neq \frac{1}{2}$). The Dutch/FPSB auction is explicitly contained in the class (it sets $\beta = 1$), and we have seen that it delivers the same equilibrium expected price as that in the 'best' equilibrium. Hence we can conclude that it is impossible to improve on that equilibrium of the Dutch/FPSB (or indeed the dominant strategy outcome of English/SPSB) auction design by trying any other design in the class of auctions where price is set as a fraction of the bid.[13]

Summary

In this chapter we have set out some stylized models of auction behaviour. We considered four specific auction designs for situations in which bidders had independent private valuations of the good up for auction. We showed that:

(1) From a strategic point of view English auctions were equivalent to 'second price sealed bid' auctions, and that Dutch auctions were equivalent to 'first price sealed bid auctions'.

(2) In the case of English/SPSB auctions we argued that bidders had a dominant strategy, which was to bid their full valuation. Play of this strategy yielded a truth-telling equilibrium in which the allocation of the good was Pareto-efficient, at a price given by the second highest valuation in the population of bidders.

(3) In the case of Dutch/FPSB auctions we argued that no such dominant strategy was available. Bidders had to weigh the benefits of a higher bid in terms of a higher probability of getting the good against the costs in terms of a lower surplus (valuation minus price) if they did get the good. We constructed an equilibrium for this kind of auction, where (risk neutral) bidders put in bid prices that were a fraction $(N-1)/N$ of their valuations. The equilibrium resulted in efficient allocation at a price given by the fraction $(N-1)/N$ times the highest valuation. We argued, however, that this predicted outcome depended on certain assumptions. In particular, if differential attitudes to risk were present amongst bidders, then the equilibrium allocation need not be efficient. Further this outcome was likely to be more fragile than that for the English/SPSB auction, since it was founded on mutual best responses that were not dominant strategies.

(4) We showed that all these auctions delivered the same equilibrium expected price for the good. Thus, from the seller's point of view there was nothing to choose between English/SPSB and Dutch/FPSB auctions, in terms of the equilibrium outcomes. Again, the predic-

tion for Dutch/FPSB auctions depended on assumptions of risk neutrality etc.

(5) Finally we used the revelation principle to search for some 'optimal' auction design. In particular, we looked at the class of auctions where the winner paid a price given by some fraction β of their bid, to ascertain whether any such auction could deliver a higher equilibrium expected price than the English/SPSB or Dutch/FPSB auction. We found that only one auction design (β = ¹/₂) yielded truth-telling as an equilibrium and that that solution generated the same expected price as the auctions analysed earlier. We concluded from this (on the basis of the revelation principle) that no equilibrium of any auction design within the class considered could improve on the equilibrium of the English, Dutch or sealed bid auctions.

Further Literature on Auction Theory

Point I   Differential risk aversion in Dutch/FPSB auctions

The more risk averse the bidder, the more he is likely to bid for the good *ceteris paribus*. This can be illustrated in terms of a simple model suggested by Cox et al. (1982). Bidder i is taken to have utility function:

$$V_i(y) = y^{1-r_i}$$

where V is utility, y is some amount of money, and $0 \leq r_i < 1$ is the coefficient of relative risk aversion for bidder i. Working through the same analysis given in the main text, but incorporating this utility function, yields equilibrium bids of the form:

$$b_i = \frac{N-1}{N-r_i} V_i.$$

The more risk averse the bidder the nearer is r to one and hence the higher the bid. The presence of risk averse bidders then implies that expected revenue equivalence between the English/SPSB and Dutch/FPSB auctions breaks down, since the latter yield higher bids, and so a higher expected price. (Bidding in English/SPSB auctions is unaffected by r, since the dominant strategy is still to bid $b_i = V_i$.)

Furthermore, if people *differ* in their degree of risk aversion then Dutch/FPSB may not yield efficient outcomes in equilibrium. To see this, take the case of two bidders, with $r_1 = 0$ and $r_2 = 0.9$, whilst $V_1 = 0.8$ and $V_2 = 0.7$. Bidder 1 is risk neutral; and he also happens to value the good most highly. Bidder 2 puts in the higher bid, however, because he is highly risk averse. Specifically, the above bidding function yields $b_1 = 0.4$ and $b_2 = 0.636$. The outcome is inefficient in that the person with the lower valuation gets the good.

Point 2   Endogenous quantities

Hansen (1988) looked at the case where the number of units to be sold is not just the one single good. This circumstance might arise in a situation where a buyer is awarding a contract for industrial procurement. Sellers of the good compete for the contract, and the price is fixed in an auction. Once the price is fixed, the buyer has the right to buy as many units at that price as she pleases. The buyer's demand decision is modelled by a demand function $Q(p)$. Each seller i has (privately observed) constant unit costs c_i.

If $Q(p)$ were fixed at some exogenous number of units, then this situation would be analogous to our auction model in the main chapter, except that here it is the sellers that put in the bids, and the higher their privately observed unit cost the less the contract is worth to them. The buyer will choose the lowest price as the winner of the auction.

Hansen considers the consequences of having quantity demanded increase as price falls ($Q'(p) < 0$). In an English/SPSB auction, each seller again has a dominant strategy, which is to bid c_i, and if he wins (c_i is the lowest bid) then he receives an equilibrium price equal to the second lowest cost ($p = SLC$) from the buyer, for each unit sold. Hence demand is given in equilibrium as $Q(p = SLC)$. The bidding strategy for these auctions is unaffected by introducing the demand function $Q(p)$. The outcome is Pareto-inefficient in that the price paid is *not* equal to the constant marginal cost of the least cost seller; $p >$ lowest unit cost, since $p =$ second lowest cost, yielding $Q(SLC) < Q(LC)$.

In a Dutch/FPSB environment, however, introducing the demand function $Q(p)$ does change bidding strategies. We know that with risk-neutral bidders and a fixed quantity the Dutch/FPSB auction yields the same equilibrium as the English/SPSB one. With $Q'(p) < 0$ (quantity increases as the price falls) however, so lowering the bid-price has an extra effect on the bidder's expected return. With two bidders this is:

$$E(R)_i = (b_i - c_i) \cdot Q(b_i) \cdot q(b_i < b_j).$$

A lower bid price b_i reduces the margin gained on a unit of sales if the auction is won $(b - c)$, but it raises the probability of winning (q). These are the same strategic considerations as in the analysis of Dutch/FPSB auctions in the main chapter. But now a lower bid also raises the number of units Q on which the margin $(b - c)$ is made if the auction is won. This gives bidders an extra incentive to lower their bid price, in Dutch/FPSB auctions.

Without that added incentive, we know that the Dutch/FPSB yields the same expected price as the English/SPSB auction. With it, the expected price in the Dutch/FPSB auction falls below that in the English/SPSB auction, yielding a higher demand. The winning bidder i still bids above unit cost c_i to make a profit from the deal, so the outcome is still not efficient, but given that the winning bid price is lower here than in the English/SPSB auction so the equilibrium outcome will be closer to Pareto-efficiency.

Hansen argued that this logic might explain why Dutch/FPSB auctions are actually quite popular in the awarding of industrial procurement contracts.

Point 3   Reserve prices

Riley and Samuelson (1981)* consider an auction environment in which the seller can post a reserve price $\sigma \geq 0$ for the good; if the bidding yields a price less than σ, then the good is not sold.[14] Setting the reserve price at a strictly positive level $(\sigma > 0)$ may affect the outcome, either:

(a)   If both bidders value the good at less than σ, in which case the good will not be sold. The reserve price proves costly to the seller in this case, in that it causes the loss of the sale of a good that is worthless to her.

(b)   If one bidder values the good at above σ and the other values it below σ (e.g., $V_1 > \sigma > V_2 > 0$), in which case the good will be sold at a price above the second highest valuation. The reserve price is of benefit to the seller here, in that it raises the sale price.

What is the likely net impact of these two opposing effects on the *expected* price from the auction? Riley and Samuelson show that effect (b) dominates effect (a) such that the expected price is maximized at a positive reserve price. To illustrate this result, consider the simplest case of a single risk neutral bidder with valuation v in a Dutch/FPSB auction. We noted earlier in our discussion of equation (14.6), that (in the absence of a reserve price) such a bidder would bid zero for the good, yielding expected revenue $E(p) = 0$. By contrast, the introduction of a reserve price $\sigma > 0$ would cause the bidder to bid the reserve price as long as $v > \sigma$, yielding $E(p) = \text{prob}(v > \sigma) . \sigma$. Expected revenue is positive in this case, as long as $\sigma \leq 1$ (where 1 is the highest possible value of v from the uniform distribution of figure 14.1). Thus the seller clearly makes more money on average with a positive reserve price, as the Riley and Samuelson result predicts.

Finally, we know from point (1) above that if buyers are risk averse then the conventional Dutch/SPSB auction yields a higher expected price than the English/SPSB auction. Riley and Samuelson further show that the optimal reserve price in such an auction is lower, the higher the degree of buyer risk aversion.

Point 4   Common values and correlated values

We noted in the main chapter that common value auctions raised quite different issues to the independent private value auctions analysed here. These are briefly discussed in the next chapter. **Milgrom and Weber (1982)*** consider an auction environment that contains elements of both common and private values. The idea is that in many auctions, bidders do not know exactly what a good is worth, and hence they must estimate their valuation. Often, these estimates have a common component across bidders, and an independent one. For example, all bidders might be able to observe certain characteristics of an antique, which causes their estimated valuations of it to be correlated with each other. The estimated valuations may differ, partly because bidders may make independent errors in their estimates and partly because each may genuinely differ in the utility they might get from the same good. (An analogous argument holds in bidding for franchises, contracts etc.)

Milgrom and Weber capture the non-independence of estimated valuations in terms of what they call 'affiliation'. This means that the higher a bidder's estimated valuation, the more likely it is from his point of view that other bidders' estimates will be high also.

The consequences of this are far-reaching, and can be summarized as follows. Dutch and FPSB auctions remain strategically equivalent, and so they deliver the same expected price. English auctions and SPSB auctions are not strategically equivalent in this context. Intuitively, this is because over the course of an English auction, each bidder observes the progress of the bidding. Since bidders are uncertain about the worth of the piece, and since (they know that) their estimates are affiliated, so observing other peoples' bids can be informative, and affect that person's bidding. In an SPSB auction, bidders do not get this information (bids are just written in sealed envelopes). Milgrom and Weber show that the consequence of this difference results in more aggressive bidding in the English auction resulting in a higher expected price in equilibrium (if there are more than two bidders).

Both English and SPSB auctions turn out also to deliver higher equilibrium expected prices than the Dutch/FBSP auctions in this context. The logic driving this result is quite subtle. In the English and SPSB auctions the price paid by the winner is given by the second highest bid, which is in turn dependent upon rivals' valuations of the good. In an 'independent value' setting, these valuations were drawn independently of the winner's valuation. Here this is no longer true, since rival bidder's valuations are affiliated with the winner's valuation. Thus the price paid is indirectly dependent on the winner's valuation, in English/SPSB auctions in this environment. This causes bidders to bid more aggressively, raising the equilibrium price. In the Dutch/FPSB auction bidding is unaffected by this change since the price paid is simply the winning bid, whether values are affiliated or not.

These arguments suggest that the English auction design is likely to be most attractive to the seller (since it yields the highest expected price). Milgrom and Weber argue that this might explain why the dominant form of auction empirically observed is the English variety.

Milgrom and Weber also consider the incentives facing a seller who has (verifiable) private information that is relevant to bidders' valuations of the good, in the context of auctions with affiliated values; should the seller adopt a policy of revealing all information? They show that a general policy of always revealing information is best for the seller as it maximises the expected price. Intuitively, winning bidders tend to extract more surplus from the auction by knowing more about the good than their rival bidders; the seller prevents that person from getting the good cheaply by adopting a policy which puts as much information as she has got about the good 'out in the open' and available to all bidders (the underlying logic for this result is related to the 'verifiable message' argument in chapter 7, where it was argued that uninformed parties would in equilibrium 'assume the worst' about any information that was not revealed).

Point 5   Rings

Graham and Marshall (1987) consider auction design from the point of view of their susceptibility to rings. So far, we have assumed no collusion amongst bidders. A ring occurs when a group of bidders collude over their bid, and then (if they get the good) re-auction the object amongst themselves. By colluding in the main auction, the ring can get the good at a lower price than in the absence of collusion. For example, in an English/SPSB auction, a representative of the ring can bid the highest valuation of all the ring members – if he gets the good, then he pays a price equal to the second highest bid of *bidders outside the ring*. The ring members get the good at a lower price, and can divide up that surplus among themselves.

Which auction designs are most susceptible to such rings? This may be considered in terms of the incentives to cheat on the ring. In an English auction, a member cannot successfully cheat, by getting a friend (say) to bid on his behalf against the ring representative – since the latter would simply keep on bidding till he reached the highest valuation of members in the group. Hence the ring is unlikely to be broken by cheating. In a Dutch/FPSB auction, however, there is much to gain by cheating on the ring – you get your friend to put in a bid a shade above the ring representative's bid, and stand a greater chance of getting the good cheaply than if the ring had not existed. Hence the ring is more likely to be destroyed by cheats in such an auction design

For that reason, one might expect Dutch/FPSB auctions to be favoured in situations where the seller has reason to suspect collusion amongst the bidders.

Point 6   Further issues

Milgrom (1989) has highlighted a variety of other issues that are relevant to auction design. One point that may matter in practice is that English auctions have the disadvantage that they require the physical presence of the bidders. If people cannot spare the time or make the effort to be present, then an English auction may not be viable. The SPSB auction shares many of the features of the English auction and does not require the presence of the bidder (you leave your bid in a sealed envelope) – but such an auction is open to manipulation by the auctioneer, who may name you as the winner but insert a false bid himself to drive up the price you pay.

On the other hand English/SPSB auctions may economize on the costs of preparing a bid. In Dutch/FPSB auctions, each bidder's best strategy depends in part on what other bidders do, and so there is an incentive to expend resources to gather information on rivals' strategies. In the English/SPSB auction by contrast, bidders have a dominant strategy which depends only on their own valuation. Hence bid preparation may be less costly.

Point 7   Optimal auctions (again)

We noted earlier in this chapter that the auction designs studied here are equivalent from the seller's point of view, and that they are also 'optimal' over an (albeit limited) class of alternative designs. Much of what we have said on 'Further Literature' may be seen to qualify that result: e.g., attitudes to risk, collusion, reserve prices, etc. all may affect auction performance. **Wilson (1992)*** surveys the literature on optimal auctions, and considers other possible designs, e.g. introducing entry fees/subsidies, or allowing sellers to reject the highest bid with some positive probability.

Milgrom (1989) notes that identification of 'optimal' auctions can yield quite outlandish and very complicated designs in certain situations. He argues that many of these designs are not 'robust' – they work optimally under certain conditions but outside of that they can work very badly. The attraction of the popular designs discussed here (English, FPSB, etc.) is that they are robust – they may not be always exactly optimal, but they rarely let you down badly.

NOTES

1   The strategy is actually *weakly* dominant, in that in some cases it may not matter what the bid is – for example, if others bid an amount more than you value the good, then your payoff is zero regardless, for any bid you make up to your valuation (since you do not get the good in any event).

2   Consider the following numerical example. You are bidding in a SPSB auction for a good which you value at $100, against one other bidder. Say you bid $70 rather than the full $100 for it. If the other bidder bids $80 then you would lose the good, even though you would gladly have paid $90 for it. If the other bidder bid $50 then your bid of $70 does get you the good, but you do not pay any less for it than if you had bid $100 (since the rules of the SPSB auction are that you pay the second highest bid which is $50 regardless of whether you bid $70 or $100). Similarly, say you bid

$120 instead of $100. If the other bidder bid $80, you would get the good for $80 either way. But if the other bidder bids $110, then your bid of $120 gets you the good for $110 when you only value it at $100.

3   In the language of game theory, the extensive forms of the two auctions differ, but the (reduced) normal forms are the same.

4   If bidding is in discrete units of money, then in an English auction the winning bid may actually pay an amount slightly greater than SHV (e.g. if the bidding is in $1 units, and the SHV = $13, then the winner may pay $14).

5   The scaling of valuations is immaterial. It would be just as easy to have valuations drawn from a uniform distribution between 0 and 100, say.

6   The vertical distance is 1 since the total area contained by the whole distribution must be 1. For this to be true we need vertical distance × (full) horizontal distance = 1, and since the full horizontal distance is 1 so the vertical distance is 1 also.

7   The reader may take it on trust throughout this chapter that the first-order conditions do indeed identify a global maximum.

8   Note the importance of the seller's precommitment to sell in this context, as mentioned in the introduction. *Without such precommitment,* the seller would have an incentive to renege on the agreement to sell at the highest price bid. After all bids were in, she would demand that the highest bidder pay *double* the amount bid (since he only bids half his valuation). But if bidders anticipate this, then they would bid differently in the first place.

9   See Milgrom (1989) or Mas Colell et al. (1995)* for further discussion of the conditions under which revenue equivalence holds.

10   The equilibrium involves truth-telling (i.e. $b_i = V_i$) by construction, therefore i wins the auction if $V_i > V_j$, since both bidders bid their valuations, and the price paid is $p = \beta b_i = \beta V_i$.

11   Fix the bid b_1 as some point in the distribution in figure 14.1. The chances that V_2 is less than that is given by the area to the left of b_1, which is given as 'horizontal distance to b_1 × vertical distance' = b_1.

12   It is only suggestive, because it rests on the assumption that bidder 2 tells the truth.

13   Indeed, the fact that there is a unique truth-telling auction design in the class ($p = \beta b$) implies that all designs in that class yield the same expected price in equilibrium. Changing the fraction of their bids that winners pay (β) causes bidders to adjust the fraction of their valuations that they bid, to leave the outcome unaffected.

14   We have assumed the seller values the good at zero. More generally, if the seller values it at $V^0 > 0$, then the reserve price may be set at some level $V^* = V^0 + \sigma$.

CHAPTER 15

Auction Design: Experimental Evidence

In this chapter we discuss the methods and findings of experimental studies on auctions with independent private values. Auctions of this kind have been the subject of extensive experimental work, much of it heavily influenced by the early study by Coppinger, Smith and Titus (1980), henceforth CST.

The next section sets out the experimental environment for studying auctions, followed by a summary of the hypotheses suggested by the theory (as discussed in chapter 14). We then discuss the CST study. This is followed by a more general account of our understanding of experimental auctions, which draws on the findings of more recent studies. The chapter concludes with a guide to further and related literature on experimental and real world auctions.

The Experimental Auction Environment

In order to test the theoretical models of auction behaviour described in chapter 14, the experimenter must induce independent private values amongst the subjects/bidders. This is done in the usual way by giving each bidder a redemption value or RV (CST actually use the term 'resale value'). The winning bidder then makes money out of the auction, given by the amount: payoff = RV − price.

Subjects are often given a sum for turning up to the experiment (e.g. $3, as in Cox et al., 1982), as an inducement to participate and also to ensure that even if bidders make losses in the auction proper they still do not end up out of pocket.

Bidders are usually privately told their own RV, but not the RVs of other bidders. Instead, they are told (in simple language) that each bidder's RV is an independent random draw from some specified distribution (this information structure accords with the assumptions of the theory). The most common distribution used is (a discrete analogue to) the uniform distribution, since this is the easiest distribution to explain to subjects and also accords with the simple versions of the theory, as set out in chapter 14. Thus, bidders' valuations might be draws from the following:

$$\$0.1, \quad \$0.2, \quad \$0.3, \ldots \quad \$9.9, \quad \$10.0$$

where each value is equally likely. Draws are made with replacement (so if *you* get a valuation of $5.00, other bidders could also draw $5.00). Each bidder usually knows the *number* of bidders in the auction.

Experiments often consist of a *series* of such auction, where the RV of each bidder changes from one auction to the next. Winnings over the series of auctions are added up and paid at the end. Often such experiments are conducted on computers, with bidders given some practise on the machines before the experiment proper begins (the CST study was largely conducted without computers).

Hypotheses

Individual bidding behaviour

According to the theory, in equilibrium bidders in English and SPSB auctions bid their full valuation. That is, we expect:

$$b_i = RV_i$$

for each bidder *i* irrespective of attitudes to risk.

In Dutch/FPSB auctions, theory predicts that in equilibrium risk neutral bidders bid:

$$b_i = \frac{N-1}{N} RV_i$$

where N is the number of bidders in the auction.

Expected revenue

Theory predicts average prices ($\bar{p}$) given as:

$$\bar{p}_{EA} = \bar{p}_{SPSB} = \bar{p}_{DA} = \bar{p}_{FPSB} = \frac{N-1}{N+1} V_{max}$$

assuming risk neutrality in the case of DA(=Dutch) and FPSB auctions. Note that we have revised the formula for expected revenue by rescaling by V_{max} (the highest valuation possible in the uniform distribution). In the earlier theory we assumed valuations were scaled between 0 and 1; in the experimental example above they were in fact scaled up to $10, and so we would have to rescale expected revenue by multiplying by $V_{max} = 10$.

Efficiency

Theory predicts that English and SPSB auctions will be efficient (the bidder with the highest RV wins the good). It predicts that Dutch and FPSB auctions will also be efficient if all bidders are risk neutral (or at least as long as they hold the same attitudes to risk).

Isomorphism

Theory predicts English and SPSB auctions are isomorphic, and that Dutch and FPSB auctions are isomorphic.

Coppinger, Smith and Titus (CST)

This early study of experimental auctions has been so influential that a proper understanding of their work is necessary before we can consider more recent material. They structured their main experimental auctions on alternating sequences, e.g., 12 English auctions, then 12 Dutch, then 12 English or vice versa. English and Dutch auctions were conducted orally, with 8 bidders in each auction. They conducted experiments using several different distributions for buyers' valuations, but we shall concentrate on those sessions (5 and 6 in their study) using the uniform distribution scaled from $0.1 to $10 as set out above.

With $N = 8$ and $V_{max} = 10$ we find the expected price in theory to be

$$\frac{8-1}{8+1} 10 = \$7.78.$$

The experimental results are given in table 15.1. These show that CST found average prices slightly below the predicted price, but the difference was not statistically significant.

Table 15.1   Coppinger, Titus and Smith auction results

	English	Dutch	FPSB	SPSB
Average price[a] (deviation from expected price)	−0.28	−0.14	0.39[c]	−0.23
Percentage of efficient matches[b] (%)	97	78	90	96

[a] The table gives the difference between the theoretically expected and the average actual prices.
[b] Efficient matches arise when the good is won by the bidder with the highest valuation.
[c] Indicates statistically significant from zero. All figures relate to the experiments using the uniform distribution, except the efficiency percentages for the sealed bid auctions, which relate to all CST sealed bid experiments.

A similar set of alternating sequences were conducted on FPSB and SPSB auctions, this time with $N = 5$, yielding expected price

$$\frac{5-1}{5+1}10 = \$6.67.$$

The results given in table 15.1 show that average prices in SPSB auctions were again insignificantly less than the predicted price. CST reported evidence that subjects tended initially to *underbid* in SPSB auctions but that with experience they learned to play the dominant strategy of bidding their full RV.

The major point to emerge from their study, however, concerned play in the FPSB auction, where CST found that bidders tended systematically to bid too much, leading to average prices significantly *above* the predicted price. Hence behaviour in FPSB auctions did not correspond to theoretical expectations.

The predicted isomorphism between English and SPSB auctions seems to hold good in these experimental results. However, the expected isomorphism between Dutch and FPSB auctions does *not* hold, since the former yields prices in line with expectations but the latter does not.

In terms of *efficiency*, CST found that English auctions allocated the good to the bidder with the highest RV 97 per cent of the time; for Dutch auctions the figure was 78 per cent; for SPSB auctions 96 per cent; and for FPSB 90 per cent. Further work generally supports the finding that English auctions are the most efficient in this sense.

Understanding FPSB Auctions

The major finding to emerge from CST was that FPSB auction behaviour does not correspond to risk neutral equilibrium theoretical predictions. Much of the subsequent literature has concentrated on explaining this finding. Some of the major ideas to emerge in the literature are considered below.

Risk aversion

A natural explanation for high prices in FPSB auctions is that they reflect risk averse bidding behaviour. Intuitively, risk averse bidders bid more (than would be expected under the assumption of risk neutrality) to reduce the risk of not getting the good. Hence the higher prices. Cox, Roberson and Smith (1982) (henceforth CRS) set out a version of the theory based on the Constant Relative Risk Aversion Model (CRRAM), briefly mentioned at the end of chapter 14. This model introduces the possibility of risk aversion in bidding behaviour; it even allows bidders to vary in their degree of risk aversion – but it constrains the form of their risk aversion. Specifically, it specifies utility of income $V(y)$ as:

$$V_i(y) = y^{1-r_i}$$

where $0 \leq r_i < 1$ is the (constant) coefficient of relative risk aversion for bidder i. Note that if $r_i = 0$ for all bidders, then we get the standard risk neutral model that we studied in the main text of chapter 14. Reworking the theory with this utility function yields the following equilibrium bidding strategy in a FPSB/Dutch auction:

$$b_i = \frac{N-1}{N-r_i} V_i.$$

This tells us that a risk averse bidder ($r_i > 0$) would bid a higher fraction of his valuation than a risk neutral bidder, consistent with the higher observed prices.

CRS conducted a series of Dutch, SPSB, and FPSB experimental auctions and interpreted the results on this basis. Once again they found FPSB auctions yielded systematically higher prices than the other auction designs, confirming the finding of CST. They conducted a series of tests which showed that bidding behaviour in the Dutch and FPSB auctions

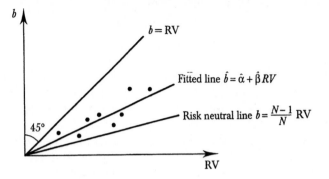

Figure 15.1   Buyer bid functions

was (in most cases) inconsistent with risk neutral bidding behaviour, and consistent with risk aversion.

Cox, Smith and Walker (1988) (henceforth CSW) further pursued these ideas in a series of FPSB auction experiments. They fitted statistical models to describe bidding behaviour for each bidder i, of the form:

$$b_{it} = \alpha_i + \beta_i RV_{it} + \varepsilon_{it}$$

where i is the bidder, t indicates the specific FPSB experimental auction, RV is the bidder's redemption value, b is their observed bid, α and β are regression parameters, and ε is a residual term which reflects unexplained behaviour. This 'bid function' is easiest to understand in terms of figure 15.1, where we plot the valuations and bids of some representative bidder. On the 45° line, we know that bids = RV; typically we would expect actual bids to lie below this. The 'risk neutral' bid line is given as

$$b = \frac{N-1}{N} RV,$$

telling us the bid expected in theory *if the bidder were risk neutral*, given the number of bidders in the auction (N). This may be compared with the actual decisions of the bidder which are indicated as dots on the diagram. The 'fitted line' gives an estimate for the above bid function, given as $b = \hat{\alpha} + \hat{\beta}RV$ where $\hat{\alpha}$ and $\hat{\beta}$ are calculated such that this line fits the actual decisions as closely as possible. If the bidder were, in reality, risk averse then we would expect the fitted line to lie above the risk neutral line, so that the estimated slope coefficient $(\hat{\beta})$ satisfies

$$\hat{\beta} > \frac{N-1}{N}.$$

Under either risk aversion or risk neutrality we would expect a bidder with a RV of zero to place a bid of zero. Thus we expect the fitted line to go through the origin, implying a value for the intercept term of $\alpha \simeq 0$.

CSW found in practice that bid functions of this form explained a very high proportion of the variation in their experimental data. Ninety-two per cent of the slope coefficients were consistent with risk aversion, 70 per cent significantly so.

CSW also found that the intercept term was significantly different from zero 22 per cent of the time, with a tendency to be negative (63 per cent). This is strong evidence in *contradiction* to the expectation of a zero intercept. They considered various possible explanations for this. They noted for example that there was some evidence of 'throw-away bids' in their data, where bidders who received a low valuation decided to bid zero (presumably bidders thought their chances of profitably winning were so small that they might as well not bother bidding seriously).

Overall, these studies suggest that the apparent misbehaviour in experimental FPSB auctions might be due to risk aversion amongst bidders. This comes through in the high average prices, as well as the observed steepness of the estimated bidding functions. Some aspects of the experimental results still appear rather difficult to explain, however, particularly the tendency for the intercept terms of the bidding functions to take on negative estimated values.[1]

The flat payoff function critique

Harrison (1989) has suggested an alternative explanation for the experimental auction results, which is based on problems in the experimental design. Harrison's basic argument was that the cash incentives used in the experiments failed to motivate the bidders. Even though bidders stood to make a reasonable amount of money out of the experiments (e.g. expected earnings were about $15 for a 1-hour session in CRS), Harrison argued that the *costs of making a mistake* were quite low.

Consider figure 15.2, where the solid black curve plots the expected monetary payoff to a bid (the 'payoff function'). The payoff is maximized in this example at a bid of $6, and yields expected returns of $1. How

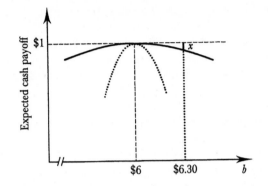

Figure 15.2 The flat payoff function critique

much would the bidder lose if they bid 30 cents more (or less) than $6? In the example, given the bidder's expected return from bidding $6.30 is $0.98. The cost of this mistake is given by distance $x = 2$ cents. The low cost of the mistake arises because the payoff function drawn in figure 15.2 is quite flat. A better experimental design would yield payoff functions more like that in the dotted curve, where the sharper peak implies more pronounced costs for a given mistake.

Harrison's argument was that this sort of problem figured quite prominently in the experimental auctions. The experimenters 'lost control' of the bidders preferences, because bidders had little to lose financially by making mistakes. Instead, other uncontrolled factors outside the experimental design would influence bidders decisions – for example, bidders might 'overbid' because they get utility from the 'thrill' of winning.

This critique drew a strong response (see the December 1992 issue of the *American Economic Review*). We shall not rehearse all the arguments. The flat payoff critique is interesting, however, partly because it gives an alternative explanation for overbidding in FPSB auctions, but more generally because it illustrates some of the problems involved in running experiments.

Why are Dutch and FPSB Auctions not Isomorphic?

In theory, bidders face exactly the same decision problem in these two auction designs, and so they ought to make the same choices. The decision problem is to choose a bid price in both cases. In practice, however, the choices made in the two auction designs diverged. People bid at around the risk neutral equilibrium level in Dutch auctions, whereas they bid above it in FPSB auctions. If overbidding is due to risk aversion in FPSB auction, for example, then one would expect the same bidders to overbid in Dutch auctions also, yet that is not what happens.

This anomaly has been less extensively discussed in the literature, but CRS suggest some explanations. The two auction designs differ in the way decisions are communicated, in that in FPSB auctions the bid is *written*, whereas in Dutch auctions it is *oral*; further the latter is conducted in 'real time', in that the subjects can watch as the asking price is progressively lowered. CRS suggest that bidders might get utility from the 'suspense of waiting' in Dutch auctions; they might get a thrill from seeing the price come down and so wish to prolong the excitement by holding off from bidding a little longer than they would have done if they had just been interested in the cash.

An alternative explanation which they suggest is that bidders might (mistakenly) revise their beliefs about their rivals' valuations of the good by observing the latters' failure to bid as the price falls. This erroneous revision of beliefs may cause them to lower their own bid during the course of the auction and so result in lower bid prices as compared to FPSB auctions. We shall consider a third possible explanation a little later.

Understanding English and SPSB Auctions

Thus far it would seem that the one area where theory and experimental evidence do agree concerns English and SPSB auctions. CST showed that in these auctions at least, experienced bidders played their dominant strategy (bid = RV) and average prices were in line with theoretical expectations. However, subsequent literature has re-opened this issue, particularly in relation to SPSB auctions. Kagel, Harstad and Levin (1987) (henceforth KHL) pointed out that in the early SPSB experiments of CST and CRS, subjects appear to have been explicitly *prohibited* from bidding *above* their valuation of the good. There is no good theoretical reason for this – bidders ought to be free to make their own mind up how much they wish to bid for the good. KHL found that when subjects were given a free choice there was a clear tendency for bidders to bid above their valuation in SPSB auctions, resulting in higher average prices as compared to English auctions. Once again, we find 'misbehaviour', and a theoretical isomorphism (this time between English and SPSB auctions) that is not supported by experimental evidence.

KHL consider some possible explanations for misbehaviour in SPSB auctions. They argue that overbidding occurs in these auctions because of the following.

(i)   *The complexity of the problem*: it is not at all obvious that the 'right' strategy is to bid your full valuation in an auction where the winner pays a price equal to the second highest bid.

(ii)   *Lack of feedback*: say your valuation of the good is $5.00 and you bid $5.20. In most cases, overbidding by 20 cents makes no difference. It only matters *to you* if (a) you win the auction, and (b) the second highest bid is more than $5.00, in which case you make a loss. Since the likelihood of this is small, bidders have little opportunity to *learn* from this kind of mistake.

(iii) *The small losses incurred*: in the unlikely event that you do suffer a loss, e.g. because someone else bids $5.10 in the above example, then bidding $5.20 causes you to lose a mere 10 cents.

It is interesting to note that the 'bottom line' emerging from these auction experiments appears to be that in the oral/real time auctions (English, Dutch) behaviour appears to accord with elementary theory, whereas in the written/sealed bid auctions (first and second price) we tend to observe systematic overbidding. This division caused Kagel (1995) to speculate that the important issue driving the results might lie in the sorts of decisions that people are asked to make. In the sealed bid auctions the decision is a monetary amount – 'do I bid $5, $6, $7 . . . ?' In the real time auctions, however, the choices are of the binary 'yes/no' variety – 'do I bid now or not?' The monetary amount is only determined indirectly from the 'yes/no' decisions. Psychologists argue that the cognitive processes involved in the two types of decisions are different, and hence may lead to different outcomes.[2]

Summary

Early experiments on private value auctions by CST suggested that whilst English, Dutch, and (with experience) SPSB auctions yielded behaviour broadly in line with the basic theory, FPSB tended to yield overbidding and average prices above the expected level. Subsequent work by CRS and by CSW attempted to explain this finding for FPSB auctions in terms of risk aversion on the part of bidders. Alternatively, Harrison suggested that the result might be due to experimental design faults.

Misbehaviour in FPSB auctions implies that the theoretical isomorphism between Dutch and FPSB auctions is not supported in practice. CRS suggested this might be because of 'suspense of waiting' or erroneous revision of beliefs in Dutch auctions.

The early experiments by CST suggested that behaviour in English and SPSB auctions was broadly in line with theory. Subsequent work by KHL has suggested, however, that this result may have been due to the inappropriate prohibition of bids above valuations in SPSB auctions. Further experiments which allowed complete freedom in bidding tended to produce overbidding in SPSB auctions. KHL suggest that this behaviour might reflect the superficial complexity of the decision problem in SPSB auctions; the limited learning opportunities in such a context; and the modest level of losses that arise from such behaviour.

The end result appears to be that the 'real-time' English and Dutch auctions yield behaviour broadly in line with theory, but that the sealed bid auctions (FPSB and SPSB) both yield overbidding. Kagel has suggested that the underlying cause of these differences may be due to the different kinds of decisions involved. In the former case bidders make binary 'yes/no' choices, whereas in the latter they choose monetary amounts. Psychologists argue that the human cognitive processes used to handle these types of decisions differ, and hence yield different choices.

Further Empirical Literature on Auctions

Further experimental evidence

There is a wealth of further studies on experimental auctions, which is extensively surveyed in Kagel (1995). Here we briefly mention some further themes and issues:

Point I   Changing the number of bidders

Theory suggests that as N increases so each bidder ought to increase their bid in FPSB auctions. **Battalio et al. (1990)** report experimental results which support this prediction.

Point 2   Uncertainty regarding the number of bidders

How do bidders behave if they do not know the number of rival bidders? **Dyer et al. (1989)** report a tendency for higher prices to emerge in FPSB experimental auctions, as a result of such uncertainty. These results appear consistent with higher bidding due to risk aversion.

Point 3   Multiple unit discriminative auctions

Say there are $Q > 1$ identical units of the good on offer in the auction, and $N > Q$ bidders. For concreteness suppose $Q = 2$ and $N = 4$. The seller can invite sealed bids and then sell the first unit to the highest bidder, and the second unit to the second highest (each bidder pays their bid price). **Cox et al. (1984)** conducted experiments on auctions of this kind. They found evidence of bidding in excess of levels expected under risk neutrality in some cases. But they also found some puzzling evidence of bidding below the risk neutral level in other cases.

Point 4   Common value auctions – 'the winner's curse'

There is a huge branch of the literature that deals with experiments on common value auctions. This literature is dominated by a phenomenon called 'the winner's curse'. Say bidders are bidding for some item which is worth the same to all (the value is 'common'), but no bidder is exactly sure what that value will turn out to be. The classic example is bidding for drilling rights to an offshore oil field – nobody knows exactly how much the field will be worth, but that value (whatever it turns out to be) will be the same whoever wins the auction.

Say each bidder first estimates the common value and, second, calculates a bid for it, in a FPSB auction. Suppose bidders are *on average* right in their estimates of the value. Then the *average* bidder would find that he made as much money from the oil field as he expected. But it is not the average bidder but the highest bidder that wins. The winner is likely to have systematically overestimated the common value, and so find that the oil field makes less money than expected (it might even make losses). The winner is cursed. (This argument was previously mentioned in chapter 9 in relation to takeover bids.)

In theory, people ought to spot this problem in advance and hence shade down their bids to ensure that if they win they will not be cursed in this way. The empirical question dealt with in experimental auctions concerns whether or not the winner's curse occurs in practice or not.

We have deliberately not dealt with this question in depth in this book because the theoretical issues are much more complex than those that arise in independent private value auctions. Early experimental work, e.g. by Bazermann and Samuelson (1983), supports the existence of such a curse in practice. Further work by Kagel and Levin (1986) suggests that the effect may be mitigated by (a) learning and (b) exclusion of 'poor' bidders through bankruptcy.

Point 5   Correlated value auctions

Kagel et al. (1987) analyse experimental auctions in which bidders have private values, but those valuations are correlated across bidders. Hence, if you value the good highly, then you can deduce that your rivals are likely to value it highly too. They found that bidders tended to play their dominant strategy in English auctions, but to overbid in SPSB auctions. Under FPSB rules, behaviour corresponded reasonably well with theory. In particular they found that introducing public information about rival bidders' values tended to increase FPSB auction prices. This qualitative result fits Milgrom and Weber's (1982)* theoretical predictions, though the size of the increase was smaller than expected.

Real-world evidence

McAfee and McMillan (1987) discuss a number of real-world studies of auction behaviour. The advantages of these studies is that they involve professional bidders in an environment where the stakes are often high. The disadvantage lies in the lack of control – the researcher has no control on the bidders valuations, or their information, it is hard to tell whether valuations are independent or correlated etc. McAfee and McMillan note, however, that these studies suggest the following broad conclusions (none of which is surprising):

(i)   bids increase with valuations;

(ii)   the price increases with the number of bidders;

(iii) better informed bidders make higher returns in common value auctions.

NOTES

1   CRS and CSW did investigate further dimensions of the problem. For example, CSW experimented with higher-order polynomials to the bid function to allow for more complex forms of risk aversion than that suggested by the

CRAMM model. Cox et al. (1985) also considered the issue of risk aversion in FPSB auctions. The interested reader is directed to the original papers for further details.

2   This kind of argument is well known in other areas of experimental economics, particularly in relation to 'preference reversals'; see, for example, Lichtenstein and Slovic (1971).

References for Part 4

Battalio, R., Kogut, C. and Meyer, D. (1990), 'The Effect of Varying Numbers of Bidders in First-price Private Value Auctions', in L. Green and J. Kagel (eds), *Advances in Behavioural Economics*, volume 2 (Norwood, NJ: Ablex).

Bazermann, M. and Samuelson, W. (1983), 'I Won the Auction but I Don't Want the Prize', *Journal of Conflict Resolution,* 27, pp. 618–34.

Coppinger, V., Smith, V. and Titus, J. (1980), 'Incentives and Behaviour in English, Dutch and Sealed Bid Auctions', *Economic Inquiry*, 43, pp. 1–22.

Cox, J., Roberson, B. and Smith, V. (1982), 'Theory and Behaviour of Single Object Auctions', in V. Smith (ed.), *Research in Experimental Economics* (Greenwich, CT: JAI Press).

Cox, J., Smith, V. and Walker, J. (1984), 'Theory and Behaviour of Multiple Unit Discriminative Auctions', *Journal of Finance*, 39, pp. 983–1010.

Cox, J., Smith, V. and Walker, J. (1985), 'Experimental Development of Sealed Bid Auction Theory', *American Economic Review*, 75 (papers and proceedings), pp. 160–5.

Cox, J., Smith, V. and Walker, J. (1988), 'Theory and Individual Behaviour of First Price Auctions', *Journal of Risk and Uncertainty*, 1, pp. 61–99.

Dyer, D., Kagel, J. and Levin, D. (1989), 'Resolving Uncertainty about the Number of Bidders in Independent Private Value Auctions: An Experimental Analysis', *Rand Journal of Economics*, 20, pp. 268–79.

Graham, D. and Marshall, R. (1987), 'Collusive Bidder Behaviour at Single Object Second Price and English Auctions', *Journal of Political Economy*, 101, pp. 119–37.

Hansen, R. (1988), 'Auctions with Endogenous Quantity', *Rand Journal of Economics*, 19, pp. 44–58.

Harrison, G. (1989), 'Theory and Misbehaviour of First Price Auctions', *American Economic Review*, 79, pp. 747–62.

Kagel, J. (1995), 'Auctions: A Survey of Experimental Research', in J. Kagel and A. Roth (eds), *The Handbook of Experimental Economics* (Princeton, NJ: Princeton University Press).

Kagel, J. and Levin, D. (1986), 'The Winner's Curse and Public Information in Common Value Auctions', *American Economic Review*, 76, pp. 894–920.

Kagel, J., Harstad, R. and Levin, D. (1987), 'Information Impact and Allocation Rules in Auctions with Affiliated Private Values: A Laboratory Study', *Econometrica*, 55, pp. 1275–304.

Kreps, D. (1990),* *A Course in Microeconomic Theory* (New York: Harvester Wheatsheaf).

Lichtenstein, S. and Slovic, P. (1971), 'Reversal of Preferences between Bids and Choices in Gambling Decisions', *Journal of Experimental Psychology*, 89, pp. 46–55.

Mas Colell, A., Whinston, M. and Green, J. (1995),* *Microeconomic Theory* (Oxford: Oxford University Press).

McAfee, R. and McMillan, J. (1987), 'Auctions and Bidding', *Journal of Economic Literature*, 25, pp. 699–738.

Milgrom, P. (1989), 'Auctions and Bidding: A Primer', *Journal of Economic Perspectives*, 3, pp. 3–22.

Milgrom, P. and Weber, R. (1982),* 'A Theory of Auctions and Competitive Bidding', *Econometrica*, 50, pp. 1485–527.

Myerson, R. (1979),* 'Incentive Compatibility and the Bargaining Problem', *Econometrica*, 47, pp. 61–73.

Myerson, R. (1991), 'Analysis of Incentives in Bargaining and Mediation', in H. Peyton Young (ed.), *Negotiation Analysis* (Ann Arbor, MI: University of Michigan Press).

Myerson, R. and Satterthwaite, M. (1983),* 'Efficient Mechanisms for Bilateral Trade', *Journal of Economic Theory*, 29, pp. 265–81.

Riley, J. and Samuelson, W. (1981),* 'Optimal Auctions', *American Economic Review*, 71, pp. 381–92.

Vickrey, W. (1961), 'Counterspeculation, Auctions, and Sealed Tenders', *Journal of Finance*, 16, pp. 8–37.

Wilson, R. (1992),* 'Strategic Analysis of Auctions', in R. Aumann and S. Hart (eds), *Handbook of Game Theory*, volume 1 (Oxford: Elsevier Science Publishers).

CHAPTER 16

Concluding Comments

This book is about the role of information in understanding lying and cheating behaviour in markets and organizations. We have argued that:

(i)   Private information underlies adverse selection problems, pre-contractual opportunism or 'lying'.

(ii) Hidden action underlies moral hazard, postcontractual opportunism or 'cheating'.

We illustrated the former in relation to private information about used-car quality, leading to the 'market for lemons'. We then considered signalling mechanism for conveying private information, in relation to the role of education in the job market.

We illustrated the latter in relation to the actions of managers which were taken to be imperfectly observed by shareholders.

At each stage we have highlighted the welfare losses that arise from the information problems. In the final section of the book we considered questions of mechanism design under imperfect information. The idea here was to design mechanisms for transacting, in the face of problems of imperfect information. The examples of bargaining and auctions were given.

There is much more to the literature on imperfect information. For example, we have said little in this book on search, information in financial markets, or regulation. Hopefully, however, we have managed to get across a flavour of the broad spectrum of ideas, and to have whetted readers' appetite for more. The 'Guides to Further Literature' provided at various points in the book should hopefully provide the interested reader with some useful pointers.

Appendix: Brief Notes on Probability Distributions, Bayes' Rule, Expected Utility, and Game Theory

In this appendix we briefly review various technical concepts used in the book. The discussion is elementary.

Probability Distributions

Say there are two types of workers – those who have productivity = 1, and those who are productivity = 2 (as in chapter 5 of this book). The probability that a worker chosen at random will be low productivity is q, and probability she will be high is $(1 - q)$; and so the probability she will be of either type is $q + (1 - q) = 1$. We have here the simplest kind of probability distribution, defined in this case over worker types. The distribution is depicted in the relative frequency diagram of figure A.1.

In certain situations we might have a finer gradation of worker types; some workers might be productivity $^1/_2$ others 1, $1^1/_2$, etc. Such a 'finer' distribution is depicted in figure A.2. Note that the sum of the probabilities must again by definition be equal to 1.

Consider now even finer gradations of worker types. Say the gradations got so fine that productivity could take on any real positive number between 0 and 2. Then we would get a continuous probability distribution of the kind depicted in figure A.3, where we have 'probability density' measured on the vertical axis instead of relative frequency. The probability that a worker has productivity between 0 and 2 must again be equal to one, by definition (the upper and lower limits could in principle be $-\infty$ and ∞). This probability is given by the total area

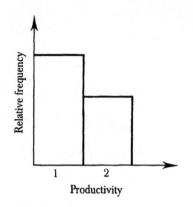

Figure A.1 Probability distribution 1

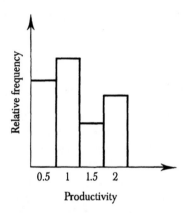

Figure A.2 Probability distribution 2

underneath the distribution in figure A.3. The probability that a worker chosen at random has productivity in some given interval (e.g. more than productivity = 0.4 but less than productivity = 1) is given as the area underneath the distribution between those two points. This is illustrated as the shaded area in the figure. Calculating that probability usually requires integral calculus.

Some classic examples of probability distributions are the normal and the log-normal distributions. In this book we use the *uniform distribution* quite extensively. An example of this is given in figure A.4. Here a worker's productivity might lie anywhere between some lower and some upper limit (taken here as 0 and 2 respectively), with any value between

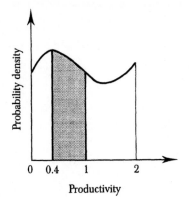

Figure A.3   Probability distribution 3

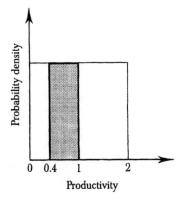

Figure A.4   Probability distribution 4

the two being equally likely. Once again, the area underneath the entire distribution must equal 1 by definition. The density may then be calculated in this case via the following formula

'vertical distance times horizontal distance' = 1
density times 2 = 1
density = $^1/_2$.

The probability that a worker's productivity will lie in some interval many in this case be calculated without recourse to integral calculus. It is the area under the distribution over that interval, and is given as the length of the interval times the density. For example, the probability that it lies between 0.4 and 1

$$\left(1 - 0.4\right) \text{ times } \frac{1}{2} = 0.3$$

Bayes' Rule

This is an important rule for interpreting statistical information. Say employers cannot observe workers' productivity prior to hiring, but they can observe their education level. Then the employers might be able to make inferences about productivity from observed education. Bayes' rule provides the appropriate way of making such inferences.

In general terms this rule says that the probability of an event E given some data D may be calculated as:

$$p\left(E|D\right) = \frac{p\left(D|E\right)p\left(E\right)}{p\left(D|E\right)p\left(E\right) + p\left(D|\text{not } E\right)p\left(\text{not } E\right)}$$

where $p(E)$ stands for 'probability of the event', $p(\text{not } E)$ is 'probability that the event does *not* happen', and the vertical line means 'given' or 'conditional on' so $p(E|D)$ means 'probability of the event given the data', for example.

By way of illustration, consider the simplest case above where workers are either low productivity (with probability q) or high productivity (with probability $(1 - q)$). Call y an index of education level. Suppose some proportion x_H of high productivity workers set education at $y = 1\frac{1}{2}$, and proportion x_L of low productivity workers also set $y = 1\frac{1}{2}$. Then the probability that the next worker who happens to have $y = 1\frac{1}{2}$ will be high productivity is given (via Bayes' rule) as:

$$p\left(\text{high}|y = 1\frac{1}{2}\right) = \frac{p\left(y = 1\frac{1}{2}|\text{high}\right)\left(1 - q\right)}{p\left(y = 1\frac{1}{2}|\text{high}\right)\left(1 - q\right) + p\left(y = 1\frac{1}{2}|\text{low}\right)q}$$

$$= \frac{x_H\left(1 - q\right)}{x_H\left(1 - q\right) + x_L q}$$

(in a signalling equilibrium (chapter 5) employers' beliefs had to be consistent with this rule.) To take some numerical examples, suppose *all* high productivity workers set $y = 1^{1}/_{2}$, and that no low productivity workers did (as happened in a separating equilibrium). Then Bayes' rule says that in that case:

$$p\left(\text{high}\big|y = 1\,^{1}/_{2}\right) = \frac{1(1-q)}{1(1-q)+0q} = 1$$

so employers' best guess is that a worker with $y = 1^{1}/_{2}$ would be high productivity for sure.

Alternatively, say *all* workers set $y = 1^{1}/_{2}$ regardless of their productivity (i.e. they 'pooled' on the same education level). Then in that case:

$$p\left(\text{high}\big|y = 1\,^{1}/_{2}\right) = \frac{1(1-q)}{1(1-q)+1q} = 1-q.$$

As one might expect, employers are no wiser in this case from observing $y = 1^{1}/_{2}$ than they were before; their best guess is that the worker is high productivity with probability $1 - q$.

Expected Utility

How are people to make choices in an uncertain world? The prevailing orthodoxy in economics is to model choice under uncertainty as the outcome of expected utility (*EU*) maximization. This framework may be derived from axioms about behaviour (e.g., see Kreps, 1990*). To see how *EU* 'works', consider an individual who has utility of income given as $U(w)$. He faces uncertainty in that there are two possible states of the world that might arise. For example, in State 1 he is lucky and gets high w; in State 2 he is unlucky and gets low w. Once the uncertainty is resolved, then we can tell his actual w and calculate his actual utility in the knowledge of the realized state of the world. But we cannot tell *beforehand* what state will occur. Say the individual believes that his probability of being lucky is p. Then we can calculate his *expected* utility as

$$EU = U\left(w \text{ if lucky}\right)p + U\left(w \text{ if unlucky}\right)\left(1 - p\right).$$

Say now that the individual faces some *decision*, which may affect the probability of being lucky and/or the income level in the two states. For

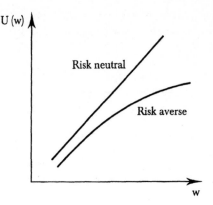

Figure A.5   Utility functions

example, he might face a choice between working hard or not (as in chapter 10). Then the individual can do a similar calculation to that above – he calculates his *EU* if he were to work hard, and his *EU* if he were not to work hard. His decision rule in this framework is then to make his choice in a way that yields highest *EU*. (If working hard yields more *EU*, for example, then so be it).

The decisions that different individuals would make in this context depend on their preferences – in particular their *attitudes to risk*. An important benchmark case arises when an individual happens to be risk neutral. In this case, his $U(w)$ function would be linear as indicated in figure A.5. That is, his marginal utility of income is constant (each extra \$ adds as much to utility as the last \$). This arises most clearly when $U(w) = w$, that is his utility is given exactly by his cash income. Suppose that such an individual receiving income of w were offered a fair bet (i.e., one which would 'break even' on average); e.g. 50 per cent chance of winning \$1000 and 50 per cent chance of losing \$1000. Then his *EU* if he accepted the bet would be:

$$EU_{\text{bet}} = \tfrac{1}{2}U\big(w+1000\big) + \tfrac{1}{2}U\big(w-1000\big)$$
$$= \tfrac{1}{2}\big(w+1000\big) + \tfrac{1}{2}\big(w-1000\big)$$
$$= w.$$

This is the *same* as his utility if he did not accept the bet. Hence a risk neutral individual is indifferent between accepting or rejecting a bet that breaks even on average.

Now compare the case of risk aversion with this benchmark 'risk neutral' case. For a risk averse individual, the function $U(w)$ would have the curved (concave) shape indicated in figure A.5. The marginal utility of income is diminishing, i.e., each extra \$ adds less to utility than the last \$. An example of such a function would be $U(w) = \sqrt{w}$. How would this person respond to the same fair bet mentioned above? Say that prior to the bet his income was $w = 5000$. Then his EU from accepting the bet would be

$$
\begin{aligned}
EU_{bet} &= \frac{1}{2}U(w+1000) + \frac{1}{2}U(w-1000) \\
&= \frac{1}{2}\sqrt{6000} + \frac{1}{2}\sqrt{4000} \\
&= 70.35.
\end{aligned}
$$

Compare this with his utility if he rejects the bet, given as $U(5000) = \sqrt{5000} = 70.71$. Clearly this person would *reject* the fair bet. Put another way, he would require a risk premium before he would be indifferent to a gamble of any kind (i.e., a bet would have to make money on average rather than just breaking even).

Game Theory

Games are strategic situations, where each person's payoff depends in part on what other people do. Games may be represented in either normal form (as in figure A.6) or in extensive form (as in figure A.7). The

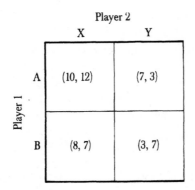

Figure A.6 A game in normal form

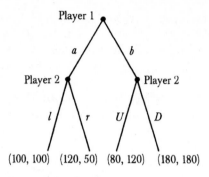

Figure A.7   A game in extensive form

normal form for a two-player game looks like a table, with the possible choices facing person 1 listed down the left side, those facing person 2 across the top, and the payoffs to each person in the brackets inside the boxes (payoff to person 1 is listed first). The choices facing players might, for example, be output levels (high output or low output), and the payoffs might be expected profits. In general, payoffs may be defined in terms of expected utility. To understand how to read figure A.6, say for example that person 1 chose A and 2 chose X; then the table indicates that person 1 will receive a payoff of 10, and person 2 a payoff of 12. We shall discuss the extensive form in figure A.7 a little later. Consider first some 'solution concepts' for games.

Dominance

Notice from figure A.6 that player 1 gets a higher payoff from choosing A rather than B, *whatever player 2 does*. The choice of A is said to *strictly dominate* the alternative of B.

Now consider player 2. Choosing X yields a higher payoff than Y to that person if *player 1 chose A*, but X yields the same payoff as Y to player 2 if *player 1 chose B*. Choice X is said to *weakly dominate* Y (note that A strictly and weakly dominates B for player 1).

Can we 'solve' the game using these dominance arguments (i.e. can we pinpoint exactly what player 1 and player 2 will do in this situation)? Suppose we worked on the basis that no player will ever play a strictly dominated strategy, which seems not unreasonable. On that basis we could rule out the play of B by player 1. That narrows the possibilities down somewhat, but it does not give us an exact prediction of play.

We could go further and work on the basis that players would not choose *weakly* dominated strategies (although this seems a little more dubious as a working assumption). If so, then player 1 will not play B, and player 2 will not play Y, and we are left with a 'solution', where 1 plays A and 2 plays X, yielding payoffs of 10 and 12 respectively.

In general, we will not always get 'solutions' like this by applying dominance concepts to games. It is quite possible that applying strict or even weak dominance will not rule out any possibilities, in some games. In other games we will be able to get part way to a solution by ruling out some possibilities but not others, using dominance relations. Applying weak dominance will always take us at least as far as strict dominance. And in some cases we will get an exact solution using strict (or if not strict then weak) dominance.

Nash equilibrium

This is an alternative solution concept to that of dominance, which may take us further down the line to finding an exact prediction of play in a game. A Nash equilibrium (NE) has the characteristic that each person in the game plays a best response to the other players' strategies. Consider a two-player game. The idea is that for a NE to hold, player 1 plays the strategy that gives him the highest payoff, given the strategy of player 2; and that player 2 plays the strategy that gives her highest payoff given the strategy of player 1. Neither player can gain from unilaterally deviating form his/her equilibrium strategy.

NE is related to the dominance concepts above. In particular, no player will play a strictly dominated strategy in an NE. Nash equilibria can be in 'pure' or 'mixed' strategies. A pure strategy is where a player makes a choice *with certainty* (e.g. A or B). An example of a pure strategy equilibrium can be found in the game in figure A.6. Say player 1 chooses A – then player 2's best response is X. Say player 2 chooses X – then player 1's best response is to play A. Hence play of A by player 1 and X by player 2 is a (pure strategy) NE.

In a mixed strategy equilibrium, players' strategies are *probabilistic*. We mention in chapter 12 the example of the game of 'taking penalties'. A very simple version of this game would run as follows. The kicker can either kick the ball right or left, and the goalkeeper can either dive right or left. If they both go the same way then we assume for simplicity that the keeper 'wins' by saving the goal; but if they go different ways then the kicker 'wins' by scoring a goal. Suppose that a player gets a payoff of 1 if he 'wins' and zero if he loses. It is easy to see that there is no pure strategy equilibrium in this game. If both players go 'the same way', then the kicker can unilaterally gain by deviating to the other strategy; if the players go 'opposite ways' then the keeper can gain by deviating to go the same way as the kicker. In both cases we do not have mutual best responses.

Say instead that the kicker chose right with probability p and the keeper chose right with probability q. For any player to 'mix' (i.e. go right with positive probability less than one) that person must be indifferent between the strategies. The expected payoffs to going left or right are

$$\text{Kicker} \quad \left\{ \begin{array}{l} \text{payoff}(R) = 0.q + 1 \cdot (1-q) = 1-q \\ \text{payoff}(L) = 1.q + 0(1-q) = q \end{array} \right.$$

$$\text{Keeper} \quad \left\{ \begin{array}{l} \text{payoff}(R) = 1.p + 0(1-p) = p \\ \text{payoff}(L) = 0.p + 1(1-p) = 1-p. \end{array} \right.$$

For the kicker to be indifferent (such that payoff(L) = payoff(R)) we need $q = {}^1\!/_2$; for the keeper to be indifferent we need $p = {}^1\!/_2$. Hence we find that if both players go right with probability ${}^1\!/_2$ then neither can gain by unilaterally changing strategy, and we have a mixed strategy equilibrium. The players keep each other guessing.

An NE always exists in any game (as long as the number of players and of pure strategies is finite). There may, however, be several such equilibria (indeed this situation occurred in the signalling game of chapter 5). Hence we may be left once again in a situation where we still do not have a unique 'solution' to a particular game. Game theorists have looked for refinements to the NE concept, in order to narrow down the set of predictions in such situations.

Subgame perfection

This is probably the most commonly used and widely accepted such refinement of NE. In order to explain this concept we need first to understand 'extensive form games' of the kind depicted in figure A.7. Whereas the normal form looks like a table, the extensive form looks like a tree. The latter allows us to depict the sequencing of decisions that lead to any particular outcome. The extensive form of the particular game in figure A.7 says that player 1 moves first by choosing either a or b; if he chooses a then player 2 follows by choosing between l or r, and if he chooses b then player 2 follows by choosing between U or D. The payoffs are listed at the end (player 1 payoff listed first).

A casual inspection of this game would suggest to most people that player 1 is likely to choose b and player 2 choose D, yielding both players their highest possible payoff of 180. This happens also to be an NE. But it is not the *only* NE. Say instead that player 2 decided that she *would choose U* if player 1 chose b, and that she would choose l if player 1 chose a. Then the best that player 1 can do (given player 2's choices) is to choose a. The best that player 2 can do after player 1's choice of a is to choose l, and they both end up with a payoff of 100. This is an NE. The fact that player 2 *would choose U* after b affects player 1's choice; but player 2 has no reason to change that decision given that 1 actually chooses a since her choice after b is never implemented and so does not affect her payoff.

Clearly, then, we are in the thorny situation alluded to above of having multiple NE. But in this case, the latter equilibrium seems suspect. It seems incredible that player 2 would choose U after b, since this would yield her a payoff of 120 as compared to 180 if she chose D. Intuitively, the former equilibrium (play of b, D yielding 180 each) seems more plausible.

It is precisely in this sort of situation where the subgame perfection (SGP) refinement comes into play. In an SGP equilibrium, not only must play of the game as a whole be an NE, but *play in every subgame of the game must also be an NE*. In the example of figure A.7, there is a (proper) subgame where player 2 chooses between l and r; and there is another where player 2 chooses between U and D. If we consider player 2's choice between U and D, the NE of this subgame is clearly for her to choose D (that is her best decision). And once she chooses D in that subgame, so player 1's best response is to choose b. Hence we end up back with the more plausible equilibrium. The rather odd equilibrium where 1 chose a and 2 chose l is ruled out by SGP.

SGP equilibria always exist; this follows because NE exist, hence an equilibrium to every subgame exists and so a SGP equilibrium to the game as a whole exists. SGP equilibria are a subset of NE. In some games, all NE are SGP (this happens in chapter 5); but in others some NE turn out not to be SGP's (this happened in chapter 3 and chapter 6).

Index